Solaris™ 10 Security Essentials

Solaris™ 10 Security Essentials

Sun Microsystems Security Engineers

Sun Microsystems Press

PRENTICE
HALL

Upper Saddle River, NJ • Boston • Indianapolis • San Francisco
New York • Toronto • Montreal • London • Munich • Paris • Madrid
Capetown • Sydney • Tokyo • Singapore • Mexico City

The publisher offers excellent discounts on this book when ordered in quantity for bulk purchases or special sales, which may include electronic versions and/or custom covers and content particular to your business, training goals, marketing focus, and branding interests. For more information, please contact:

U.S. Corporate and Government Sales
(800) 382-3419
corpsales@pearsontechgroup.com

For sales outside the United States please contact:

International Sales
international@pearsoned.com

Visit us on the Web: informit.com/ph

Library of Congress Cataloging-in-Publication Data
Solaris 10 security essentials / Sun Microsystems security engineers.
    p.   cm.
  Includes index.
  ISBN 978-0-13-701233-6 (pbk. : alk. paper)
  1. Solaris (Computer file) 2. Computer security 3.
Operating systems (Computers). I. Sun Microsystems.
  QA76.9.A25S65524 2009
  005.8—dc22

                                    2009034603

ISBN-13: 978-0-13-701233-6
ISBN-10:   0-13-701233-0
Text printed in the United States on recycled paper at RR Donnelley in Crawfordsville, Indiana.
First printing, November 2009

Contents

Preface

Solaris™ 10 Security Essentials

Solaris™ 10 Security Essentials is the first book in the new series on Solaris system administration. It covers all of the features of the Solaris 10 Operating System that make it the best choice for meeting the present-day challenges to robust and secure computing. Other books in the series are *Solaris™ 10 System Administration Essentials* and *Solaris™ 10 ZFS Essentials*. The former covers all of the breakthrough features of the Solaris 10 Operating System in one place. *Solaris™ 10 ZFS Essentials* provides a hands-on look at the revolutionary new ZFS file system introduced in the Solaris 10 OS.

The Solaris OS has a long history of innovation. The Solaris 10 OS is a watershed release that includes features such as:

- **Zones,** which provide application isolation and facilitate server consolidation
- **ZFS,** the file system that provides a new approach to managing your data with an easy administration interface
- The **Fault Management Architecture,** which automates fault detection and resolution
- The **Service Management Facility,** a unified model for services and service management on every Solaris system
- **Dynamic Tracing (DTrace),** for troubleshooting OS and application problems on production systems in real time

Security has long been a core strength of the Solaris OS and it has been significantly enhanced in the Solaris 10 version in areas such as:

- Zones virtualization security
- System hardening
- Trusted Extensions
- Privileges and Role-Based Access Control (RBAC)
- Cryptographic services and key management
- Auditing
- Network security
- Pluggable Authentication Modules (PAM)

The strength of Solaris operating system security is its scalability and adaptability. It can protect a single-user system with login authentication to Internet and intranet configurations.

This book is the work of the engineers and architects who conceptualized the services, wrote the specifications, and coded the Solaris OS's security features. They bring a wide range of industry and academic experience to the business of creating and deploying secure operating systems. These are the people who know Solaris 10 security best. They have combined to write a book that speaks to readers who want to learn Solaris or who want to use Solaris for the first time in their company's or their own environment. Readers do not have to be experienced Solaris users or operating system developers to take advantage of this book.

Books in the Solaris System Administration Series

Solaris™ 10 System Administration Essentials

Solaris™ 10 System Administration Essentials covers all of the breakthrough features of the Solaris 10 Operating System in one place. It does so in a straightforward way that makes an enterprise-level operating system accessible to system administrators at all levels.

Solaris™ 10 System Administration Essentials provides a comprehensive overview along with hands-on examples of the key features that have made Solaris the leading UNIX operating system for years and the significant new features of Solaris 10 that put it far ahead of its competitors. These features include Zones, the ZFS file system, Fault Management Architecture, Service Management Facility, and DTrace, the dynamic tracing tool for troubleshooting OS and application problems on production systems in real time.

Solaris™ 10 ZFS Essentials

Solaris™ 10 ZFS Essentials presents the revolutionary Zettabyte File System introduced in Solaris 10. It is a file system that is elegant in its simplicity and the ease with which it allows system administrators to manage data and storage.

ZFS is an all-purpose file system that is built on top of a pool of storage devices. File systems that are created from a storage pool share space with the other file systems in the pool. Administrators do not have to allocate storage space based on the intended size of a file system because file systems grow automatically within the space that is allocated to the storage pool. When new storage devices are added, all file systems in the pool can immediately use the additional space.

Intended Audience

The books in the Solaris System Administration Series can benefit anyone who wants to learn more about the Solaris 10 operating system. They are written to be particularly accessible to system administrators who are new to Solaris, and people who are perhaps already serving as administrators in companies running Linux, Windows, and/or other UNIX systems.

If you are not presently a practicing system administrator but want to become one, then this series, starting with *Solaris™ 10 System Administration Essentials*, provides an excellent introduction. In fact, most of the examples used in the books are suited to or can be adapted to small learning environments like a home setup. Even before you venture into corporate system administration or deploy Solaris 10 in your existing IT installation, these books will help you experiment in a small test environment.

OpenSolaris

In June 2005, Sun Microsystems introduced OpenSolaris, a fully functional Solaris operating system release built from open source. While the books in this series focus on Solaris 10, they often incorporate aspects of OpenSolaris. Now that Solaris has been open-sourced, its evolution has accelerated even beyond its normally rapid pace. The authors of this series have often found it interesting to introduce features or nuances that are new in OpenSolaris. At the same, many of the enhancements introduced into OpenSolaris are finding their way into Solaris 10. Whether you are learning Solaris 10 or already have an eye on OpenSolaris, the books in this series are for you.

About the Authors

This book benefits from the contributions of numerous experts in Solaris security technologies. Below are brief biographies of each of the contributing authors.

Glenn Brunette is a Distinguished Engineer, Global Systems Engineering Director, and Chief Security Architect at Sun Microsystems, where he leads a global team focused on information security and assurance. Glenn is the founder of Sun's Systemic Security approach; an OpenSolaris Security Community Leader; the co-founder of the Solaris Security Toolkit software; and a frequent author, contributor, and speaker at both Sun and industry events. Externally, Glenn has served in leadership positions at the National Cyber Security Partnership, the Enterprise Grid Alliance, and the Center for Internet Security.

Hai-May Chao is a Staff Engineer at Sun Microsystems in the Solaris Security Technologies group. For the past six years, she has been participating in the design and development of the cryptographic framework and key management framework for the Solaris OS. Hai-May started at Sun in the Trusted Solaris group, developing security features for Trusted Solaris software and the Solaris Management Console. Before joining Sun, Hai-May was a firmware developer at Amdahl, working on IBM-compatible features such as the Multiple Domain Facility (MDF).

Martin Englund is a Principal Security Engineer in the Web Engineering organization at Sun Microsystems. He has over sixteen years of experience in data and network security. Web Engineering itself operates the majority of Sun's external Web presence to the Internet and operationally comes under hourly attack. Martin is responsible for the operational security of over 500 Solaris systems that collectively provide the platform for Sun's external Web presence. Prior to this role, Martin worked in Java Security Engineering and the Sun IT Security Office, where he was responsible for creating the standards and tools used by Sun IT to secure its servers. He has also authored numerous technical papers on security, including Sun Blueprints. Before joining Sun, Martin completed studies in Computer Science and Mathematics and worked as a research engineer at the University of Umeå in Sweden.

Glenn Faden is a Distinguished Engineer in the Solaris Security Technologies group and has worked at Sun for nineteen years. He is currently the architect for Solaris Trusted Extensions and was one of the architects for the Trusted Solaris OS and role-based access control (RBAC). He designed Sun's multilevel desktops based on Open Look, CDE, and GNOME and holds a patent for the underlying X11 security policy. Glenn has made extensive contributions to the Solaris security foundation, including access control lists, auditing, device allocation, and OS virtualization. He also developed the RBAC and process rights management tools for the Solaris Management Console. He has authored several articles for Sun's Blueprints Web site and the Solaris Developer Connection. Glenn previously worked for Qubix, OmniCad, and Gould Computer Systems in Desktop Publishing and OS development. He has a Master of Science in Computer Science from the Florida Institute of Technology.

Mark Fenwick is a Developer in the Solaris Security Technologies group. His current focus is IPsec and IKE. With over two decades of hardware and UNIX software experience, he has extensive knowledge of firewalls, VPN technology, encryption, and networking protocols. Mark has taught technical classes and presented technical papers to Sun support staff and customers. He closely follows key Sun technologies such as ZFS, Sun Ray, and OpenSolaris, both at work and in his UNIX-only home. In his spare time, he enjoys riding one of his many bicycles and cooking.

Valerie Anne Fenwick is a Staff Engineer at Sun Microsystems with over a decade of experience in computer security. She helped to design and develop the cryptographic framework for the Solaris OS. In addition, she chaired the team responsible for code revisions to the Operating System and Networking consolidation for OpenSolaris. Valerie has a Bachelor of Science in Computer Science from Purdue University. In her spare time, she enjoys performing at community theaters, riding her bike, and skiing.

Wyllys Ingersoll is a Senior Staff Engineer at Sun Microsystems in the Solaris Security Technologies group. He has been working in the UNIX security field for thirteen years. Since 2000, he has worked on many of the security features in the Solaris OS: Kerberos, the cryptographic framework, and the key management framework, to name a few. Prior to working at Sun, he developed application firewall software for MCI Worldcom and AOL. He received a Master of Science in Computer Science from Virginia Tech in 1996 and a Bachelor of Science in Computer Engineering from Lehigh University in 1988. He lives and works from his home in northern Virginia today.

Wolfgang Ley received his diploma in computer science at the German Technical University of Clausthal-Zellerfeld. From 1994 to 1999, he worked at the DFN-CERT (German Computer Emergency Response Team) to build up this new service. During that time, he was also active in the Forum of Incident Response and Security Teams (FIRST). He then joined Sun Microsystems, working as Backend Support Engineer and is dealing with network, security, and kernel internals such as crashdump analysis.

Darren Moffat is a Senior Staff Engineer at Sun Microsystems in the Solaris Security Technologies group. Darren is the architect for the Solaris cryptographic framework and Solaris encrypted storage projects. He is also involved in various other OpenSolaris security-related technologies and features. He is an OpenSolaris Security Community leader. Before joining Solaris engineering, Darren worked in SunServices supporting the Trusted Solaris OS, NFS, name services, and Kerberos. Before joining Sun, Darren worked as an analyst/programmer for the UK Ministry of Defence. He is a graduate of the Computing Science Department of Glasgow University.

Pravas Kumar Panda received his engineering degree from Biju Patnayak University of Technology in Orissa, India, in 2003 and joined Sun Microsystems soon after that. He has been working on security technologies for the past three years. During this time, he has focused on Kerberos, SSH, PAM, and packet capturing. He has delivered talks on OpenSolaris, secure programing, and security technologies at various universities in India. Pravas enjoys playing the keyboard. He lives in Bangalore with his wife Bobby and their young daughter Avishi.

Jan Pechanec works at Sun Microsystems in the Solaris Security Technologies group. At the moment, he works mostly with technologies around the SSH protocol and the PKCS #11 standard. He graduated in 2001 from the Faculty of Mathematics and Physics at Charles University in Prague, where he majored in operating systems and computer networks. For the last few years, he has also been working at Charles University, lecturing on UNIX and UNIX C programming.

Mark Phalan works at the Prague office of Sun Microsystems for the Solaris Security Technologies group. He works on Kerberos-related technologies for the Solaris OS and for OpenSolaris. He graduated in 2003 from the Computer Science department of Trinity College Dublin with a BA(Mod) in Computer Science.

Scott Rotondo is a Principal Engineer at Sun Microsystems who works as a security architect for the Solaris operating system. He also serves as President of the Trusted Computing Group (TCG), an industry consortium that defines open standards for hardware-enabled trusted computing. In addition to his work on other security features, Scott leads Sun's development effort to support TCG technologies in Solaris. Scott has over twenty years of technical and management experience in UNIX operating system development. For more than a decade, his focus has been on security issues and features in the Solaris operating system.

Christoph Schuba studied mathematics and management information systems at the Universität Heidelberg and at the Universität Mannheim in Germany. As a Fulbright scholar, he earned his Master of Science and Doctor of Philosophy degrees in Computer Science from Purdue University in 1993 and 1997, respectively, performing most of his dissertation research in the Computer Science Laboratory at the Xerox Palo Alto Research Center (PARC). Christoph has taught undergraduate and graduate courses in computer and network security, cryptography, operating systems, and distributed systems at San Jose State University, USA; at the Universtität Heidelberg, Germany; at the International University in Bruchsal, Germany; and at Linkopings universitet in Linköping, Sweden, where he held the chair in information security. Since 1997, Christoph has been working at Sun Labs and most recently in the Solaris Software Security Organization at Sun Microsystems, Inc. He holds 13 patents and is author and co-author of numerous scientific articles in computer and network security.

Sharon Read Veach is a Technical Writer at Sun. She specializes in documenting inherent security features of the Solaris OS, such as auditing, cryptography, and IPsec. As part of a team of writers, she worked on the Trusted Solaris OS, the predecessor to the Trusted Extensions software in the Solaris 10 release.

Darren Reed is a Senior Systems Engineer in the Solaris Networking group. He is the principal engineer for IPfilter in Solaris.

Joep Vesseur is a Staff Engineer working for the Solaris Security Technologies group. His main focus areas are PAM, secure programming practices, and OS and network security in general. He has co-authored Solaris 9 and Solaris 10 Security exams, several Sun Blueprints, and he is a leader of the Dutch OpenSolaris User Group. His background is in digital forensic science and high-performance computing.

Paul Wernau is a member of the Solaris Security Technologies group. He started his career in Sun Microsystems doing technical support over the phone for enterprise customers, specializing in networking, firewalls, encrypting gateways, and VPNs. Now an IPsec developer, he tries to remember to focus on observability and meaningful error messages, keeping in mind his experience with debugging problems with system administrators.

Solaris Security Services

The Solaris Operating System (Solaris OS) offers a variety of security services, from single-user login authentication to network protections. In the Solaris 10 release, Sun expands its Solaris OS security offerings to provide containment, encryption, PKCS #11 functionality, Trusted Extensions (labeling), and other advanced security features. Many features are based on open industry standards, such as Kerberos and PKCS #11.

This book is written by the engineers and architects who conceptualized the services, wrote the specifications, and coded the security software. This book is intended for users who are interested in maintaining security on a single system and for users who administer a network of systems.

1.1 A Solaris Security Story

In 1988, the Morris worm attacked UNIX systems on the Internet, replicated itself, and brought the network down. This was the first Internet worm.[1] Many of the network systems were Sun systems. The Morris worm gained remote access by trying common passwords, using the debug mode of `sendmail`, and exploiting a buffer overflow in the `fingerd` program. Countermeasures were complex, because UNIX systems were constructed for openness and connectivity, not security. Today, security is part of Sun's DNA. The kernel and installation are designed to protect Solaris systems from attack.

Fast forward to 2007, after Sun distributed Solaris OS code to external developers and users under an OpenSolaris license. An early scrutinizer of the code reported a previously unknown vulnerability in Solaris' telnet program. Because the code was open sourced, the report could and did include a pointer to the lines in the code that were responsible. The report was posted on a Sunday afternoon. By Monday, Sun engineers and testers in Australia, the United Kingdom, and the United States determined how the telnet -f -l root command could compromise a system, posted a Sun Alert, and provided a temporary fix. By Tuesday, Sun issued a patch.[2]

Sun's countermeasures were not complex. Since 1988, Sun has implemented many security features that limit the damage that an attack can inflict. A Secure By Default (SBD) installation closes the telnet port. If the port is open, a simple svcadm command disables the telnet service. Containers, called zones, can limit the effect of an attack, so the system can be reached and fixed by an administrator with the proper privileges.

So, unlike the Morris worm, the telnet worm required a small patch for the specific bug. Solaris security features were already in place. The patch was required on all systems that were running the Solaris 10 version of the OS. Solaris administrators were urged to install the patch, and until they could patch the system, they were urged to disable the telnet program.

The danger of a telnet worm attack appeared to be averted due to a solid Solaris kernel, external eyes that pinpointed the offending code, a global response by Sun engineers, and the creation, testing, and distribution of a patch by Sun services. That was the engineering part of the fix; then came the applying part of the fix. The patch needed to be applied. Humans, or scripts that were run by humans, needed to patch all affected systems.

Two weeks after the patch was released, hackers launched a telnet worm. The worm infected thousands of unpatched systems on the network of the most extensive installation of Solaris machines—SWAN, the Sun-wide area network of Sun Microsystems.

Sun engineers install and re-install their machines to test code. For the most part, these systems are administered by the individual engineer. When the worm invaded these systems, network traffic increased noticeably. Administrative disruption was minimal. The worm could not gain root access, so the SWAN was accessible and systems could be repaired remotely.

Within six hours of detecting the worm at Sun, a process was implemented to help Sun engineers both report and repair infected systems. Within 24 hours of the initial outbreak, over 7000 systems had been inoculated by Sun IT and lab network volunteers, and the worm propagation had been controlled on SWAN.

The process needed to handle systems that were not managed by Sun IT, such as systems in lab environments, individually managed systems, and systems that had been offline when the repairs were effected. Such systems could get infected upon going online and then spread the worm from within SWAN. Similarly, systems that were subsequently reinstalled with existing JumpStart scripts would re-infect Sun from within SWAN. The inoculation script handled this chaotic environment by locating every newly booted system and configuring it so that the worm could not re-infect. For systems that allowed root login, it disabled the `telnet` program and because root compromise was possible, advised the administrator in LARGE TYPE to patch the system.

So, the Solaris security story is a series of short stories.

- Limit the attack surface—use an OS with built-in security.
- Find vulnerabilities quickly—provide the code as open source for more eyes on the code.
- Create a patch—the underlying security enables quick creation.
- End a vulnerability—apply the patch.
- Prevent the attack from being re-introduced—provide comprehensive network management, which might require scripts or firewalls between LANs at a site.

1.2 Security Services in the Solaris OS

Solaris OS security features protect network packets from being snooped on the wire, protect the system from rogue programs, and limit the damage from denial of service (DoS) attacks. Many features are in place at installation. Some features must be configured and then activated. Other features can be strengthened to meet more stringent requirements. This security strategy enables you to configure your system to have the smallest footprint with the largest security benefits. You decide.

Table 1.1 describes the default security configuration and points to the chapters that cover the feature or its use in concert with other features.

Table 1.1 Security Features, Default Configurations, and Chapters in Which They Are Covered

Security Feature	Default Configuration	Chapter
Passwords	Are required, and failures are logged after five attempts. Passwords must have at least two alphabetic characters and one non-alphabetic character. A new password must differ from an existing password by at least three characters.	Chapter 6, "Pluggable Authentication Modules (PAM)"

continues

Table 1.1 Security Features, Default Configurations, and Chapters in Which They Are Covered (*continued*)

Security Feature	Default Configuration	Chapter
User authentication	The Pluggable Authentication Module (PAM) authenticates users attempting to log in to the system.	Chapter 6, "Pluggable Authentication Modules (PAM)"
Authorizations	For some administrative commands, the user must be authorized. Device-related commands, batch job-related commands, printer-administration commands, and audit commands are checked for user authorization.	Chapter 5, "Privileges and Role-Based Access Control"
Cryptographic services	User-level services (encryption and decryption) are immediately available. If hardware that supports encryption or key storage capabilities is attached to your system, the framework automatically detects it.	Chapter 7, "Solaris Cryptographic Framework"
Privilege	Many Solaris administrative commands are protected by privileges, not by file permissions or by the UID of the invoking process. For example, Kerberos commands, network commands, file commands, and commands that control processes are privileged. Some Solaris daemons run as the user daemon with privileges, rather than as root, such as `lockd`, `nfsd`, and `rpcbind`. Device policy and device access is controlled by privileges, not by file permissions.	Chapter 5, "Privileges and Role-Based Access Control"
Remote login	Is limited. The root user cannot log in remotely, either by using SSH or through the console. Is encrypted. Non-root users can log in remotely through an encrypted SSH connection.	Chapter 10, "Solaris Network Security"
Key Management Framework (KMF)	KMF provides central storage capability on your system for keys for NSS, OpenSSL, and PKCS #11 applications.	Chapter 8, "Key Management Framework (KMF)"
File protection	Files that you create can be modified by you or a user in your group. No users can create files or subdirectories in directories that you create. Administrative directories are read-only except to the superuser (root).	Chapter 4, "File System Security"
Service Management Facility (SMF)	SMF provides a general mechanism for the control and configuration of system services. The profile of each system is stored in a repository, so at reboot the system's set of services is restored.	Chapter 2, "Hardening Solaris Systems" Chapter 3, "System Protection with SMF"

1.3 Configurable Security Services in the Solaris OS

By editing configuration files and enabling services, you can customize the security profile of the system to match your site's requirements. Some features, such as ACLs and KMF, are easily configured on the command line. Table 1.2 lists the features that can be customized, the reasons why you might customize them, and the chapters where the features are covered.

Table 1.2 Configurable Security Services

Security Feature	Reasons to Configure	Chapter
File permissions and ACLs	Access Control Lists (ACLs) can protect files at a more fine-grained level than standard UNIX permissions	Chapter 4, "File System Security"
Service Management Facility (SMF)	You can customize Solaris services to invoke only the appropriate set of services for each system. A service profile returns the system to the customized state if problems occur.	Chapter 3, "System Protection with SMF" Chapter 5, "Privileges and Role-Based Access Control"
NFS	When you mount files from a central server, files that must not be modified can be mounted read-only. You can limit access to the central server.	Chapter 4, "File System Security"
Network	You can easily limit which ports listen or are open for two-way traffic on the network. For example, you might open the ftp port only on those systems that serve files. You can configure IP filter to reduce unwanted traffic. You can filter network packets to respond to unrecognized systems' requests with little or no information. You can encrypt and authenticate all traffic over the net by configuring IPsec on the gateways that forward traffic from your LAN. Secure, automated key exchange is provided by IKE (Internet Key Exchange). For single sign-on and a central repository for a network of users and systems, you can configure Kerberos.	Chapter 10, "Solaris Network Security" Chapter 3, "System Protection with SMF"

continues

Table 1.2 Configurable Security Services (*continued*)

Security Feature	Reasons to Configure	Chapter
Roles and superuser	You can limit root's capabilities and prevent root access. A user can be assigned an administrative role to handle part of the total set of administrative tasks. You can assign all the administrative tasks to a set of discrete roles whose duties do not overlap. Users log in by providing their own user name, and then assume a role to perform their administrative tasks. Also, you can make root a role instead of a user, so that direct login as root is denied. To become root, a user who is assigned the root role logs in as a regular user, and then assumes the role.	Chapter 5, "Privileges and Role-Based Access Control"
Containers	You can partition the system into containers, or zones. When you run an application from a zone, attacks on the application are confined to that zone. The rest of the system is not affected. In addition, if you are using roles to administer the system, the attacker cannot set up the system to distribute more attacks. Zones have fewer permitted privileges than the OS. You can configure a zone to have even fewer, which further limits the effects of an attack. You can set quotas on disk space and on CPU usage. You can create projects that formalize disk space, CPU usage, and other allowed parameters. Besides increasing efficiency, these features further limit the effects of an attack.	Chapter 11, "Zones Virtualization Security"
Monitoring	With Solaris auditing, you can identify and track intruders. You can select system events to be audited. Auditing keeps a record of every transaction. You can request a truncated text record to read as the audit records are generated, but the full record is available only to the administrator who is authorized to read the audit trail. With the Basic Audit Reporting Tool (BART), you can verify that the current set of files on your system is what it should be. The Solaris Fingerprint Database (SFD) can help you determine that the binaries in your system's public directories all originated from Sun, and that the files are the latest versions.	Chapter 6, "Pluggable Authentication Modules (PAM)" Chapter 2, "Hardening Solaris Systems"

Table 1.2 Configurable Security Services (*continued*)

Security Feature	Reasons to Configure	Chapter
Passwords	You can specify a strong encryption algorithm for passwords. You can also enforce password complexity requirements in the software so that poor passwords are rejected. You can require that the password be changed at a specified interval, and be changed so that the new password is not a variant of past passwords.	Chapter 6, "Pluggable Authentication Modules (PAM)"
User authentication	PAM can be extended to authenticate users who want to use an application.	Chapter 6, "Pluggable Authentication Modules (PAM)"
Execution protection	You can set a variable to prevent the user of a shell from executing code within the stack. You can prevent executables from being added to mounted file systems. You can identify rogue programs by using monitoring programs such as BART and the Solaris Fingerprint Database (SFD).	Chapter 2, "Hardening Solaris Systems" Chapter 4, "File System Security" Chapter 7, "Solaris Crypto-graphic Framework"
Trusted Extensions	You can protect your data and network with multilevel security. By default, the software defines the levels Public, Confidential: Internal Use Only, Confidential: Need to Know, and Confidential: Restricted.	Chapter 12, "Configuring and Using Trusted Extensions"

Notes

1. For more information, see Spafford, Eugene. *The Internet Worm Program: an analysis.* Purdue Technical Report CDS-TR-823. 1988.

2. For a fuller account, see the Sun blogs, `http://blogs.sun.com/drscholl/` and `http://blogs.sun.com/tpenta/entry/the_in_telnetd_vulnerability_exploit`.

2

Hardening Solaris Systems

Solaris systems are highly configurable. Even before installing additional software, the administrator has the opportunity to make hundreds of choices about how to set up the operating system itself. These choices include which services to enable, the specific configuration settings of each service, and additional settings that apply to the system as a whole.

There is no single "right answer" to any of these configuration choices. If there were, that choice could be set permanently in the operating system, and there would be no need for it to be configurable. Indeed, the process of hardening a computer system is one of making choices and trade-offs that maximize security, while still supporting the intended uses of the system. Beyond the basic techniques presented here, the publications listed at the end of this chapter provide a great deal of specific information to guide the administrator in selecting configuration settings to harden a system.

Once the necessary configuration choices have been made and implemented, the system requires regular monitoring to ensure that the system remains in the hardened state. The latter half of this chapter describes tools in the Solaris OS and elsewhere that help to simplify this task.

2.1 Securing Network Services

Traditionally, many UNIX-based systems have made a wide variety of services available to remote clients over the network. By default, Solaris 10 OS installation enables a large number of network services. This open approach is convenient because it makes services available with minimal setup, and it may provide adequate security in environments where access to the network is limited to a known and trusted set of users. However, many Solaris systems are attached to the Internet or to other networks that cannot be fully trusted. In such an environment, it is prudent to limit the set of services provided to remote clients.

Of course, a service that listens to the network for requests and provides responses is not necessarily insecure. Such services are typically designed to authenticate the identity of the client in some way before performing a requested operation or divulging any non-public information. However, sometimes even the "public" information that is provided without authentication can be useful to an attacker. More importantly, the programs that implement these services, like all programs, may contain bugs, and accepting input from the network makes it easier for an attacker to exploit remotely and anonymously any vulnerabilities that may exist.

To reduce this risk to an acceptable level, the guiding principle is to minimize the set of opportunities available to an attacker, sometimes called the "attack surface," by providing only the services that are necessary for the purpose of the system. Furthermore, it is important to disable unnecessary services from the moment the system is connected to the network. If a vulnerable service is enabled briefly after installation or each time the system is booted until the service is disabled, then a window of opportunity exists for an attacker to exploit the vulnerability until the service is disabled.

2.1.1 Minimizing Installed Software

One approach to limit the network services that are provided by a system is to avoid installing the software that provides unneeded services. All of the programs that are delivered with a Solaris release are divided into *packages*, with related programs grouped together in the same package. Of course, if a package is not installed, the programs it contains cannot run, and therefore they cannot provide any services that are accessible from the network.

Beginning in the Solaris 9 release, the common network services provided by inetd(1M) were divided among several new packages; for example, the packages related to the telnet program are shown below. Discrete packaging allows the administrator to limit the network services provided by customizing the installation to leave out some packages. Individual packages can also be removed after installation using pkgrm(1M).

```
# pkginfo SUNWtnetc SUNWtnetd SUNWtnetr
system      SUNWtnetc Telnet Command (client)
system      SUNWtnetd Telnet Server Daemon (Usr)
system      SUNWtnetr Telnet Server Daemon (Root)
```

The Solaris 10 release expanded upon this idea by adding a Reduced Networking selection at install time to complement the existing Core, End User, Developer, and Entire Distribution choices. Each of these options is an install *metacluster*, which defines the set of packages to be installed. The Reduced Networking metacluster eliminates as many networking services as possible while leaving the system operational enough to allow further configuration. Of course, this configuration must be done by an administrator at the system console, because there are no services running to allow for remote access and administration.

In most cases, a system installed with the Reduced Networking metacluster is too limited to be useful without adding additional packages. Completely eliminating network services has a severe impact on local users as well; for example, a Reduced Networking system does not allow local users to log in via the window system. Rather than using the installed system as-is, the Reduced Networking metacluster is intended to serve as a foundation to which the administrator can add only those packages that are desired for the particular system.

While removing packages is an effective way to eliminate network services, this approach has several practical drawbacks. The first is that the level of granularity may be insufficient. Although services are divided among more packages than in the past, it is still common to have several related services provided by a single package, and choosing to install a package means installing all of the services it provides. Second, it is inconvenient to add services later to adapt to changing requirements, since this requires access to the original installation media in order to add the relevant packages. Finally, packages that are added some time after installation will not have the benefit of any bug fixes contained in patches that may have been applied to the system after installation.

For details about Sun's support for minimized systems, refer to http://www.opensolaris.org/os/community/security/files/minimization-support-rules-ext.pdf.

2.1.2 Using SMF to Control Network Services

The Solaris *Service Management Facility* (SMF), introduced in the Solaris 10 OS, provides a general mechanism for the control and configuration of system services. The fundamental unit of administration in SMF is the *service instance*. An instance is a specific configuration of a service. For example, a Web server is a service. A single Web server daemon that is configured to accept Web service requests on port 80 is an instance of that service. Multiple instances of the same service can run on a single Solaris OS. Each service instance is given a *Fault Management Resource Identifier* (FMRI). The FMRI includes the service name and the instance name. When you list a service using the svcs(1) command, the listing includes the status, date, service name, and service instance. In the next case, "network/dhcp-server" identifies the service, and "default" identifies the instance.

```
# svcs -a | grep dhcp
disabled    Apr 10 svc:/network/dhcp-server:default
```

Because SMF separates configuration of a service from its installation, it is possible to install the entire Solaris OS but enable only the services that are needed on the particular system. To simplify the management process, SMF bundles together the configuration settings for many services into a *profile*. Solaris includes two generic predefined profiles in /var/svc/profile called generic_open.xml and generic_limited_net.xml. The open profile provides the traditional Solaris configuration with many network services enabled. The limited_net profile provides no services to remote clients except for the Secure Shell daemon sshd(1M).

An exception is made for sshd because it is frequently necessary to have some mechanism that allows the administrator to log in and administer the system remotely. Since the need to administer the system remotely may occur at unpredictable times, it is impractical to enable sshd only when it is needed. For this reason, sshd is left enabled by default. Secure Shell is a safer choice for remote administration than telnet or rlogin because it protects the privacy and integrity of the communication session. An administrator who does not want to leave sshd enabled can disable this service individually using the svcadm(1M) command as follows:

svcadm disable ssh

The goal of the limited_net profile is to avoid providing network services to remote clients without affecting the normal activities of local users. The services affected by the limited_net profile are shown in Table 2.1.

Table 2.1 Services Affected by the limited_net Profile

Service	Action Taken
X window server	limited to local system
Dtlogin	limited to local system
Dtprintinfo	disabled
Dtcm	limited to local system
CDE process subcontrol	disabled
ToolTalk	limited to local system
X font server	disabled
Rpcbind	limited to local system

Table 2.1 Services Affected by the `limited_net` Profile (*continued*)

Service	Action Taken
Syslog	limited to local system
Sendmail	limited to local system
WBEM	limited to local system
Smcwebserver	limited to local system
BSD print server	limited to local system
Internet print protocol	disabled
SVM remote metaset, mediator, and mutihost disk	disabled
Berkeley r-comands: rsh, rlogin, rstat, rusers	disabled
Telnet	disabled
NFS client and server (including lockd, statd, rquotad)	disabled
FTP	disabled
Finger	disabled
Standard Type Services	disabled
DMI	disabled
SNMP	disabled
Solstice Enterprise Agent	disabled

For services that are normally used only by remote clients, it is straightforward for the profile to simply disable those services. Other services, including several that are associated with the window system, are also needed by local users. For these services, SMF *properties* are used to configure the services to respond only to requests originating from the local system. Two examples of properties that control the response to remote requests are shown below.

```
# svcprop -t -p config/local_only rpc/bind
config/local_only boolean true
# svcprop -t -p config/log_from_remote system-log
config/log_from_remote boolean false
```

The first example, for the `rpcbind` service, is typical of services where a new Boolean "local_only" property has been added. When this property value is set to `true`, the service only accepts requests from the local system. The `syslog` service, shown in the second example, already contained a "log_from_remote" property in previous releases of the Solaris OS. To limit `syslog` to accepting data from the local system, this property is set to `false`.

SMF profiles are normally applied by using the `svccfg`(1M) command. However, while the `generic_limited_net` profile disables services, it does not set the service properties needed to configure local-only operation. Therefore, the Solaris OS provides the `netservices`(1M) command that applies the SMF profile and also sets the necessary SMF service properties to restrict services to local requests only.

2.1.3 Selecting Profiles at Install Time and Afterwards

When a system is upgraded from a previous release of Solaris, the system continues to provide the same services to the network that it did before the upgrade.

On the other hand, an initial install presents the opportunity to select the limited networking configuration at install time. During an interactive installation, the user is prompted to choose whether or not to enable the traditional networking services. This choice can also be made automatically during a Jump-Start installation. Currently, a non-interactive installation defaults to the traditional, or open, configuration, but this default may change to the limited networking configuration in future releases of the Solaris OS.

As described later in this chapter, a different SMF profile can be applied at any time after installation. However, the advantage of selecting the `limited_net` profile during installation is that the system is protected from potentially hostile network traffic from the first time that it boots. If the system boots with services that accept requests from the network, then there is at least a brief period during which the system is vulnerable before the administrator can disable services or limit them to local requests only.

For a system that is running in the open configuration, either because of a choice at install time or because it was upgraded from a previous Solaris release, the limited networking configuration can be applied at any time afterwards using the `netservices` command.

```
# netservices limited
```

2.1.4 Results of Applying Network Profiles

A system that is running the traditional open configuration shows a large number of enabled `inetd` services.

```
# inetadm | grep enabled
enabled    online    svc:/application/x11/xfs:default
enabled    online    svc:/application/font/stfsloader:default
enabled    offline   svc:/application/print/rfc1179:default
enabled    online    svc:/network/rpc/calendar-manager:udp
enabled    online    svc:/network/rpc/ttdbserver:tcp
enabled    online    svc:/network/rpc/mdcomm:default
enabled    online    svc:/network/rpc/meta:default
enabled    online    svc:/network/rpc/metamed:default
enabled    online    svc:/network/rpc/metamh:default
enabled    online    svc:/network/rpc/gss:default
enabled    online    svc:/network/rpc/smserver:default
enabled    online    svc:/network/rpc/rstat:default
enabled    online    svc:/network/rpc/rusers:default
enabled    online    svc:/network/dtspc:default
enabled    online    svc:/network/nfs/rquota:default
enabled    online    svc:/network/security/ktkt_warn:default
enabled    online    svc:/network/telnet:default
enabled    online    svc:/network/ftp:default
enabled    online    svc:/network/finger:default
enabled    online    svc:/network/login:rlogin
enabled    online    svc:/network/shell:default
enabled    online    svc:/network/rpc-100235_1/rpc_ticotsord:default
```

Similarly, the SMF properties for syslogd(1M) and rpcbind(1M) show that they are configured to accept requests from the network.

```
# svcprop -t -p config/local_only rpc/bind
config/local_only boolean false
# svcprop -t -p config/log_from_remote system-log
config/log_from_remote boolean true
```

After the limited-networking profile is applied, the set of enabled inetd services is dramatically reduced.

```
# netservices limited

# inetadm | grep enabled
enabled    online    svc:/application/font/stfsloader:default
enabled    offline   svc:/application/print/rfc1179:default
enabled    online    svc:/network/rpc/gss:default
enabled    online    svc:/network/rpc/ttdbserver:tcp
enabled    online    svc:/network/rpc/smserver:default
enabled    online    svc:/network/security/ktkt_warn:default
enabled    online    svc:/network/rpc-100235_1/rpc_ticotsord:default
```

The syslogd and rpcbind services are still enabled for local clients, but these services are configured to ignore requests from the network.

```
# svcprop -t -p config/local_only rpc/bind
config/local_only boolean true
# svcprop -t -p config/log_from_remote system-log
config/log_from_remote boolean false
```

The difference can also be seen by examining the output of the nmap[1] command, which shows the open ports that are visible to another system on the network. With the open configuration, we see the following open ports:

```
PORT        STATE SERVICE        VERSION

21/tcp      open  ftp            Solaris ftpd
22/tcp      open  ssh            SunSSH 1.1 (protocol 2.0)
23/tcp      open  telnet         BSD-derived telnetd
25/tcp      open  smtp           Sendmail 8.13.8+Sun/8.13.8
79/tcp      open  finger?
111/tcp     open  rpcbind          2-4 (rpc #100000)
513/tcp     open  rlogin
514/tcp     open  tcpwrapped
587/tcp     open  smtp           Sendmail 8.13.8+Sun/8.13.8
898/tcp     open  http           Solaris management console server
(Java 1.5.0_14; Tomcat 2.1; SunOS 5.10 sparc)
4045/tcp    open  nlockmgr         1-4 (rpc #100021)
6112/tcp    open  dtspc?
7100/tcp    open  font-service Sun Solaris fs.auto
32779/tcp   open  status           1 (rpc #100024)
```

After applying the limited networking configuration, the only open ports are for sshd and rpcbind. Although the rpcbind port is visible to a network scan, it does not accept connections from remote clients due to the setting of the config/local_only property.

```
PORT        STATE SERVICE  VERSION
22/tcp      open  ssh      SunSSH 1.1 (protocol 2.0)
111/tcp     open  rpcbind  2-4 (rpc #100000)
```

2.2 Configuration Hardening

Disabling or restricting access to network services is just one aspect of operating-system hardening. Once the network attack surface has been minimized and unnecessary services have been disabled, you may want to turn inward and look at how the configuration of the operating system and the remaining operational services can be adjusted to improve the overall security of the system.

This section highlights a number of ways in which you can adjust the default configuration to improve the overall security of the system. The degree to which you harden the OS is wholly dependent upon your operational and environmental conditions, but as a general rule the following are generally accepted operating system security recommendations.

- Protect the OpenBoot PROM
- Enable Solaris Non-Executable Stacks
- Log Core Dumps
- Lock Out Accounts

This list is not intended to be complete, but rather is representative of the types of steps often taken by organizations to further lock down their systems. Each of the steps described in this section changes a Solaris OS default value. Note that systems already in deployment must be evaluated to ensure that even the security settings provided by default are still in place or that any changes are understood and well documented.

2.2.1 Protect the OpenBoot PROM

Sun's SPARC hardware provides console-security features that can prevent EEPROM changes, hardware command execution, and even system startup without the appropriate password. This password protection only works while the system is at the OpenBoot PROM level (when the operating system is stopped) or immediately after the system is powered on before the operating system is started.

The OpenBoot PROM password is not related to the Solaris OS root password, and it should not be set as the same password. Once set, the OpenBoot PROM password is not displayed, but can be retrieved in clear text form. When changing the OpenBoot PROM password, the system does not ask for the old password prior to changing it to the new one. In some environments, it may make more sense to set the OpenBoot PROM password to something known to the hardware technicians. The two security modes available are command and full.

Unless an authorized user has the correct password, the command security mode prevents EEPROM changes and hardware-command execution while at the OpenBoot PROM level. The full security mode provides the restrictions of the command mode and, in addition, does not allow the system to boot without the correct OpenBoot PROM password. The full security mode requires operator interaction to boot the system; the system will not boot without first entering the correct password. Do not use the `full` security mode on servers or other systems that must boot quickly without manual intervention.[2]

Use the `/usr/sbin/eeprom` command to set the OpenBoot PROM security mode and password. In this example, the OpenBoot PROM security mode is set to `command`.

```
# eeprom security-mode=command
Changing PROM password:
New password: <password>
Retype new password: <password>
```

2.2.2 Enable Solaris Non-Executable Stacks

Non-executable stacks provide a very useful technique for thwarting certain kinds of buffer overflow attacks. Initially developed for the SPARC platform, non-executable stack protection is also now available on x64 systems supporting either the Execute Disable (XD) bit on Intel platforms or the No Execute (NX) bit on AMD platforms.

As with other kernel parameters, the non-executable stack state is configured (enabled or disabled) by a setting in the `/etc/system` file. For example, the following statement added to the `/etc/system` file would enable this feature:

```
set noexec_user_stack=1
```

Once this setting has been made, the system must be rebooted for the change to take effect. It is also possible to compile a program so that it runs with a non-executable stack regardless of the system configuration. For more details applicable to both developers and system administrators, see `http://blogs.sun.com/gbrunett/tags/noexstk`.

2.2.3 Log Core Dumps

The operating system writes out a core file for a process when the process is terminated due to receiving certain signals. Such signals can be generated when the process is unable to handle an unexpected condition. Core dumps can provide an early warning of an attacker attempting to overflow a buffer in a running process.

A core file is a disk copy of the contents of the process address space at the time the process received the signal, along with additional information about the state of the process. The Solaris OS allows you to adjust quite a few parameters that are related to the capture and logging of core dumps files.

One configuration change often implemented is to send a notice to the system logging service when a program "dumps core." This kind of notification can be used to trigger administrative action to determine if there is a problem with the service or if the system may be under attack.

To enable the logging of core dump events, simply run the `/usr/bin/coreadm` command:

```
# /usr/bin/coreadm -e log
```

After this command is run, future core dump events are logged to the `syslog` facility.

2.2.4 Lock Out Accounts

Another system-wide parameter that is often used is account lockout. Often referred to as a "three strikes policy," account lockout offers you a way of locking individual user accounts after a specified number of consecutive, failed authentication attempts (note that this number does not have to be three!).

Account lockout can be enabled on a per-user basis or globally where it impacts all users on the system who are not specifically excluded from the policy. Account lockout is also service agnostic, in that the consecutive failed authentication attempts need not be from the same service. In this way, the operating system can detect brute-force authentication attempts that could start with Secure Shell and move to other services like TELNET or FTP.

To enable account lockout globally, you set the `LOCK_AFTER_RETRIES` parameter to `YES` in the `/etc/security/policy.conf` file. By default, the `root` account is excluded from this policy. If you want to have other exclusions or simply want to specify a different per-user policy, you must edit the `/etc/user_attr` file and/or each impacted user, set the `lock_after_retries` parameter to either `yes` or `no` based on your intent. To specify how many consecutive failed authentication attempts are permitted before an account is locked, set the `RETRIES` parameter in the `/etc/default/login` file. By default, this value is `5`.

Note that once an account is locked, it can only be unlocked by administrative intervention. A system administrator must unlock the account using the `-u` option to the `/usr/bin/passwd` command before that account can be successfully accessed.

For more information, see `http://blogs.sun.com/gbrunett/entry/solaris_10_account_lockout_three`.

2.2.5 Other Security Configuration Ideas

This section has provided just a small window into the various security hardening configuration settings that exist in the Solaris OS. There are many more system-wide as well as service-specific configuration settings that can be adjusted if necessary. As a general rule, the default values provided in the Solaris OS are suitable for most organizations, but particular cases might require additional configuration changes. Beyond the Solaris product documentation, we recommend that you review the publications that are listed at the end of this chapter for specific hardening suggestions.[3]

2.3 Basic Audit and Reporting Tool

The Basic Audit and Reporting Tool (BART) provides a quick and easy way to collect information on filesystem objects and their attributes so that, at a later time, you can determine whether there have been any changes. While this kind of functionality is clearly useful for security incident detection, BART is also often used as part of a larger change management process to validate approved changes and to detect those that may have occurred outside of an approved process.

The BART tool, `/usr/bin/bart`, collects such information as an object's UID, GID, permissions, access control lists, modification time, size, and type. In addition, for files, BART generates an MD5 fingerprint from the contents of the file so that the integrity of a file's contents can also be verified. The exact attributes that are collected depend on the type of object being evaluated. For a full list of the attributes that can be collected, see the `bart_rules`(4) manual page.

BART has two primary modes of operation: `create` and `compare`.

2.3.1 Collecting Filesystem Object Attributes (Create Mode)

When run in create mode, BART collects file system object information from a system. You can control the scope of collection on a system. You can include the entire system, all files under a specified directory, or just a subset of files. You can even define a more granular policy by using a rules file that can be customized to meet your organization's requirements.

When you use BART in create mode, BART reads its rules file from either standard input or from a regular file. As BART processes individual file system objects, it records its results in a manifest file. This manifest is directed to standard output by default, although you can easily redirect the output to a file or to another process.

For example, to create a BART manifest called `/root/bart.control` based upon the files under `/usr/lib/nis`, the following command could be used:

```
# find /usr/lib/nis | bart create -I > /root/bart.control
```

2.3.2 Comparing Filesystem Object Attributes (Compare Mode)

To use BART in compare mode, you need two BART manifests and, optionally, a rules file.

- The first (and original) manifest, called the control manifest, is used as your baseline.
- The second manifest, called the test manifest, is then compared against the control. The manifests are compared in accordance with a set of rules, if supplied.
- If a rules file is specified, then BART uses the rules to determine how to make the various comparisons. One of the benefits of rules files is that they can help eliminate any false alarms in your reports, thereby allowing you to better focus your efforts on the remaining alarms.

You can also use BART to compare any two independent BART snapshots to determine whether the objects being assessed have been changed. For example, with BART, you can quickly and easily answer the question: "Has this file changed since yesterday?"

For example, building upon the last example, create a test manifest for the `/usr/lib/nis` directory:

```
# find /usr/lib/nis | bart create -I > /root/bart.test
```

Once both the control and test manifests have been created, you can compare them to look for any differences:

```
# bart compare /root/bart.control /root/bart.test
/usr/lib/nis/foo:
 add
/usr/lib/nis/nisping:
 uid control:0 test:2
```

In this case, the `/usr/lib/nis/foo` file has been added to the `/usr/lib/nis` directory, and the `/usr/lib/nis/nisping` program has had its owner changed from `root` (uid 0) to `bin` (uid 2). These changes happened after the control manifest was first created.

Using the cron(1M) command, you can generate BART manifests every minute, hour, day, week, or month. How often you actually run BART to generate new manifests is based on how critical your need is to detect change. Because one size does not fit all, you might even want to consider having different BART rules or policies. For example, you might have two policies:

- A smaller policy, targeting a few key files, that runs every minute or hour
- A larger policy, collecting information across the entire system, that runs only once a day or once a week

Use common sense when deciding how often to generate manifests. You need to balance your detection priorities with the I/O load that the collection process generates on the system. For more information on automating the collection and processing of BART manifests, see the Sun BluePrint article titled "Automating Solaris 10 File Integrity Checks," which can be found at http://www.sun.com/blueprints/0305/819-2259.pdf.

2.3.3 Determining Whether a Filesystem Object Is Genuine

Regardless of the selected time intervals, however, BART is still not able to definitively answer the question: "Is this a genuine object that Sun shipped?" BART cannot answer this question because you need to manually create the control manifest after the system has been installed. Someone or something could have changed a Sun-provided file from its default before you performed your first BART snapshot, particularly if the first BART manifest is generated well after installation. Remember that, if your control manifest is somehow corrupt, then all of the later comparisons against the original manifest are suspect.

2.4 Signed ELF Filesystem Objects

To determine if a filesystem object is indeed genuine, you can query its cryptographic signature. Starting in the Solaris 10 OS, most operating system Executable and Linkable Format (ELF) objects have been cryptographically signed by Sun. The signatures on these files can be validated by using the elfsign(1) command.

```
# elfsign verify -e /usr/bin/su
elfsign: verification of /usr/bin/su passed.
```

While this is a very strong way of validating the integrity of a file, this approach is only applicable to ELF objects such as binaries, libraries, device drivers, and other compiled code. Also, due to license or other restrictions, some binaries that are shipped in a Solaris release cannot be modified and therefore the signature cannot be added to those files. Last, text-based configuration and log files and other non-binary content are not protected in this manner. The Solaris Fingerprint Database, discussed in the next section, can validate files that are not signed.

2.5 Solaris Fingerprint Database (sfpDB)

The Solaris Fingerprint Database (sfpDB) is a free SunSolve Online service that enables organizations to verify the integrity of files that are distributed with the Solaris OS. Organizations can, at any time, query the sfpDB to determine whether an operating system file did indeed come from Sun.

The sfpDB is a powerful tool for organizations that want to validate the integrity of their operating systems, baseline snapshots, and patches—or even to assist during digital forensic investigations in which the integrity of objects might be called into question.

The Solaris Fingerprint Database is itself a collection of file fingerprints that have been created from the contents of Solaris OS media kits, unbundled software, and patches. These fingerprints are created as part of the release process in order to ensure that the fingerprints are current and reflect actual shipping versions of files provided by Sun. By submitting fingerprints to the Solaris Fingerprint Database service, organizations can then determine which, if any, of the submitted fingerprints belongs to an actual file supplied by Sun.

2.5.1 How the sfpDB Tool Works

The Solaris Fingerprint Database is a collection of file fingerprints that are generated by using the MD5 Message Digest Algorithm, which is defined in RFC 1321:

The algorithm takes as input a message of arbitrary length and produces as output a 128-bit "fingerprint" or "message digest" of the input. It is conjectured that it is computationally infeasible to produce two messages having the same message digest, or to produce any message having a given pre-specified target message digest.

By using this algorithm, it is expected that no two different files will share the same fingerprint. While this assurance is not necessarily as strong as a cryptographic signature, it is virtually impossible to modify a file in such as way as to retain its original MD5 fingerprint. Note that, in September 2004, researchers announced that the MD5 algorithm was "broken." That is, they had developed a method to produce two pre-images (for example, files) with the same MD5 hash value. While the announcement is important, this breakthrough does not impact the validity of the Solaris Fingerprint Database. As of the publication of this book, no feasible method exists to produce a pre-image (such as a text or binary file) that matches a given hash value. That is, no file could be replaced with another, different file and still retain its original MD5 hash value. For more information about the resistance of hash functions to attack, see, for example, http://www.schneier.com/crypto-gram-0409.html#3.

To use the Solaris Fingerprint Database service, you calculate MD5 fingerprints for the files you want to check, and then submit them to the database service for processing. The sfpDB service evaluates the submitted fingerprints and determines if a match exists for any of the objects.

For each fingerprint match, the information shown in Table 2.2 is provided.

Table 2.2 Fingerprint Database Fields

Field	Description
canonical-path	Absolute path name of the file delivered by Sun matching the supplied fingerprint. This field is often examined to determine whether a valid Solaris OS program has been renamed or moved to a new location.
package	Solaris OS package name associated with this file. With this information, the Solaris OS packaging tools can be used to gather additional information. Further, the package name can be compared with the packages that are actually installed on the system to determine whether an unauthorized package had been installed, or if a file (from that package) has been added to the system.
version	Version of the Solaris OS package associated with this file. This information can be used to determine whether the file was supplied as part of the initial Solaris OS distribution, or whether it was made available in a patch. This value must match the one returned by the following command: `pkgparam <package_name> VERSION` Version information is useful in detecting downgrade attacks in which a program is replaced with an older, potentially vulnerable (but otherwise valid) version of itself.
architecture	Hardware architecture that is associated with the package that delivered the file.
source	Original product that delivered the file. Just as with the version information, this value can be used to identify discrepancies between what is installed and what is supposed to be installed on the system. For example, source would flag a Solaris 2.5.1 binary that had been installed on a Solaris 10 system.

Note that a single file fingerprint can result in several matches. Text files often generate several matches because they do not depend on the underlying operating system version or hardware platform. Examples of text files are configuration files and shell scripts.

2.5.2 Creating an MD5 File Fingerprint

The Solaris 10 OS contains a program that can be used to generate MD5 fingerprints: /usr/bin/digest. The following example uses the digest program to create an MD5 fingerprint:

```
# digest -v -a md5 /usr/bin/su
md5 (/usr/bin/su) = bab18f089705c1628ccdc177b802d571
```

2.5.3 Testing an MD5 File Fingerprint

Once the MD5 fingerprints have been computed, they can be submitted to the Solaris Fingerprint Database to determine whether they correspond to values associated with valid Sun operating system files. To test the collected fingerprints:

1. Visit the Solaris Fingerprint Database page at http://sunsolve.sun.com/pub-cgi/fileFingerprints.pl.
   After connecting to this URL, the Solaris Fingerprint Web form is displayed. Scroll to the bottom of the page to find the text window where the collected fingerprints can be entered.

2. Type or copy and paste one or more MD5 fingerprints into the Web form. For example, to verify the su command fingerprint that was generated in the preceding example, paste the MD5 value into the Web form:
   bab18f089705c1628ccdc177b802d571

3. Click the Submit button to view the results.
   For this example, the following result is returned:

```
Results of Last Search
bab18f089705c1628ccdc177b802d571 -        - 1 match(es)
    * canonical-path: /usr/bin/su
    * package: SUNWcsu
    * version: 11.10.0,REV=2005.01.21.15.53
    * architecture: sparc
    * source: Solaris 10/SPARC
```

The Solaris Fingerprint Database query properly identified the `/usr/bin/su` program as the object to which the fingerprint belonged. It is important to not only examine the name and canonical path when evaluating the results, as there are many possible outcomes such as multiple data mismatches, matches indicating an upgrade or downgrade attack, and of course, a failure where the fingerprint that you provided was not found in the database. Each of these cases, along with a more in-depth treatment of the Solaris Fingerprint Database, is provided in the Sun BluePrint article titled *The Solaris Fingerprint Database: A Security Tool for Solaris Operating Environment Files (Updated for Solaris 10)*, which can be found at `http://www.sun.com/blueprints/0306/816-1148.pdf`.

It is good practice to use together both of the tools discussed in this chapter: the Basic Audit and Reporting Tool and the Solaris Fingerprint Database. More information on this integration can be found in the Sun BluePrint article titled "Integrating BART and the Solaris Fingerprint Database in the Solaris 10 Operating System," which can be found at `http://www.sun.com/blueprints/0405/819-2260.pdf`.

References

The following publications provide specific guidance for hardening Solaris systems for various purposes. As always, you must consider the intended uses of your system before deciding which advice to follow. Evaluate any potential changes to ensure that they are appropriate for your environment, your applications, and your management practices.

Center for Internet Security, *Solaris 10 Benchmark*,
> `http://www.sun.com/security/docs/CIS_Solaris_10_Benchmark_v4.pdf`
> This is a set of recommended hardening practices produced by the independent Center for Internet Security, with input from Sun.

Sun Microsystems, *An Overview of Solaris 10 Operating System Security Controls*,
> `http://www.sun.com/security/docs/s10-cis-appendix-v1.1.pdf`
> This guide is designed to be used as an appendix to the preceding CIS benchmark.

OpenSolaris Security Community Library,
> `http://www.opensolaris.org/os/community/security/library`
> This page contains the preceding two links, as well as others that were submitted by the OpenSolaris community. It also includes links to Sun BluePrints and other documents on individual security topics.

Notes

1. nmap is an open-source network scanning tool available in OpenSolaris or at `http://www.insecure.org/nmap`.

2. This passage was adapted from the Solaris OS Security BluePrint Article by Alex Noordegraaf at `http://www.sun.com/blueprints/1202/816-5242.pdf`.

3. Sun Microsystems works closely with the Center for Internet Security to develop and publish security configuration guidance for the Solaris operating system. See `http://www.cisecurity.org/bench_solaris.html`. The CIS Benchmark is also discussed in the CIS document included in the "References" section earlier in this chapter.

System Protection
with SMF

All services on a Solaris 10 system are controlled by the Service Management Facility (SMF). Among the advantages of SMF, which include automatic starting of dependent services and the ability to recover easily from a service outage, is the ability to use the power of role-based access control (RBAC) in an SMF manifest. With RBAC, programs can run with the precise privileges and authorizations that the program needs, and no more. This chapter shows you how to configure four programs—NFS, IP filter, FTP, and the Apache2 Web server—as SMF services.

3.1 Service Management Facility (SMF)

SMF provides a more powerful administrative interface for Solaris services than the traditional UNIX run-control scripts.

Solaris services are executables such as system processes, daemons, applications, and scripts. Database software, Web server software, and site-specific scripts can be controlled by SMF. SMF provides simple, fast, and visible administration through the following features.

- Services can be enabled, disabled, or restarted with one administrative command, `svcadm`.

- Failed services are restarted automatically in dependency order. The source of the failure does not affect the automatic restart.

- Service objects can be viewed and managed with commands such as `svcs`, `svcadm`, and `svccfg`.

- Services are easy to debug. The `svcs -x` command provides an explanation of why a service is not running. Per-service log files also simplify debugging.

- Services are easy to test, back up, and restore to a particular configuration because configuration states are preserved in service manifests.

- Systems boot and shut down faster because services are started and stopped according to the dependencies between services. Services can be started in parallel.

- Administrators can securely delegate tasks to non-root users who have permissions to administer particular services through RBAC rights profiles, roles, authorizations, or privileges.

- SMF *milestones* correspond to system init states such as the multiuser run level.

- SMF can be used on a system that is also using traditional UNIX `rc` scripts. While this practice is not recommended, you can use traditional scripts for some services and use SMF for others. For more information, see the `smf`(5), `svcadm`(1M), `svcs`(1), and `svccfg`(1M) man pages.

Manifests, or snapshots of each service, are in a central repository. This overall snapshot initializes the system at reboot. You can define a number of manifest collections, which are called *profiles*. The limited profile was discussed in Chapter 2, "Hardening Solaris Systems." The `svccfg apply` *profile* command configures your system with *profile*.

3.2 How SMF Configuration Works

A service is shipped together with an SMF manifest. The manifest's format is an XML file in the */var/svc/manifest/* directory. The manifest contains the information about dependencies, if the service is enabled or disabled, and other basic configuration and default information. During system boot, the manifests are imported into the SMF repository. The repository is a database in the */etc/svc/* directory.

You can have multiple manifests or snapshots of each service. At boot, a profile is selected. A profile enables or disables every Solaris service. After the profile initializes the system during boot, an administrator can further customize the configuration by using SMF commands. These commands directly modify the repository and the profile, and the changed configuration is restored at the next boot.

3.3 Modifying Solaris Services Defaults

On a Solaris system that is hardened by the limited profile, network services that you might want to run on particular systems are disabled (hardening is discussed in Chapter 2, "Hardening Solaris Systems"). For example, the `ftp` service is disabled, as is NFS file sharing. Services that require configuration, such as IPfilter and IPsec, are disabled by default.

The following sections provide examples of using SMF to configure a system for a particular purpose. Once you have configured the system, the manifest is in the repository. When the system reboots, that configuration is restored. The examples illustrate the following points.

- Services that must be configured in configuration files are enabled after the files are configured. If you did not configure the file, or if the file cannot be read, the problem is recorded in the log file.

- You might want to try different configurations of a service. By using different configuration files, you can create testing environments. The final configuration state is restored at reboot.

- Some services, such as FTP, are necessary but might require monitoring. You can set up monitoring services before bringing them online, thereby ensuring that the service is in compliance with site security policy for its first use.

- You might want to limit the attack surface on a network service. The Apache2 Web service can be configured to use RBAC to limit the privileges that the service uses. You can also require a more limited account than `root` to run the service.

3.3.1 Configuring the NFS Service

To configure a service that requires you to customize a configuration file, you perform the following steps.

1. List the status of the service.
2. Modify or create the configuration file.
3. Enable the service.
4. Verify that the service is online.
5. If the system reports an error, read the service log and then fix the error.
6. Test and use the service.

In the following example, you configure a system to serve help documents. The files must be shared read-only.

```
# svcs -a | grep nfs
...
disabled        Jan_10 svc:/network/nfs/server:default
# vi /etc/dfs/dfstab
...
share -F nfs -o ro /export/helpdocs
...
# svcadm enable svc:/network/nfs/server
# svcs -x svc:/network/nfs/server:default
State: online since Tue Jan 20 5:15:05 2009
  See: nfsd(1M)
  See: /var/svc/log/network-nfs-server:default.log
Impact: None
```

If you try to enable a service without its supporting files, view the log file to determine the problem:

```
# svcs -x svc:/network/nfs/server:default (NFS server)
 State: disabled since Tue Jan 20 5:10:10 2009
Reason: Temporarily disabled by an administrator.
   See: http://sun.com/msg/SMF-8000-1S
   See: nfsd(1M)
   See: /var/svc/log/network-nfs-server:default.log
Impact: This service is not running.
# vi /var/svc/log/network-nfs-server:default.log
...
No NFS filesystems are shared
...
```

3.3.2 Configuring the IP Filter Service

Like the NFS service, the IP filter service cannot be enabled until you create a configuration file. Your site's security requirements dictate what configuration rules you place in the file. Some services, such as IPsec, require that each communicating system has a configuration file. To enable a service that requires a configuration file involves the following steps.

1. Create the configuration file. Use the man page for the service name if you do not know the name of the configuration file. Then read the configuration file man page for the syntax.

2. If syntax verification is available, verify the syntax of the file.

3. If the service needs to run on both systems, such as the IPsec service, configure the second system.

4. Enable the service on one or both systems.

5. Enable the service.

6. Verify that the service is running.

In the following examples, you protect a system that includes non-global zones. The IP filter rules protect the global zone and the Web server zone. You first create and add rules to the `/etc/ipf/ipf.conf` configuration file.

```
# vi /etc/ipf/ipf.conf
set intercept_loopback true;
# *** GLOBAL ZONE: (IN: TCP/22, OUT: ANYTHING)
pass in quick proto tcp from any to global-zone port = 22
keep state keep frags
pass out quick from global-zone to any keep state keep frags
# *** Web Server ZONE: (IN: TCP/80, OUT: NOTHING)
pass in quick proto tcp from any to websvc port = 80
keep state keep frags
block out quick from websvc to any

# *** DEFAULT DENY
block in log all
block in from any to 255.255.255.255
block in from any to 127.0.0.1/32
```

Then you verify the syntax of the configuration file before enabling the service.

```
# ipf /etc/ipf/ipf.conf
# svcs -a | grep ipf
disabled       Dec_10    svc:/network/ipfilter:default
# svcadm enable svc:/network/ipfilter:default
# svcs ipfilter
enabled        Jan_10    svc:/network/ipfilter:default
```

To test a different configuration, you create another configuration file, verify the syntax of the file, and change the `config/entities` property to point to the new file. This test file adds rules for the Web data zone.

```
# vi /etc/ipf/testipf.conf
set intercept_loopback true;
# *** GLOBAL ZONE: (IN: TCP/22, OUT: ANYTHING)
pass in quick proto tcp from any to global-zone port = 22
keep state keep frags
pass out quick from global-zone to any keep state keep frags

# *** Web Server ZONE: (IN: TCP/80, OUT: NOTHING)
pass in quick proto tcp from any to websvc port = 80
keep state keep frags
```

continues

```
block out quick from websvc to any
# *** Web Data ZONE: (IN: TCP/22, OUT: ANYTHING)
pass in quick proto tcp from any to webdat port = 22
keep state keep frags
pass out quick from webdat to any keep state keep frags
# *** DEFAULT DENY
block in log all
block in from any to 255.255.255.255
block in from any to 127.0.0.1/32
# ipf /etc/ipf/testipf.conf
# svcprop ipfilter | grep config
config/entities fmri file://localhost/etc/ipf/ipf.conf
config/grouping astring require_all
config/restart_on astring restart
config/type astring path
# svccfg -s /network/ipfilter \
setprop config/entities=file://localhost/etc/ipf/testipf.conf
```

After you refresh and restart the service, you then verify that the property has been set.

```
# svcadm refresh ipfilter
# svcadm restart ipfilter
# svcprop ipfilter | grep etc
config/entities fmri file://localhost/etc/ipf/testipf.conf
```

After testing is complete, you can restore the original file.

```
# svccfg -s /network/ipfilter \
setprop config/entities=file://localhost/etc/ipf/ipf.conf
# svcadm refresh ipfilter
# svcadm restart ipfilter
# svcprop ipfilter | grep etc
config/entities fmri file://localhost/etc/ipf/ipf.conf
```

3.3.3 Configuring the `ftp` Service

The `ftp` service is controlled by the `inetd` command. Often, site security policy requires that an FTP server log detailed records of all FTP connections. In the following two examples, you configure properties of the `ftp` service that log transactions and turn on debugging.

To configure a service that requires you to change service properties, you perform the following steps.

1. List the status of the service.

2. List the properties of the service.

3. Change one or more properties of the service.

4. Verify that the service property is changed.

5. Enable the service.

6. Verify that the property change is effective.

In the first part of this example, you configure FTP to log every login on System A, the FTP server. Note that the `ftp` service is initially disabled on System A.

```
A # svcs ftp
STATE          STIME     FMRI
disabled       Jan_10    svc:/network/ftp:default
A # inetadm -l svc:/network/ftp:default
SCOPE    NAME=VALUE
         name="ftp"
         endpoint_type="stream"
         proto="tcp6"
         isrpc=FALSE
         wait=FALSE
         exec="/usr/sbin/in.ftpd -a"
         user="root"
...
default  tcp_trace=FALSE
default  tcp_wrappers=FALSE
default  connection_backlog=10
```

The login log property for the `ftp` service is `tcp_trace`. You change the value from FALSE to TRUE, then enable the service and verify that the service is online.

```
A # inetadm -m svc:/network/ftp:default tcp_trace=TRUE
A # inetadm -l svc:/network/ftp:default
SCOPE    NAME=VALUE
         name="ftp"
...

         tcp_trace=TRUE
...
A # svcadm enable svc:/network/ftp:default
A # svcs ftp
STATE          STIME     FMRI
online         07:07:07  svc:/network/ftp:default
```

Then, as a regular user, run the `ftp` command from machine B.

```
B $ ftp A
Connected to A.
220 A FTP server ready.
Name (A:testftp):
331 Password required for testftp.
Password:
230 User testftp logged in.
Remote system type is UNIX.
Using binary mode to transfer files.
ftp>
```

As superuser, examine the login record in the log file on machine A.

```
A # tail -1 /var/adm/messages
Jan 10 07:20:20 A inetd[16208]: [ID 317013 daemon.notice] ftp[6036] from B 49822
```

To continue with this example, disable the service. You want to establish monitoring before the service is online.

```
A # svcadm disable ftp
A # svcs -x ftp
svc:/network/ftp:default (FTP server)
 State: disabled since January 20, 2009  07:20:22 AM PST
Reason: Disabled by an administrator.
   See: http://sun.com/msg/SMF-8000-05
   See: in.ftpd(1M)
   See: ftpd(1M)
Impact: This service is not running.
```

The exec property for the ftp service contains the command that is executed to start the service. The man page for that command describes the arguments that the command accepts. You can select arguments to add to the exec property so that the command runs with those arguments when the service starts. Therefore, to modify the command that runs a service, you perform the following steps.

1. List the exec property of the service.
2. From the man page, determine the arguments to the service's exec command.
3. Add selected arguments to the exec property of the service.
4. Verify that the exec property is changed.
5. Enable the service.
6. Test and use the service.

In the following example, you modify the ftp service to provide debugging information and a detailed log of each transaction. To modify the exec property of the ftp service, first list the exec property, then read the man page of the exec command to determine which arguments to pass to the command.

```
# inetadm -l svc:/network/ftp:default | grep exec
        exec="/usr/sbin/in.ftpd -a"
# man in.ftpd
```

From the `in.ftpd`(1M) man page, select the options that provide detailed information.

- `-v` Write debugging information to `syslogd`(1M).
- `-w` Record each user login and logout in the `wtmpx`(4) file.
- `-i` Log the names of all files received by the FTP Server to `xferlog`(4).

Modify the `exec` property for the service and verify that the property is changed.

```
# inetadm -m ftp exec="/usr/sbin/in.ftpd -a -i -v -w"
# inetadm -l ftp | grep exec
      exec="/usr/sbin/in.ftpd -a -i -v -w"
```

Test that the property change is effective. First, enable the service. Then, as a regular user, transfer a file. Finally, verify that the log file was updated.

```
A # svcadm enable svc:/network/ftp:default
A # svcs ftp
STATE          STIME       FMRI
online         07:07:07 svc:/network/ftp:default
```

As a regular user, try to put a file in the FTP repository.

```
B $ ftp A
Connected to A.
220 A FTP server ready.
Name (A:testftp):
331 Password required for testftp.
Password:
230 User testftp logged in.
Remote system type is UNIX.
Using binary mode to transfer files.
ftp> mput design.tar
mput design.tar? y
200 PORT command successful.
150 Opening BINARY mode data connection for design.tar.
226 Transfer complete.
^D
ftp> 221-You have transferred 0 bytes in 0 files.
221-Total traffic for this session was 361 bytes in 0 transfers.
221-Thank you for using the FTP service on A.
221 Goodbye.
B $
```

As superuser, examine the record in the `xferlog` file. The log indicates that the user's attempt to transfer the `design.tar` file from B to A was unsuccessful.

```
A # cat /var/log/xferlog
Sat Jan 20 07:18:10 2009 1 B.mydomain.com 0 /home/test/design.tar b _ i r test ftp 0 * c
```

3.3.4 Configuring the Apache2 Web Service

The Apache2 Web server program is offered as part of the Solaris OS. Web servers are frequently the targets of attackers. You can use RBAC to limit the server's vulnerability to attack. Other Solaris features, such as zones, are also useful when setting up network services.

To configure a service with RBAC, you perform some of the following steps.

1. List the properties of the service.
2. Create a rights profile, or a role, or authorizations for the service.
3. Add privileges to or remove privileges from the service.
4. Verify that the service properties are changed.
5. Enable the service.
6. Verify that the property change is effective.

The Apache2 Web server program is provided in the SUNWapch2r and SUNWapch2u packages. By default, the Apache2 service is disabled.

```
# svcs apache2
disabled 11:11:10 svc:/network/http:apache2
```

By default, services are started with the `root` account. However, the `http.conf` file for the Apache2 service creates a daemon, `webservd`, to run the service. When you configure the service with the default files, the service starts under the `root` account, switches to the `webservd` account, and runs with all privileges.

To reduce the privileges of the Apache2 server and start the service with `webservd`, do the following.

- Remove basic privileges that the service does not need, `proc_session`, `proc_info`, and `file_link_any`.
- Add the network privilege the service needs to use a privileged port, `net_privaddr`.
- Do not change the limit set.
- Set the user and group to `webservd`. When the user and group are set in the SMF manifest, the service starts as `webservd`, not as `root`.

```
# svccfg -s apache2
... apache2> setprop start/user = astring: webservd
... apache2> setprop start/group = astring: webservd
... apache2> setprop start/privileges = astring:
basic,!proc_session,!proc_info,!file_link_any,net_privaddr
... apache2> end
# svcadm -v refresh apache2
Action refresh set for svc:/network/http:apache2.
```

To verify that this configuration has been set, examine the service's start properties.

```
# svcprop -v -p start apache2
start/exec astring /lib/svc/method/http-apache2\ start
...
start/user astring webservd
start/group astring webservd
start/privileges astring
basic,!proc_session,!proc_info,!file_link_any,net_privaddr
start/limit_privileges astring :default
start/use_profile boolean false
...
```

Note

If you had created a rights profile that included the privileges for the service, you could type the name of the rights profile as the value for the use_profile property, rather than setting the privileges.

You can now enable the service. Verify that the service starts under webservd and has a limited set of privileges.

```
# svcadm -v enable -s apache2
svc:/network/http:apache2 enabled.
# svcs apache2
STATE STIME FMRI
online 12:02:21 svc:/network/http:apache2
# ps -aef | grep apache | grep -v grep
webservd 5568 5559 0 12:02:22 ? 0:00 /usr/apache2/bin/httpd -k start
...
# ppriv -S 5559
5559: /usr/apache2/bin/httpd -k start
flags = <none>
E: net_privaddr,proc_exec,proc_fork
I: net_privaddr,proc_exec,proc_fork
P: net_privaddr,proc_exec,proc_fork
L: limit
```

For more examples of using RBAC in SMF manifests, see Chapter 5, "Privileges and Role-Based Access Control."

Further Reading

For a fuller account of setting up an Apache2 Web server, see the following:

Limiting Service Privileges in the Solaris™ 10 Operating System,
  `http://www.sun.com/blueprints/0505/819-2680.pdf`

Understanding the Security Capabilities of Solaris Zones Software,
  `http://www.sun.com/offers/details/820-7017.html`

Eliminating Web Page Hijacking Using Solaris 10 Security,
  `http://www.sun.com/software/solaris/howtoguides/`
  `s10securityhowto.pdf`

4

File System Security

File system security is one of the most basic security features in the Solaris OS. These features have evolved quite a bit over time, from the traditional UNIX security mechanisms to ACLs on NFSv4 and ZFS file systems.

4.1 Traditional UNIX File System Security

The basics of file system security start with the three modes for files and directories: *user, group,* and *other*. These modes have been around since the birth of UNIX. The *other* mode is also called *world* or *everyone*.

The *user* mode is the permissions that are granted to the file or directory owner, the *group* mode is the permissions that are granted to those who are members of the same group as the group that owns the file or directory, and *other* is the permissions that are granted to users who are neither the owner of the file or directory nor a member of the group that owns the file or directory.

Modes can be either symbolic or absolute. Symbolic are **r**ead, **w**rite, and **exe**cute, and are listed per mode. Absolute is an octal number constructed by adding the bits for user, group, and other. The values are shown in Table 4.1.

So, to compute the octal value, you add the numbers that correspond to the symbolic mode. For example, `rwxrw-r--` corresponds to 400 + 200 + 100 + 40 + 20 + 4 = 764.

The execute bit on a directory gives permission to search the directory.

Table 4.1 Modes

User			Group			Other		
r	w	x	r	w	x	r	w	x
400	200	100	40	20	10	4	2	1

Consider the following two examples. You want to make a script that you own readable, writable, and executable by you, readable and executable by group members, and with no permissions for others. In symbolic mode, you run the following command:

```
$ chmod u=rwx,g=rx,o= /path/to/file
```

The absolute notation is much shorter and has the same effect as the above example:

```
$ chmod 750 /path/to/file
```

The symbolic notation allows you to add and subtract. For example, if you have created a shell script that has mode 644 and you want to make it executable for you only, run the following command:

```
$ chmod u+x /path/to/file
```

To make it executable for everyone, you run the following command:

```
$ chmod a+x /path/to/file
```

In symbolic notation, a indicates *all*.

With the execute bit, the script can be run as any other program. Without the execute bit, the script can be run if it is readable by passing the script as an argument to the appropriate shell. The following command runs a readable script that does not have the execute bit set:

```
$ sh /path/to/script.sh
```

4.1.1 `setuid`, `setgid`, and Sticky Bit

In addition to the user bit, the group bit, and the other bit, a fourth bit field is used for the purposes listed in Table 4.2.

Table 4.2 Bit Field Description

	setuid	setgid	Sticky Bit
File	Execute with user ID (uid) of the owner of the file instead of the uid of the current process	Execute with group id (gid) of the group of the file instead of the gid of the current process	n/a
Directory	n/a	Causes all files and directories created in the directory to have gid of the group	Causes files in writable directories to only be removed/renamed if at least one of the following is true: • the user owns the file • the user owns the directory • the file is writable by the user • the user is a privileged user
Octal value	4000	2000	1000

Note

This section ignores combinations that do not have security implications.

The setgid bit on directories can only be set by using the symbolic mode. The following command sets the setgid bit on the directory. All files and directories that are created in this directory are assigned the same group as the directory.

```
$ id
uid=100(martin) gid=10(staff)
$ mkfile file
$ ls -l file
-rw-r--r--   1 martin    staff      512 Aug  8 08:15 file
$ chmod g+s .
$ ls -ld .
drwxr-sr-x   2 martin    sysadmin   512 Aug  8 08:15 .
$ mkfile new-file
$ ls -l new-file
-rw-r--r--   1 martin    sysadmin   512 Aug  8 08:16 new-file
```

When files and directories are created, they are created with the same group as the process that invokes the command. By default, the system assigns the primary group that is specified in /etc/passwd. When you use the newgrp command to change the user's primary group, files and directories that you create are then assigned the new group.

```
$ id -a
uid=100(martin) gid=10(staff) groups=10(staff),14(sysadmin)
$ newgrp sysadmin
$ id -a
uid=100(martin) gid=14(sysadmin) groups=10(staff),14(sysadmin)
```

The sticky bit is used on temporary directories like /tmp and /var/tmp to allow users to share common (world-writable) directories. However, when you create temporary files in a common directory, you need to be aware of a possible race condition. If an attacker can guess the name of the file that you are going to create, the file can be created by the attacker with permissions to allow both of you to read and write to the file. Files that are created by a script are especially susceptible to this kind of attack.

Consider the following script:

```
#!/bin/sh
#
TMPFILE=/tmp/root.$$

who > $TMPFILE
awk '{print $1}' $TMPFILE
```

An attacker can create a few hundred files in /tmp that begin with root.*x*, where *x* is the current process ID (pid), and the script above will happily use a file that is owned by the attacker. The attacker is then able to rapidly overwrite the contents of legitimate files with the attacker's malicious content.

To prevent this kind of attack, you should use the mktemp(1) command instead. This command allows you to safely create temporary files (and directories) in world-writable directories with the setuid bit. If mktemp can successfully generate a unique name, it creates a file or directory with permissions that allow only the owner to read and write to it.

```
#!/bin/sh
#
TMPFILE=`mktemp /tmp/file.XXXXXX`

if [ -z "$TMPFILE" ]; then
    echo "unable to create temporary file"
    exit 1
fi

who > $TMPFILE
awk '{print $1}' $TMPFILE
```

4.1.2 `chown`/`chgrp`

The `chown` and `chgrp` commands are used to change the owner or the group of a file or directory. However, the commands have restrictions.

To use the `chgrp` command to change the group of a file or directory, you must be a member of the new group.

```
$ ls -l /path/to/file
-rw-r--r--   1 martin    sysadmin        0 Jul  8 08:12 /path/to/file
$ chgrp staff /path/to/file
$ ls -l /path/to/file
-rw-r--r--   1 martin    staff           0 Jul  8 08:12 /path/to/file
```

To change the ownership of a file or directory you own, you need the `file_chown_self` privilege. This privilege is not granted to users by default. Once the privilege has been granted by your administrator, you can change the ownership of a file to another user by running the following command:

```
$ ls -l /path/to/file
-rw-r--r--   1 martin    staff           0 Jul  8 08:12 /path/to/file
$ chown someone /path/to/file
$ ls -l /path/to/file
-rw-r--r--   1 someone   staff           0 Jul  8 08:12 /path/to/file
```

4.1.3 Default `umask`

When you have logged in to a Solaris system, your shell process gets a default `umask`. `umask` is a bit mask that determines the permissions on new files and directories. The mask is written in absolute mode. The value of the mask is subtracted from the mode bits specified when the file is created to determine the permissions. For the Solaris OS, the default `umask` is `022`. With this `umask`, creating a file with mode `666` (readable and writeable by everyone) results in absolute permissions of `644`. Creating a directory with mode `777` results in absolute permissions of `755`.

To change the system default `umask`, you edit the `/etc/default/login` file and explicitly set the mask.

UMASK=002

This value of `umask` affects all processes that are started through the `login(1)` command. Another file that sets the `umask`, `/etc/profile`, is read by shells such as `/bin/sh`, `/bin/ksh`, and `/bin/bash` when those shells are invoked as a login shell.

If you are using the `setuid` bit on a directory to share files with colleagues, the default `umask` prevents them from writing to files and directories that you create. By setting the `umask` to 002, members of your group can write to those directories.

```
$ umask 002
```

4.1.4 `setfacl/getfacl`

Due to the limitations of regular UNIX file modes, the Solaris OS added Access Control Lists (ACLs) to UFS. ACLs allow more fine-grained control than traditional UNIX permissions. You can add permissions for individual users and also extra groups.

For instance, to grant a specific user the same rights as you, when the two of you do not share any group memberships, you can add an ACL that specifies the user:

```
$ ls -l foo
-rw-r--r--  1 martin  staff  0 28 Jun 17:47 foo
$ setfacl -m user:danny:rw- foo
```

To determine if an ACL has been added to a file, use `ls -l` on that file:

```
$ ls -l foo
-rw-r--r--+ 1 martin  staff  0 28 Jun 17:47 foo
```

The plus sign (+) indicates the existence of one or more ACLs. Use the `getfacl` command to inspect the file's permissions:

```
$ getfacl foo

# file: foo
# owner: martin
# group: staff
user::rw-
user:danny:rwx          #effective:rw-
group::r--              #effective:r--
mask:rw-
other:r--
```

You can also use the `find`(1) command to determine which files have ACLs.

```
$ find /usr/bin -acl -ls
```

> **Note**
>
> The getfacl and setfacl commands only apply to files on a UFS file system. For setting ACLs on a ZFS file system, see Section 4.2, "ZFS/NFSv4 ACLs."

4.1.5 Extended Attributes

In the Solaris 10 release, extended attributes were added to files. Extended attributes enable you to tie optional attributes to a file. This functionality is similar to the resource fork in Apple's HFS. While extended attributes are not a security feature, they can be exploited by an attacker to hide files.

To view the extended attributes of a file, you must create a context in which to view the attributes. The simplest way is to spawn a new shell within the target file. You use the runat command, as the following example shows:

```
$ runat /path/to/file
```

The runat command spawns a new shell where you can run normal commands to explore any extended attributes that might exist. You can also pass a command to be run within the file attribute context:

```
$ runat /path/to/file ls -l
total 2
-rw-r--r--   1 martin   staff        24 Jul  8 23:41 notes
```

To find all files with extended attributes, use the xattr option to the find command:

```
$ find /path/to/directory -xattr
```

You can prevent the use of extended attributes on a file system. See Section 4.4, "UFS and NFSv4 Mount Options" for details.

4.1.6 Promiscuous Execution

If you change the default Solaris permissions and ownerships, or if you add directories to root's PATH, those files and directories must not be writable by anyone but root. Files that are modifiable by other users can change programs to execute malicious commands.

For example, if you add a new script to /usr/bin that is writable by anyone, a malicious user can edit the script to add commands that grant the user extra privileges. This extra privilege compromises the system. The execution of a program with insecure mode is often referred to as *promiscuous execution*.

4.2 ZFS/NFSv4 ACLs

ZFS and NFSv4 ACLs address several limitations with the UFS ACLs, such as not being able to revoke permissions and being coarse-grained.

4.2.1 Access Permissions

As with UFS ACLs, use the `ls -l` command to determine if ACLs are present. Again, a plus sign (+) after the file mode indicates that an ACL is present. Use the `ls -v` command to view the actual permissions:

```
$ ls -v /path/to/file
-rw-r--r--   1 root       root            156 Apr 17 15:59 /path/to/file
     0:owner@:execute:deny
     1:owner@:read_data/write_data/append_data/write_xattr/write_attributes
        /write_acl/write_owner:allow
     2:group@:write_data/append_data/execute:deny
     3:group@:read_data:allow
     4:everyone@:write_data/append_data/write_xattr/execute/write_attributes
        /write_acl/write_owner:deny
     5:everyone@:read_data/read_xattr/read_attributes/read_acl/synchronize
        :allow
```

In ZFS and NFSv4, ACLs are made up of three parts: one part for the owner, one part for the group, and one part for everyone (other/world). These parts correspond to the traditional UNIX permissions. The difference is that each part has an allow list and a deny list, and the permissions are much more granular.

The permissions listed in Table 4.3 can be allowed or denied with ZFS and NFSv4 ACLs.

Table 4.3 Possible Values for ZFS ACLs

Permission	Description
read_data	Permission to read the data of the file
list_data	Permission to list the contents of a directory
write_data	Permission to modify the file's data anywhere in the file's offset range. This includes the ability to grow the file or write to an arbitrary offset.
append_data	The ability to modify the data, but only starting at EOF
add_file	Permission to add a new file to a directory
add_subdirectory	Permission to create a subdirectory to a directory

Table 4.3 Possible Values for ZFS ACLs (*continued*)

Permission	Description
read_xattr	The ability to read the extended attributes of a file or to do a lookup in the extended attributes directory
write_xattr	The ability to create extended attributes or write to the extended attributes directory
execute	Permission to execute a file
delete_child	Permission to delete a file within a directory
delete	Permission to delete a file
read_attributes	The ability to read basic attributes (non-ACLs) of a file. Basic attributes are considered the stat(2) level attributes.
write_attributes	Permission to change the times associated with a file or directory to an arbitrary value
read_acl	Permission to read the ACL
write_acl	Permission to write a file's ACL
write_owner	Permission to change the owner or the ability to execute chown(1) or chgrp(1)
synchronize	Permission to access a file locally at the server with synchronous reads and writes

In addition to the default three parts, you can add ACLs for individual users and for specific groups. Traditionally, to prevent a user from executing /usr/bin/su, you remove the world permissions. When world permissions are removed, a user must be a member of the group that owns /usr/bin/su to be able to execute the command.

With ZFS and NFSv4 ACLs, you can revoke the right of a particular user to execute the command.

```
# chmod A+user:danny:execute:deny /usr/bin/su
# ls -v /usr/bin/su
-r-sr-xr-x+  1 root     sys       34624 Feb 26  2007 /usr/bin/su
    0:user:danny:execute:deny
    1:owner@:write_data/append_data:deny
    2:owner@:read_data/write_xattr/execute/write_attributes/write_acl
      /write_owner:allow
    3:group@:write_data/append_data:deny
    4:group@:read_data/execute:allow
    5:everyone@:write_data/append_data/write_xattr/write_attributes
      /write_acl/write_owner:deny
    6:everyone@:read_data/read_xattr/execute/read_attributes/read_acl
      /synchronize:allow
```

You can prevent a malicious process from altering previously written contents in a log file by allowing processes to only append to the file. You revoke all write privileges except `append_data`, which allows the process to write to the file, but only at the end. The ACL display is similar to the following:

```
# chmod A+user:martin:append_data:allow /app/log
# ls -v /app/log
-rw-r-----+  1 root      root       34624 Feb 26  2007 /app/log
     0:user:martin:append_data:allow
     1:owner@:write_data/append_data:deny
     2:owner@:read_data/write_xattr/execute/write_attributes/write_acl
       /write_owner:allow
     3:group@:write_data/append_data:deny
     4:group@:read_data/execute:allow
     5:everyone@:write_data/append_data/write_xattr/write_attributes
       /write_acl/write_owner:deny
     6:everyone@:read_data/read_xattr/execute/read_attributes/read_acl
       /synchronize:allow
```

4.2.2 Inheritance Flags

Inheritance flags on directories enable you to specify how ACLs on new files and directories are treated. Table 4.4 runs down the inheritance flags.

Table 4.4 Inheritance Flags

Inheritance Flag	Description
file_inherit	Indicates that this ACE (Access Control Entry) will be added to each new non-directory file created.
dir_inherit	Indicates that this ACE will be added to each new directory created.
inherit_only	Placed on a directory, but does not apply to the directory itself, only to newly created files and directories. This flag requires the file_inherit or the dir_inherit flag to indicate what to inherit.
no_propagate	Indicates that ACL entries can only be inherited to one level of the tree. This flag requires the file_inherit or the dir_inherit flag to indicate what to inherit.

For example, inheritance flags can be used to allow a user to create new log files in a directory and only append to them:

```
# chmod A+user:martin:append_data::file_inherit:allow /app/log
# chmod A+user:martin:add_file:allow /app/log
```

4.2.3 ZFS per Filesystem ACL Properties

ZFS has two property modes that control the behavior of ACLs for each file system.

The `aclinherit` property determines ACL inheritance. Table 4.5 describes the possible values.

Table 4.5 Possible Value for the `aclinherit` Property

Value	Description
discard	For new objects, no ACL entries are inherited when a file or directory is created. The ACL on the file or directory is equal to the permission mode of the file or directory.
noallow	For new objects, only inheritable ACL entries that have an access type of deny are inherited.
secure	For new objects, the write_owner and write_acl permissions are removed when an ACL entry is inherited.
passthrough	For new objects, the inheritable ACL entries are inherited with no changes. In effect, passthrough mode disables secure mode.

The `aclmode` property modifies ACL behavior whenever a file or directory's mode is modified by the `chmod` command or when a file is initially created. Table 4.6 describes the possible values.

Table 4.6 Possible Values for the `aclmode` Property

Value	Description
discard	All ACL entries are removed except for the entries that are needed to define the mode of the file or directory.
groupmask	User or group ACL permissions are reduced so that they are no greater than the group permission bits, unless it is a user entry that has the same UID as the owner of the file or directory. Then, the ACL permissions are reduced so that they are no greater than the owner-permission bits.
passthrough	For new objects, the inheritable ACL entries are inherited with no changes.

To use UNIX file permissions only, no ACLs, on a ZFS file system, modify the `aclmode` and `aclinherit` properties on the ZFS file system as follows:

```
$ zfs set aclmode=discard z0/db
$ zfs set aclinherit=discard z0/db
```

4.3 Maintaining File System Integrity

One of the harder problems in maintaining a system is to prevent "security decay." When the system is first installed, the security is usually at its best. As time goes by, file permissions are modified, new security vulnerabilities are discovered, configuration files are edited, and so on. Such changes can inadvertently lead to an insecure system.

To battle this slow but steady decay, it is important to manage changes in the file system objects. Sun provides three tools to manage file changes: the Solaris fingerprint database, Basic Audit Reporting Tool (BART), and signed Executable and Linking Format (ELF) objects.

4.3.1 Solaris Fingerprint Database (SFD)

Sun publishes cryptographic checksums of all files that Solaris software has released, starting with the Solaris 2.0 release. These checksums are computed for patches and all bundled and most unbundled software media.

These cryptographic checksums can be used to verify the authenticity of a file. You compute the hash, and then type the result in a form on the `http://sunsolve.sun.com/fileFingerprints.do` Web site.

The SFD input form accepts either the MD5 hash or the longer canonical MD5 output format:

```
$ digest -a md5 /usr/bin/su
2a88e945cc84a70f79b221ba110a2bca
$ digest -v -a md5 /usr/bin/su
md5 (/usr/bin/su) 2a88e945cc84a70f79b221ba110a2bca
```

The result lists all files that match the MD5 hash:

```
2a88e945cc84a70f79b221ba110a2bca -  - 1 match(es)
     canonical-path: /usr/bin/su
     package: SUNWcsu
     version: 11.10.0,REV=2005.01.21.15.53
     architecture: sparc
     source: Solaris 10/SPARC
     patch: 119574-02
```

The result identifies the file and helps you determine if something fishy is going on. For example, you might find a `setuid` program called `/usr/bin/bd` and submit its hash to the SFD. If the result is `/usr/bin/su`, you must look up the newest version of the `su` binary to determine if you have been subjected to a downgrade attack. In a downgrade attack, an attacker adds an old, exploitable file as a back door. For example, an older binary might have more vulnerabilities than the latest version. By hiding the older binary (`bd`) on the system, the attacker can exploit it to gain elevated privileges even when the original file (`su`) is patched.

The SFD Web page accepts only 256 signatures at a time. If you have more than 256 files to check, you can make multiple submissions.

4.3.2 Solaris Fingerprint Database Command Line Tool

Sun provides a command line tool to help you access the SFD on your system. The `sfpC.pl` tool can be downloaded from the `http://opensolaris.org/os/project/forensics/Tools/sfpdb-tools/` Web page.

With this tool, you can integrate file checks into scripts that you write. You can also use the tool on the command line like the one below to determine if all `setuid` programs are found in the Fingerprint Database:

```
$ find /usr/sbin -perm -4000 | xargs digest -v -a md5 | ./sfpC.pl | grep '0 match'
b68df0fefe594d5d86462db16d6ffff5 -  - 0 match(es)
```

The command reports one `setuid` file that does match a file in the SFD. To locate the file, examine the full report.

4.3.3 Basic Audit Reporting Tool (BART)

BART is a tool that collects file and directory attributes into a manifest, and then lets you compare the manifest to a manifest that you previously created. This comparison can detect attribute changes to files, such as permission changes, file content changes, new files being added, and so on.

While BART is clearly useful for security incident detection, it is also handy for your change management process because the tool enables you to validate approved changes and detect changes that might have occurred outside of your approved process.

The `bart` command is used to track changes in the following file and directory attributes:

- `acl`—ACL(s) for the file
- `contents`—checksum value of the file
- `dest`—destination of symbolic link
- `devnode`—value of a device node (character device files and block device files only)

- `dirmtime`—directory modification time
- `gid`—group id of file or directory
- `lnmtime`—creation time for link
- `mode`—file or directory permission
- `mtime`—file modification time
- `size`—file size
- `type`—type of file
- `uid`—user id of file or directory

4.3.3.1 Creating a BART Rules File

The first step in using BART is to create your rules file. A rules file defines which files and directories are to be validated and which attributes are to be checked or ignored. Two directives, CHECK and IGNORE, along with a subdirectory directive, accomplish these aims.

A rules file starts with a global block whose directives apply to all subsequent blocks. The global block is followed by zero or more local blocks that can override the previous CHECK and IGNORE directives. The order of the CHECK and IGNORE directives is important because the directives are processed according to their order in the file. The following is a sample rules file:

```
# global rules
CHECK all

# don't check the size or the contents
/etc passwd shadow
IGNORE contents size

# skip all core files
/export/home1 core
/export/home2 core
IGNORE all
```

4.3.3.2 Creating a BART Manifest

A manifest is the result of running the `bart` command. A manifest is a description of the contents of a managed host, and consists of a header and a number of entries, which represent the files and directories. You never deal directly with the contents of the manifest. Instead, the `bart` command creates and compares manifests for you.

When your rules file is ready, you create your initial control manifest by using the `bart create` command:

```
$ bart create -r /path/to/rules > control.manifest
```

> **Note**
>
> You must protect the control manifest. Do not store it on the system that it describes. An attacker who manages to gain extra privileges and then modifies files on your system can then update the control manifest with the new data to mask the modifications.

One way around the problem of control manifest modification is to create a Message Authentication Code (MAC) for the manifest. The MAC lets you verify that the manifest has not been altered. To use a MAC, you need a secret key, which you use later when you want to verify that the manifest has not been tampered with.

```
$ mac -a sha256_hmac /path/to/control.manifest
Enter key:
b1389d57c99548bc2ebff9113784282e432197ee35bbfc81686db76f7e9bbd19
```

Note that it is still best practice to store a copy of the manifest on another system in case an attacker deletes the manifest and then you have no initial manifest for comparison.

The resulting MAC can be stored with the control manifest. To verify later that the manifest has not been altered, run the `mac` command again with the same secret key and confirm that the output is the same. An attacker who alters the manifest will not be able to produce the same MAC value because he does not know the secret key.

4.3.3.3 Comparing a Current Manifest to a Stored Manifest

After you create a control manifest, you can start comparing it to test manifests, that is, manifests that reflect the current state of the system.

First, create the test manifest with the same rules file that you used to create the control manifest:

```
$ bart create -r /path/to/rules > test.manifest
```

Then, run the `bart compare` command to compare the two manifests:

```
$ bart compare control.manifest test.manifest
/usr/bin/su:
  mtime  control:4873fc20  test:4873fc59
  contents  control:3371371f52471ea05bc841d71bcc6fcb
test:eb11034e9183ce07cc3800401b6d6ee9
/usr/bin/bd:
  add
```

The result is a list of files and directories which have changed between the two manifests. In this case, the su file has been modified and the bd file has been added.

> **Tip**
>
> Remember to create a new control manifest when you have patched, added new software, or otherwise changed the system. The new control manifest provides a valid snapshot of the system for future comparison.

4.3.4 Integrating BART and the Solaris Fingerprint Database

Both BART and the Solaris fingerprint database (SFD) use MD5 checksums on files. Therefore, you can use the checksums to verify that the objects in a BART manifest are genuine Sun files.

In the following example, you extract the MD5 information from the manifest, then use the SFD command line tool, sfpC.pl, to check that the BART files are matched in the SFD.

```
$ awk '$1 ~ /^\// && $2 == "F" { printf "MD5 (%s) = %s\n", $1, $NF; }' /path/to/
control.manifest | sfpC.pl | grep '0 match'
0dad1b8dbf58a779088ef3463c8f55ed - (/usr/bin/bd) - 0 match(es)
```

In addition to BART results, this test informs you that the bd file did not originate from Sun.

4.3.5 Signed ELF Objects

Starting with the Solaris 10 release, Executable and Linking Format (ELF) binary objects (commands, libraries, kernel modules, and so on) are cryptographically signed. Digital signatures, among other benefits, eliminate the need to be online to validate system files.

Signed ELF objects speed up system file comparison to files in the SFD, because all the information needed to validate a file is available on the system. The signature is in the ELF object and the certificate is in the /etc/certs directory.

The elfsign sign command is used to sign ELF objects and the elfsign verify command is used to verify the digital signature. Note that a signature does not include the path to the file, so elfsign might validate a renamed file. Renamed files provide an opportunity for downgrade attacks. Because elfsign only validates the contents of a file, it does not detect either of these conditions.

- The file now has a different name.
- A newer version of the file is available.

To work around this limitation, it is important to keep track of `setuid` and `setgid` files to detect any new files.

4.3.5.1 Verifying Solaris ELF Objects

When you verify the signature of an ELF object, there are three possible outcomes.

- The signature is correct:

```
$ elfsign verify /path/to/file
elfsign: verification of /path/to/file passed
```

- The signature does not match the contents of the ELF object, which is an indication that the file has been tampered with:

```
$ elfsign verify /path/to/file
elfsign: verification of /path/to/file failed
```

- The ELF object did not contain a signature, which indicates that this is not a Sun provided file:

```
$ elfsign verify /path/to/file
elfsign: no signature found in /path/to/file
```

4.4 UFS and NFSv4 Mount Options

In the Solaris OS, you mount local files over UFS and remote files over NFS. The most recent version of NFS is NFSv4. The Solaris OS provides four options that affect the security of a mounted file system.

- `nosuid`—Disallows `setuid` and `setgid` execution.
- `noexec`—Disallows execution of programs in the file system. Also disallows `mmap(2)` with `PROT_EXEC` of files within the file system.
- `nodevices`—Disallows opening of device special files.
- `noxattr`—Disallows the creation and manipulation of extended attributes.

The `nosuid` and `nodevices` options are especially important because these options prevent a privileged user on the NFS file server from gaining additional privileges on your system.

You can specify mount options on the command line when you mount a file system:

```
$ mount -o noxattr /dev/dsk/c0t0d0s5 /data
```

You can also specify mount options permanently in the `/etc/vfstab` file. You create an entry for the file system that you are mounting, and use the mount options field to set the options. The following line is an entry in the `vfstab` file for a UFS file system:

```
/dev/dsk/c0t0d0s5 /dev/rdsk/c0t0d0s5 /data ufs 1 yes noxattr
```

4.5 ZFS Mount Options

ZFS provides the same mount options as NFS and UFS, but the syntax is different. In ZFS, you set a property on the ZFS file system. The properties are named:

- devices
- exec
- setuid
- xattr

For example, to disallow the use of extended attributes on the `z1/db` file system, you run the following command. Because the property is on the file system, the setting persists across reboots.

```
$ zfs set xattr=off z0/db
```

To list the ZFS file systems that have the property set, you can run the `zfs get` *property* command:

```
$ zfs get xattr
NAME                            PROPERTY   VALUE              SOURCE
z0                              xattr      on                 default
z0/app                          xattr      on                 default
z0/db                           xattr      off                local
```

4.6 ZFS Delegated Administration

As of Solaris 10 update 6, it is possible to delegate ZFS administrative tasks to ordinary users.

Two styles of permissions are supported. The individual permission(s) can be explicitly specified, or the administrator can define a permission set. A permission set can then later be updated and all of the consumers of the set will automatically pick up the change.

Permission sets all begin with the symbol @ and are limited to 64 characters in length. Characters after the @ sign in a set name have the same restrictions as normal ZFS file system names. Table 4.7 shows the possible values for delegated permissions.

Table 4.7 Possible Values for Delegated Permissions

Value	Description
create	Create descendent datasets. (Must also have mount permission)
destroy	Destroy datasets.
snapshot	Take snapshots.
rollback	Rollback dataset.
clone	Create clone of any of the dataset's snapshots (must also have create permission in clone's parent)
promote	Promote dataset (must also have promote permission in origin file system)
rename	Rename a dataset (must also have create and mount permission in new parent).
mount	Mount and unmount dataset
share	Share and unshare dataset
send	Send any of the dataset's snapshots.
receive	Create a descendent with ZFS receive (must also have create permission).
allow	Allows users to grant permissions they have to another user.
userprop	Allow user properties to be modified.

You can also delegate setting the following ZFS properties: `aclinherit`, `aclmode`, `atime`, `canmount`, `checksum`, `compression`, `copies`, `devices`, `exec`, `mountpoint`, `quota`, `readonly`, `recordsize`, `reservation`, `setuid`, `shareiscsi`, `sharenfs`, `snapdir`, `volsize`, and `xattr`.

If you want to let users take snapshots and rollback changes on their home directories (provided the home directories are ZFS file systems), you can delegate that to them by first creating a permission set like this:

```
# zfs allow -s @snapper snapshot,mount,rollback,snapdir z0
# zfs allow martin @snapper z0/home/martin
# zfs allow z0/home/martin
-----------------------------------------------------------------
Local+Descendent permissions on (z0/home/martin)
      user martin @snapper
-----------------------------------------------------------------
Permission sets on (z0)
      @snapper mount,rollback,snapdir,snapshot
-----------------------------------------------------------------
```

The user can now take snapshots of the file system:

```
$ zfs snapshot z0/home/martin@20081204
$ zfs list | grep z0/home/martin
z0/home/martin              152M    4.2T 120.5M  /home/martin
z0/home/martin@20081201 18.5K       -    25M  -
z0/home/martin@20081202 1.04M       -    93.1M  -
z0/home/martin@20081203 3.80M       -    94.8M  -
z0/home/martin@20081204  348K       -    110M  -
```

With the rollback permission, the user can roll back the state of the file system to a previously taken snapshot:

```
$ ls -a
.               .bash_history  .bashrc         .ssh
..              .bash_profile  .hgrc
$ zfs rollback z0/home/martin@20081202
$ ls -a
.               .bash_history  .bashrc         .ssh
..              .bash_profile  .hgrc           src
```

Instead of doing a rollback, it is possible to recover deleted and modified files using the ZFS `snapdir` property to make the snapshot directories visible. If the `.bashrc` file accidentally was overwritten, an old copy can be recovered like this:

```
$ zfs set snapdir=visible
$ ls -a
.               .bash_history  .bashrc         .ssh        src
..              .bash_profile  .hgrc           .zfs
$ cp .zfs/snapshot/20081203/.bashrc .
```

If you quickly want to disable all delegations in a zpool, you can turn it off with the following:

```
# zpool set delegation=off z0
```

Privileges and Role-Based Access Control

Traditionally, UNIX has two levels of security: ordinary users and administrators. Administrators are all-powerful and ordinary users are not. In Solaris 10, the Solaris OS has done away with this division of power and now implements a much finer-grained scheme called "privileges," which can be used to delegate small pieces of "superuser power" to ordinary processes and users.

Since Version 8, the Solaris OS has also implemented an administrative model that allows for finer-grained control than the traditional UNIX root model: "roles." Solaris roles can be used to define a specific set of tasks ("profiles") for a specific type of administrator. Using profiles, you can define "Network Administrators" or "Tape Library Administrators" and assign those profiles to roles. These roles can subsequently be assumed by administrators to perform a role-specific task. There are large benefits from using this model, as we will describe in this chapter.

5.1 Traditional UNIX Security Model

Since the inception of UNIX in the late sixties, UNIX systems have relied on the concept of an all-powerful administrative account called root. All the other accounts are pretty much powerless. System accounts such as daemon, uucp, bin, and sys, do not have any powers beyond those of normal user accounts. The root account or, more precisely, the account with user ID zero[1] is the only account with extra privileges—make that "all privileges."

Only the root account is able to override file permissions, mount file systems, add users, reset passwords, read raw data from the network, access raw disks, or allow processes to provide services on privileged ports (network ports below 1024). The root account also owns most, if not all, of the system configuration files.

In the heart of the operating system, the kernel, all privileged operations are protected by checks to verify that the process trying to perform that particular privileged operation has a UID of zero. Only processes operating with UID 0 can perform those privileged operations; to processes operating with a non-zero UID, the operation will be denied and fail with an error code like EPERM or EACCES.[2]

In order to allow non-root users to perform certain well-defined privileged operations, the setuid bit was introduced in the file system; if an executable file has the setuid bit set, the kernel will run the program with the UID set to the owner of the executable file. With this trick, normal users can, for example, run the ping(1M) command, which needs extra privileges to send out special packets on the network. ping(1M) is installed with the following file permissions:

```
$ ls -l /usr/sbin/ping
-r-sr-xr-x   1   root      bin      60092 Nov  4 17:19 /usr/sbin/ping

$ ls -ln /usr/sbin/ping
-r-sr-xr-x   1   0         2        60092 Nov  4 17:19 /usr/sbin/ping
```

Since the setuid bit is set on this executable (the letter normally indicating that the file is executable by the owner has changed from 'x' to 's'), the kernel runs this program with the UID set to 0, the owner of the ping file. Because of this user-ID switching, the program will be allowed to send its special type of packets on the network.

This, in brief, is the administrative model that has been commonplace in UNIX systems for over three decades; there is one administrative, all-powerful user, the one with UID zero. If normal users need some or all of that power, they need to switch user (su(1M)) to the root account or rely on setuid bits in the file system. For this discussion, this illustration provides enough information. If you want more detail about the traditional UNIX security model, see Section 5.1.2, "Real and Effective IDs in the Traditional UNIX Model," later in this chapter.

5.1.1 Shortcomings of the Traditional UNIX Security Model

The model described above is beautiful in its elegance and simplicity. However, this model is not good enough in today's complex world, where systems are managed by large groups of possibly contracted-in administrators with a wide variety of experience amongst them. Organizations want a better match between the function performed by an employee and the powers of that employee. No one likes to worry that a junior help-desk employee might type the wrong command as superuser, or might browse through the company's confidential materials.

Another shortcoming of the all-or-nothing approach that the traditional UNIX model uses is that many system programs ("daemons") run with superuser powers. Oftentimes, a daemon needs some additional privilege during startup or during certain periods of its lifecycle. A daemon almost never needs all the superuser powers all the time, but the traditional model grants the daemon those powers. As a result, programming errors in daemons lead to system compromises because the privileges granted to the daemon (UID 0) are used to gain control of the system.

Finally, the traditional model does not allow for much accountability or attributability. If administrators log in to the system as root, how does one tell which administrator was responsible for which action? Even when administrators log in as themselves and then su(1M) to root, there is little evidence as to who did what.

These shortcomings are overcome in the Solaris OS with improvements in the Solaris security model that were introduced over several releases. This chapter first describes how Solaris tackles the all-or-nothing privilege model with Solaris fine-grained privileges. Section 5.3, "Solaris Role-Based Access Control," describes the Solaris role-based access control (RBAC) model of subdividing administrative tasks into profiles and roles. Finally, Section 5.4, "Privileges for System Services," describes how to configure system services by using the principle of least privilege.

5.1.2 Real and Effective IDs in the Traditional UNIX Model

For each process, the UNIX kernel keeps track of three user IDs: the "real" user ID, the "effective" user ID, and the "saved" user ID. The real and effective IDs are used in policy decisions. The saved ID is used for transitioning between IDs.

Upon login to the system, the login process uses the UID listed in the password database to set the user's login shell with a real and effective UID. Policy checks by the kernel, for example when the user's process requests to open a file, use the process's effective ID to verify that access is allowed.

The only way for a user to gain additional privileges is to execute a setuid binary. The new process has its effective UID set to the owner of the setuid file, in most cases root (UID 0), but other examples exist, like uucp.

With the effective UID set to another user, the process still runs with the real UID set to the original UID of the logged-in user. Permission checks inside the kernel use the effective ID, allowing actions that would not have been allowed to the process's real UID.

Setuid processes often need the extra privileges for just a short while; for example, to read a configuration file on startup or to obtain access to a resource. Once the information is read or the resource obtained, the extra privileges are not needed anymore and can be dropped. In traditional UNIX systems, such a process would call the setreuid(2) system call to set its effective UID back to its real UID.

In some cases, setuid processes need to be able to switch between being privileged and not being privileged. For example, a print spooler process runs all the time, but only needs privileges to create a spool file from time to time. Such processes usually start with the effective UID set to a privileged ID (in most cases UID 0), but set the effective ID to their real ID. When a privileged operation is to occur, the process regains the extra privilege by setting its effective UID back to the privileged UID. The process can do so because the saved UID is still set to the privileged UID; a user process can set its effective UID to either the real UID or the saved UID. For example, consider `xscreensaver`, the Solaris X11 screensaver. This process runs with the user's privileges most of the time, but requires extra privileges to read the password file when it needs to verify an entered password.

With the `pcred(1)` command, you can observe the different UIDs for Solaris processes:

```
# pcred `pgrep xscreensaver`
3514: euid=113369 ruid=113369 suid=0 e/r/sgid=10
```

Notice the value of `suid`, the saved UID. The `xscreensaver` process sets its effective UID to this saved UID to read the password file.

Another thing shown by the above example is that UNIX not only keeps three user IDs for each process, but it also keeps three *group* IDs per process. Just like the user IDs, the group IDs for each login process are set from the values found in the password database. These values are augmented with values found in the group database (`/etc/group` for the local database). Each process can have one primary group and up to 32 supplementary groups. For compatibility reasons, 16 supplementary groups is a common maximum. The effective group ID can be set to any of the groups that the process belongs to. Just as with user IDs, the saved group ID can be used to switch back and forth between privileged and non-privileged IDs.

5.2 Solaris Fine-Grained Privileges

To improve the all-or-nothing UNIX security model, the Solaris OS introduced the concept of fine-grained privileges. Starting with Solaris 10, the kernel no longer validates privileged operations by verifying that the user performing the operation has a UID of zero. Instead, each privileged operation is validated by verifying that the user performing the operation has been assigned the specific privilege to perform the operation.

All the operations that were previously guarded by checks for UID zero have been investigated and categorized. This resulted in a breakdown of superuser powers into a large number of operation-specific privileges—68 in Solaris 10 5/08. These privileges are used to guard the privileged operations. As you can see in Table 5.1, the privileges have names that are constructed from two parts: the type of object that is to be accessed (file, net, proc, and so on) and the type of operation that is guarded by the privilege (read, write, exec, rawaccess, etc.).

Table 5.1 Solaris 10 5/08 Privileges

contract_event	contract_observer	
cpc_cpu		
dtrace_kernel	dtrace_proc	dtrace_user
file_chown	file_chown_self	file_dac_execute
file_dac_read	file_dac_search	file_dac_write
file_downgrade_sl	file_link_any	file_owner
file_setid	file_upgrade_sl	
graphics_access	graphics_map	
ipc_dac_read	ipc_dac_write	ipc_owner
net_bindmlp	net_icmpaccess	net_mac_aware
net_privaddr	net_rawaccess	
proc_audit	proc_chroot	proc_clock_highres
proc_exec	proc_fork	proc_info
proc_lock_memory	proc_owner	proc_priocntl
proc_session	proc_setid	proc_taskid
proc_zone		
sys_acct	sys_admin	sys_audit
sys_config	sys_devices	sys_ipc_config
sys_ip_config	sys_linkdir	sys_mount
sys_net_config	sys_nfs	sys_res_config
sys_resource	sys_suser_compat	sys_time
sys_trans_label		
win_colormap	win_config	win_dac_read
win_dac_write	win_devices	win_dga
win_downgrade_sl	win_fontpath	win_mac_read

The names indicate how these privileges work. For example, a process that is granted the net_rawaccess privilege is allowed raw access to the network. Similarly, a process that holds the proc_exec privilege is allowed to execute other programs by calling the exec(2) family of system calls. A detailed description of

each privilege that is implemented in your Solaris release is given in the
privileges(5) man page and by running the command ppriv -l -v.

From the list in Table 5.1, you can also see that a number of formerly unrestricted operations are now privileged operations. For example, fork(2) and exec(2)
have never been restricted to the root user. In Solaris 10, these operations are still
allowed to all users by default, but they *can* be taken away by an administrator.

The historically unrestricted privileges are grouped together in what is
called the *basic set*. This set contains these five privileges: file_link_any,
proc_exec, proc_fork, proc_info, proc_session. By default, ordinary
users are assigned this basic set.[3] From the user's perspective, the introduction of
privileges is completely transparent; everything that used to work in the traditional UNIX security model still works.

To see which privileges a process has, you can use the ppriv(1) command:

```
$ ppriv 28394
28394:  -sh
flags = <none>
        E: basic
        I: basic
        P: basic
        L: all
```

For compatibility reasons, the user with UID zero is granted all privileges by
default. Therefore, similar to normal users, for root the transition is mostly transparent as well.

So if everything works as before, you might wonder, why go through all this
trouble of introducing these privileges? The answer is that this compatibility feature is an *option*. Even though this option is enabled by default, you can specify
the privileges that normal users get when they log in or change the privileges that
daemons run with. By restricting the privileges that you assign to users or daemons, you can harden the system by removing attack vectors that are not needed
by the users or daemons anyway.

As an example of restricting privileges, note the privileges that have been
assigned to the NFS daemon:

```
# pcred `pgrep nfsd`
871:    e/r/suid=1  e/r/sgid=12
# ppriv `pgrep nfsd`
871:    /usr/lib/nfs/nfsd
flags = PRIV_AWARE
        E: net_bindmlp,sys_nfs
        I: none
        P: net_bindmlp,sys_nfs
        L: none
```

The precise semantics of all these different privilege sets (E, I, P, L) is explained in the next section. For now, note that the NFS daemon runs with UID 1 (daemon), GID 12 (also daemon), and it runs with only the sys_nfs privilege.[4] The daemon is not allowed to create new processes using fork(), and it is not allowed to execute other programs using exec(). Breaking into this system by using the powers that are assigned to the NFS daemon has become much more difficult.

Many of the Solaris system services have been rewritten as daemons that have all unneeded privileges removed, making the system safer to deploy.

5.2.1 Solaris Privilege Sets

As shown in the previous examples, the Solaris OS uses privilege sets. Privilege sets can be empty, or they can contain a number of privileges. An example of a privilege set is the *basic set*, containing the privileges file_link_any, proc_exec, proc_fork, proc_info, and proc_session. Other examples are the *empty set*, containing no privileges at all, and the *full set*, containing all privileges.

For each process running on a Solaris 10 system, the kernel maintains a record of the process's credentials. Apart from the traditional user and group IDs, this record also contains four privilege sets called the *Effective set (E)*, the *Permitted set (P)*, the *Inheritable set (I)*, and the *Limit set (L)*.

The privileges in the effective set are the privileges that the process is allowed to exercise, analogous to the effective UID in the traditional model. The privileges in the permitted set are the privileges that the process is allowed to put in effect. The permitted set is thus the maximum set of privileges for the process. The combination of the effective and permitted set enables *privilege bracketing*, which is discussed in the next section.

The inheritable set contains all the privileges that can be carried over to a child process. The limit set contains an upper set of the privileges a process and its offspring is ever allowed to obtain. The limit set can never grow.

For unprivileged processes, the E, P, and I sets are typically equal to the basic set of privileges. The L set is typically the full set of privileges.

When a process executes another program, the new process gets the following privilege sets:

$$E' = P' = I' = L \cap I$$
$$L' = L$$

In other words, the new effective, permitted, and inheritable sets (E', P' and I') are initialized to the intersection of the old process's limit and inheritable set. The new limit set (L') is unchanged from the old limit set.

Processes can remove privileges from all four sets. Privileges removed from the permitted set cannot be restored by the process. Privileges removed from the inheritable set cannot be carried over to the process child processes. Privileges removed from the process's limit set can never be obtained by any of the process's children nor the process itself. For example, consider setting a shell's limit set to the basic set:

```
$ ppriv -s L=basic $$
$ ppriv $$
8105:  bash
flags = <none>
 E: basic
 I: basic
 P: basic
 L: basic
$ ping 127.0.0.1
ping: socket Permission denied
```

Even though the ping(1M) program is setuid root, the process is not able to acquire the new privileges it would normally get assigned since the limit set restricts the process and all of its offspring to an upper limit of the privileges in the basic set.

5.2.2 Privilege Bracketing

For privileged programs (daemons or setuid programs), it is important to limit the amount of code that runs with elevated privileges. The smaller the section that runs with extra privileges, the smaller the attack surface. In general, limiting the privileged code happens in one of two ways.

- The process performs its privileged operation at startup (for example, opening configuration files or opening a reserved network port) and then drops the extra privileges permanently.
- The process lowers its effective privilege for most of the time, enabling the extra privileges only when privileged operations are to occur.

In the traditional UNIX model, the first scenario is implemented by resetting the real and effective UID. The second scenario is implemented by switching the effective UID between UID zero and an unprivileged UID (daemon, or the user starting the program).

Using Solaris privileges, programs can either remove privileges from their permitted and effective set (removing privileges from the permitted set also removes them from the effective set) to implement the first scenario. The second scenario is implemented by removing privileges from the effective set. The privileges are added back for the privileged pieces of code.

Using this technique, programmers can *bracket* the privileged operations.

5.2.3 Preventing Privilege Escalation

The Solaris OS introduces several mechanisms to prevent a process from obtaining more privileges than it is explicitly assigned. First of all, the process's limit set can never grow. The other sets (E, P, I) can never grow beyond the limit set.

The next feature is that a process cannot control processes that have more privileges. Control includes sending signals to, reading memory from, or attaching to another process. A process cannot influence a process that is more privileged.

The final feature is that to change objects owned by UID zero, a process must have all privileges assigned. All privileges are required because many critical system files are owned by UID zero, as are raw disc images and kernel memory. Without this requirement, a process could gain privileges by editing one of the system files or by manipulating /dev/kmem directly.

The rule of thumb for preventing privilege escalation is: "an operation needs at least as many privileges to be performed as can be gained by executing it." This translates directly to rules like "you need all privileges in order to be able to edit /dev/kmem."

5.2.4 Restricting Process Privileges

Normal user processes run with E, P and I set to the basic set, and L to *all*, the set containing all privileges. These processes can fork off children, execute other processes, observe other processes (using the ps(1m) command, for example) and create hard links to files owned by other UIDs. Normal users can also gain privileges by executing setuid programs because the limit set *(all)* does not restrict the privileges that a user can obtain.

What privileges are assigned to normal user processes is controlled by two variables in /etc/security/policy.conf: PRIV_DEFAULT and PRIV_LIMIT. See the policy.conf(4) man page for more information on these variables.

Preceding examples showed how to view a process's privilege sets with the ppriv(1) command. The following example shows how this command can be used to manipulate process privilege sets:

```
$ ppriv $$
29549:  sh
flags = <none>
        E: basic
        I: basic
        P: basic
        L: all
$ ppriv -s I-proc_info $$
$ ppriv $$
29549:  sh
flags = <none>
        E: basic
        I: basic,!proc_info
        P: basic
        L: all
$ truss -p $$
truss: permission denied: 29549
```

By manipulating the inheritable set of the shell, the shell's subprocess is not allowed to control the parent shell anymore; the subprocess (truss) has fewer privileges in its permitted set than the parent process has, because the proc_info privilege has been removed from the permitted set of the truss process.

Section 5.3, "Solaris Role-Based Access Control," examines ways to assign privileges to users, roles, and profiles. Section 5.4, "Privileges for System Services," shows how to limit the privileges with which system daemons are started.

5.2.5 Solaris Privileges Implementation Details

Programmers who want to create applications that are privilege-aware by manipulating the privilege sets of the application are strongly encouraged to study the implementation details that are covered in the relevant online manual pages, such as privileges(5), and in the chapter on "Developing Privileged Applications" in the *Solaris Security for Developers Guide*.

5.3 Solaris Role-Based Access Control

Today, Solaris servers are often maintained by a small army of system administrators. Some of them might be junior administrators, some more senior. Some administrators are employed by the owner of the system. Quite often, the administrators are contracted employees. This situation is quite different from "the old days," when a UNIX administrator was an experienced UNIX guru (in the case of a male employee, often bearded and wearing sandals) who knew every nook and cranny of the system. In those days, accountability was not as important as it is today.

In today's systems, it is important to have different levels of access for different types of administration, and record who performed what action. For this reason, the old UNIX model of an all-powerful root user no longer suffices.

The solution for this deficiency in the Solaris OS is to use *roles* for specific administrative tasks. *Rights profiles* are created and assigned to roles to specify which tasks a role can perform. Roles and profiles are examined in the following sections.

5.3.1 Solaris Roles

A role, in principle, is a normal user account with one extra restriction: a role cannot log in to the system. A role can only be assumed by a user who is already logged in to the system. That is, you can only su(1M) to a role. To perform an administrative task, an ordinary user logs into the system, switches to a role that can perform the task, and only then performs that task. Because of this login restriction, auditors can always deduce which physical user performed an administrative task. This accountability is much better than "someone named root logged in from 10.16.117.1 and removed the directory containing the customer billing records."

Roles can be shared amongst users. Therefore, you no longer need to share the root password with someone who does printer management. Instead, you share the password for the role that has been created to perform printer management.

Roles can be created and managed by using either the command line tools roleadd(1M) and rolemod(1M) or using the graphical management tool, Solaris Management Console. To enable users to assume a role, their accounts must be modified to reflect this permission. Unauthorized users cannot assume a role, not even if they know the role's password.

In the following example, superuser creates a printer administration role "prtadm" and assigns the right to assume this role to user "bob":

```
# roleadd -c "Printer Administration" prtadm
# passwd prtadm
New Password:
Re-enter new Password:
passwd: password successfully changed for prtadm
# usermod -R prtadm bob
```

Next, user "bob" supplies the role password and assumes the role "prtadm":

```
$ id -a
uid=102(bob) gid=1(other) groups=1(other)
$ su prtadm
Password:
$ id -a
uid=232939(prtadm) gid=1(other) groups=1(other)
```

Until now, the role prtadm has not been assigned any rights profiles, so the role has no administrative capabilities. In the next section, superuser assigns this role's extra capabilities by using a rights profile.

5.3.2 Solaris Rights Profiles

To assign privileges to a role, the Solaris OS defines *rights profiles* that specify what privileged actions a role is allowed to perform. Two types of privilege attributes can be assigned by using rights profiles.

- *Execution Attributes*: A set of specific executables that run with extra privileges. An executable can be any binary or shell script on the system. The extra privileges can be specified by using either the real or effective user ID, the real or effective group ID, or a collection of privileges. Examples of execution attribute specifications are:

```
Printer Management:suser:cmd:::/usr/lib/lp/local/lpadmin:uid=lp;gid=lp
Network Management:solaris:cmd:::/sbin/route:privs=sys_ip_config
Process Management:solaris:cmd:::/usr/bin/kill:privs=proc_owner
```

These lines define that a role that has the "Printer Management" profile assigned to it can execute the /usr/lib/lp/local/lpadmin command with the real UID and real GID set to "lp". Roles that have the "Network Management" profile assigned can execute /sbin/route with the extra privilege sys_ip_config added to the process's credentials. Similarly, roles that have the "Process Management" profile assigned can kill other users' processes[5] because they can run the /usr/bin/kill command with the proc_owner privilege added to the credentials.

Execution attributes are defined in the exec_attr(4) database. This database can be defined on the local system in the /etc/security/exec_attr file or in a network repository like NIS. The exact syntax for defining these execution attributes are described in the man page for the execution attribute database, exec_attr(4).

At present, it is not possible to specify command options in the exec_attr(4) database. To control the options allowed by a particular profile, you create a wrapper script that performs the necessary option handling.

- *Authorizations*: Special privileges, checked and enforced by privileged programs, allow an even finer-grained model of privilege assignment than Solaris privileges do. Authorizations are represented by fully qualified names like the Java class names. Examples of authorizations include:

  - solaris.admin.usermgr.manage or
    solaris.admin.usermgr.audit

  - solaris.admin.printer.read or
    solaris.admin.printer.modify

  - solaris.device.mount.removable or
    solaris.device.mount.fixed

As the names imply, authorizations describe types of operations on classes of objects. When these authorizations are granted to a role, that role is allowed to perform the associated operations.

Authorizations are specified much like execution attributes are specified. For each profile, you specify a list of authorizations that are granted to the role that has the profile assigned. The following example shows the authorizations that are assigned to the Printer Management profile:

```
Printer Management:::Manage printers, daemons, spooling:
    auths=solaris.print.*,solaris.label.print,
    solaris.admin.printer.read,solaris.admin.printer.modify,
    solaris.admin.printer.delete;help=RtPrntAdmin.html
```

Authorizations are defined in the auth_attr(4) database, which can be on the local system in the /etc/security/auth_attr file, or in a network repository like NIS.

Authorizations and execution attributes together make up the Solaris rights profiles. The rights profile database, prof_attr(4), describes the profiles. The complete definition of the profile combines the prof_attr(4) database with the exec_attr(4) database.

Consider the definition of the Printer Management profile. The `prof_attr(4)` database defines the profile as:

```
Printer Management:::Manage printers, daemons, spooling:
    auths=solaris.print.*,solaris.label.print,
    solaris.admin.printer.read,solaris.admin.printer.modify,
    solaris.admin.printer.delete;help=RtPrntAdmin.html
```

The authorizations that are assigned to the Printer Management profile are listed in the `auth_attr(4)` database. The `solaris.print.*` notation expands to the following authorizations:

```
solaris.print.admin:::Administer Printer::help=PrintAdmin.html
solaris.print.cancel:::Cancel Print Job::help=PrintCancel.html
solaris.print.list:::List Jobs in Printer Queue::help=PrintList.html
solaris.print.nobanner:::Print without Banner::help=PrintNoBanner.html
solaris.print.ps:::Print Postscript::help=PrintPs.html
solaris.print.unlabeled:::Print without Label::help=PrintUnlabeled.html
```

The rest of the authorizations in the Printer Management profile are fully qualified. Again, from the `auth_attr(4)` database:

```
solaris.label.print::
    :View Printer Queue at All Labels::help=LabelPrint.html
solaris.admin.printer.read::
    :View Printer Information::help=AuthPrinterRead.html
solaris.admin.printer.modify::
    :Update Printer Information::help=AuthPrinterModify.html
solaris.admin.printer.delete::
    :Delete Printer Information::help=AuthPrinterDelete.html
```

The commands in the Printer Management profile are specified in the `exec_attr(4)` database:

```
Printer Management:suser:cmd:::/usr/lib/lp/local/lpadmin:uid=lp;gid=lp
Printer Management:suser:cmd:::/usr/sbin/lpfilter:euid=lp;uid=lp
Printer Management:suser:cmd:::/usr/sbin/lpforms:euid=lp
Printer Management:suser:cmd:::/usr/sbin/lpusers:euid=lp
Printer Management:suser:cmd:::/usr/sbin/ppdmgr:euid=0
```

The combination of the `prof_attr(4)` database with the `exec_attr(4)` database provides the full definition of the Printer Management profile's privileges. The `profiles(1)` and `auths(1)` commands can be used to inspect what profiles or authorizations a role has been granted. For example, the `prtadm` role is defined as follows:

```
$ profiles prtadm
Printer Management
Basic Solaris User
All
$ profiles -l prtadm

    Printer Management:
        /usr/lib/lp/local/lpadmin      uid=lp, gid=lp
        /usr/sbin/lpfilter     euid=lp, uid=lp
        /usr/sbin/lpforms      euid=lp
        /usr/sbin/lpusers      euid=lp
        /usr/sbin/ppdmgr      euid=0
    All:
        *
$ auths prtadm
solaris.print.*,solaris.label.print,solaris.admin.printer.read,
solaris.admin.printer.modify,solaris.admin.printer.delete,
solaris.device.cdrw,solaris.profmgr.read,solaris.jobs.users,
solaris.mail.mailq,solaris.admin.usermgr.read,
solaris.admin.logsvc.read,solaris.admin.fsmgr.read,
solaris.admin.serialmgr.read,solaris.admin.diskmgr.read,
solaris.admin.procmgr.user,solaris.compsys.read,
solaris.admin.prodreg.read,solaris.admin.dcmgr.read,solaris.snmp.read,
solaris.project.read,
solaris.admin.patchmgr.read,

solaris.network.hosts.read,solaris.admin.volmgr.read
```

Note that the definition of a rights profile can include other rights profiles, thereby combining several profiles into a larger profile. Consider the definition of the "Operator" profile:

```
Operator:::Can perform simple administrative tasks:
    profiles=Printer Management,Media Backup,All;
help=RtOperator.html
```

With this definition, the security attributes of the Printer Management profile and the Media Backup profile are combined into the Operator profile.

5.3.3 Managing Solaris Rights Profiles with the Solaris Management Console

The preceding examples have shown several commands that manage the RBAC databases. The examples have shown what these databases look like in plain text. The Solaris Management Console provides a GUI to administer these profiles. For example, the description of the Printer Management profile is displayed in the GUI as shown in Figure 5.1.

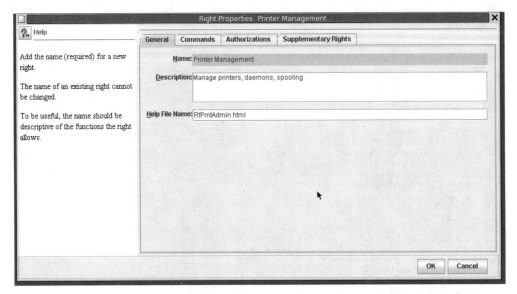

Figure 5.1 The Printer Management Profile

The commands in the Printer Management profile are displayed under the Commands tab (see Figure 5.2).

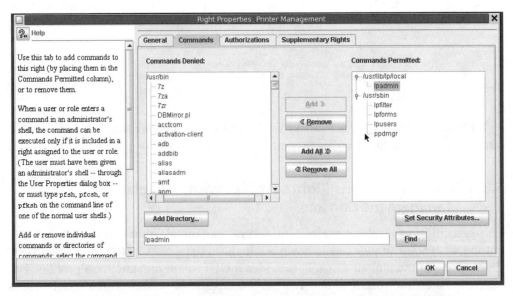

Figure 5.2 Commands Are Displayed Under the Commands Tab

The security attributes of the commands in the Printer Management profile are displayed after selecting the command and then the Security Attributes button (see Figure 5.3).

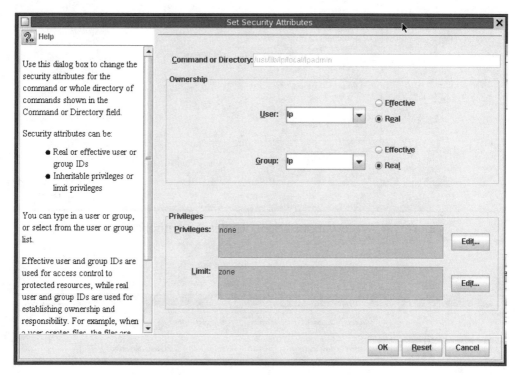

Figure 5.3 Security Attributes

The authorizations in the Printer Management profile are displayed under the Authorizations tab (see Figure 5.4).

The Printer Management profile does not include other rights profiles in its definition (see Figure 5.5).

The Solaris Management Console presents all the information about the defined profile in a GUI, and adds online help for the administrator.

5.3.4 Solaris Predefined Rights Profiles

The Solaris OS provides a number of default rights profiles. You can define your own profiles, possibly based on the Solaris profiles. Changing the Solaris default profiles is not recommended, because your changes might get overwritten by system patches or upgrades. To extend or change a Solaris supplied profile, copy the profile definition using a new profile name and edit the copy.

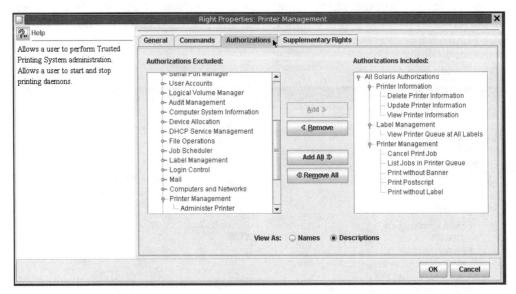

Figure 5.4 Authorizations Appear Under the Authorizations Tab

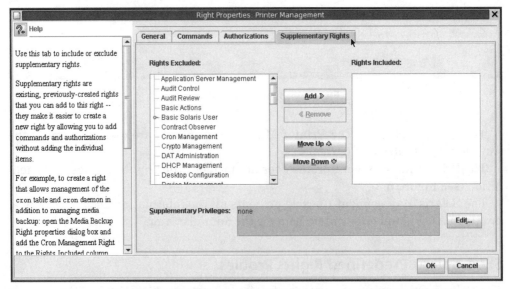

Figure 5.5 The Printer Management Profile Shows Only Printer Rights

The following Solaris profiles illustrate the possible scopes of profiles.

- **Primary Administrator**—This profile grants rights that are equivalent to the rights of the traditional root user.
- **System Administrator**—This less powerful profile is for administration that is not related to security. Roles with this profile can manage file systems, mail, and software installation. However, these roles cannot set passwords.
- **Operator**—This limited profile is for a junior administrator to perform operations such as backups and printer management.
- **Basic Solaris User**—This profile provides basic authorizations that are useful in normal operations. This profile is automatically assigned to all normal users through the PROFS_GRANTED variable in the `policy.conf`(4) database.
- **All**—This profile provides access to all commands that are not explicitly assigned to other profiles by specifying a wildcard to include all commands. Without the All profile or other profiles that use wildcards, a role can use explicitly assigned commands only. Such a limited set of commands is not very practical. The All rights profile, if used, must be the final rights profile that is assigned. This last position ensures that explicit security attribute assignments in other profiles are not overridden.

5.3.5 Assigning Rights Profiles to Roles

This section describes how to add the powers in a rights profile to a role. On the command line, the glue that holds them together is the `-P` option to the `roleadd`(1) and `rolemod`(1) commands. In the GUI, role creation prompts you for existing profiles to add to the role, and for existing users who can assume the role. The example continues with the prtadm role and the Printer Management profile.

The following command assigns the Printer Management profile to the `prtadm` role:

```
# rolemod -P "Printer Management" prtadm
```

To verify that the role has the correct profile, run the `profiles` command:

```
# profiles prtadm
Printer Management
Basic Solaris User
All
```

Note that the rolemod(1) command has added the profile to the top of the list. The other two profiles are assigned by default. The Basic Solaris User profile is defined in the policy.conf(4) file, and the All profile is included in the Basic Solaris User profile.

In fact, the rolemod(1) command has *replaced* the profile entry for the prtadm role, not added the entry. To *add* a profile, you must list the profiles for the role. For example, consider the effects of the following rolemod commands:

```
# rolemod -P "Media Backup" prtadm
# profiles prtadm
prtadm :
        Media Backup
        NDMP Management
        Basic Solaris User
        All
# rolemod -P "Printer Management,Media Backup" prtadm
# profiles prtadm
prtadm :
        Printer Management
        Media Backup
        NDMP Management
        Basic Solaris User
        All
```

The following examples show you how to use the Solaris Management Console to create the role prtadm with the Printer Management profile and assign the role to bob as part of one administrative action.

1. First, you create the role (see Figure 5.6).

2. You provide basic account information (see Figure 5.7).

3. You are prompted to add a rights profile to the role (see Figure 5.8).

4. And you provide a path to the role's home directory (see Figure 5.9).

5. You can assign an existing user to the role (see Figure 5.10).

6. Finally, you verify the account details of the role (see Figure 5.11).

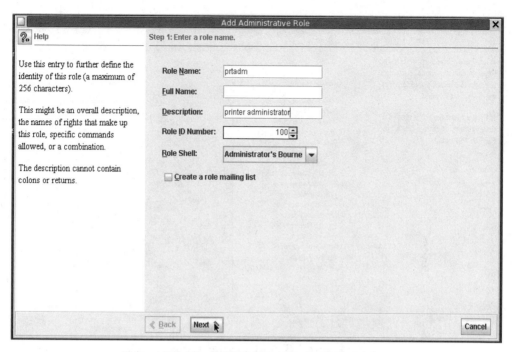

Figure 5.6 The Add Administrative Role Dialog

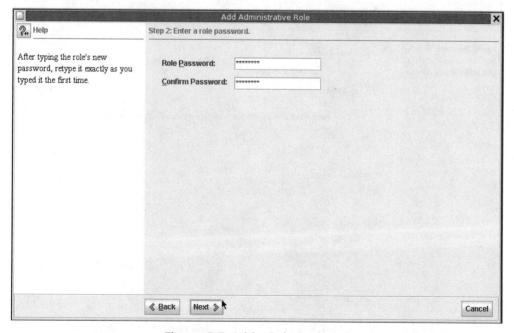

Figure 5.7 Add a Role Password

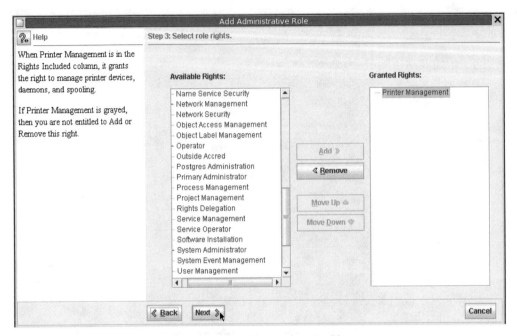

Figure 5.8 Add a Rights Profile

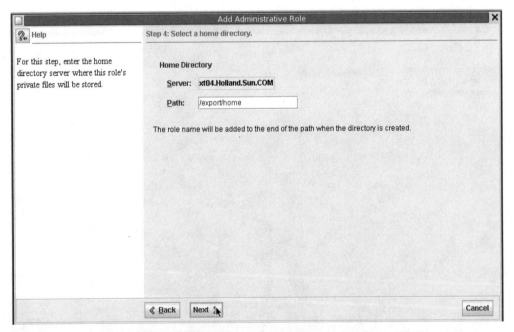

Figure 5.9 Provide a Path to The Role's Home Directory

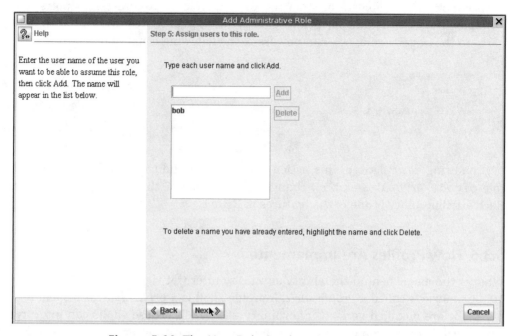

Figure 5.10 The User Bob Can be Assigned the Role

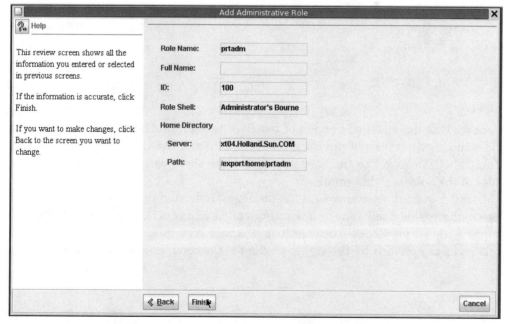

Figure 5.11 Verify the Account Details of the Role

User `bob` is now able to assume the `prtadm` role to administer printers. For example, to set the default for printing on printer LaserWriter to "print with banners," in the `prtadm` role, `bob` can now issue the following commands:

```
$ su prtadm
Password:
$ /usr/sbin/lpadmin -p LaserWriter -o banner
$
```

If auditing is configured, this action generates an audit record that states that role `prtadm`, original user `bob`, changed the options of the printer LaserWriter. Such attributability is one of the features of RBAC.

5.3.6 How Profiles Are Implemented

What is the magic behind the ability of roles to interpret rights profiles? In Solaris 10, this magic is called a *profile shell*. A profile shell is a privilege-aware shell. Profile shells are modified versions of ordinary user shells. These shells can interpret the Solaris rights profile databases and can execute programs with privileges. When you create a role such as the `prtadm` role, the `roleadd(1)` command creates the role with a profile shell:

```
$ finger prtadm
Login name: prtadm
Directory: /home/prtadm          Shell: /bin/pfsh
Never logged in.
No unread mail
No Plan.
```

`pfsh(1)` is the modified version of the Bourne shell (`sh(1)`). The Solaris OS provides modified versions of the Korn Shell (`pfksh`) and the C Shell (`pfcsh`) as well. These shells behave like the base versions of the shell, with the additional knowledge of the Solaris rights profiles.

In order to start programs with the privileges indicated in the rights profile databases, the profile shell relies on a utility called `pfexec(1)`. The `pfexec(1)` utility starts with all privileges (because it is a setuid root program) and initializes its privileges as specified by the rights profile for the command it needs to start. This can be shown by a truss(1) of the profile shell that is used by the prtadm role to execute the command /usr/sbin/lpusers -q 20 -u alice:

```
# truss -fatexec -p 2055
2055:   psargs: -pfsh
2059:   execve("/usr/bin/pfexec", 0x0003B410, 0x0003AA20)  argc = 6
2059:      *** SUID: ruid/euid/suid = 100 / 0 / 0  ***
2059:   argv: /usr/bin/pfexec /usr/sbin/lpusers -q 20 -u alice
2059:   execve("/usr/sbin/lpusers", 0xFFBFFE78, 0xFFBFFE90)  argc = 5
2059:      *** SUID: ruid/euid/suid = 100 / 71 / 71  ***
2059:   argv: /usr/sbin/lpusers -q 20 -u alice
```

The preceding truss output shows the profile shell pfsh (PID 2055) executing pfexec (PID 2059) with arguments "/usr/sbin/lpusers -q 20 -u alice", the command that was typed to the profile shell by the prtadm role (ruid 100). Next, pfexec executes /usr/sbin/lpusers with its effective UID set to 71 (lp) as specified by the execution attribute from the exec_attr(4) database:

Printer Management:suser:cmd:::/usr/sbin/lpusers:euid=lp

5.3.7 Rights Profiles and Normal Users

The preceding discussion outlines the way that RBAC is designed to be used. However, some organizations do not need to use all parts of the RBAC implementation. Some organizations skip creating roles, and instead assign rights profiles to normal users.

In the ongoing example, the prtadm role is assigned the Printer Management profile, and the role is then assigned to the user bob. The assignment of the profile is reflected in the user_attr(4) database:

```
...
prtadm::::type=role;profiles=Printer Management
bob::::type=normal;roles=prtadm
```

However, the implementation of rights profiles also permits you to assign rights profiles to normal users:

```
# usermod -P "Network Management" alice
# cat /etc/user_attr
...
prtadm::::type=role;profiles=Printer Management
bob::::type=normal;roles=prtadm
alice::::type=normal;profiles=Network Management
```

Here the `alice` account has been assigned the Network Management profile. She can execute the privileged commands that are defined by that profile. To interpret the security attributes in the rights profile applied, she must do one of the following:

- Be assigned a profile shell as her default shell
- Start a profile shell before she runs the network management commands
- Run each network command using the `pfexec` utility.

The following example shows her use of the `pfexec` utility:

```
alice$ /usr/sbin/ifconfig bge1 plumb
ifconfig: plumb: bge1: Permission denied
alice$ pfexec /usr/sbin/ifconfig bge1 plumb
alice$
```

The first invocation of `ifconfig` failed, because `alice`'s shell, a normal Bourne shell, did not apply the rights profile. By using the `pfexec(1)` utility, her rights profiles are applied.

5.3.8 Solaris RBAC Components Put Together

The illustration shown in Figure 5.12 puts the Solaris RBAC components together in five easy steps.

5.3.9 Using Solaris RBAC Locally

Table 5.2 lists the commands that are available for local Solaris RBAC administration. You can also use the Solaris Management Console.

Preceding examples showed how to create a role, add rights profiles to the role, and assign the role to a user. Another common use of RBAC is to change the root user to a role. This change prevents remote logins as root, and enables you to specify which users are allowed to assume the root role.

The following example creates a new user `carol`, changes the root user into a role, and assigns the right to assume the role to `carol`. You perform these steps as `root` or as an account that is assigned the Primary Administrator profile.

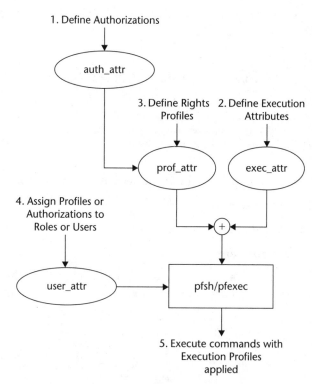

Figure 5.12 Solaris RBAC Components

Table 5.2 Solaris RBAC Commands for Local Databases

Command	Description
`auths(1)`	Lists authorizations for user.
`pfexec(1)`	Execute commands with privileges specified in the user's profile.
`profiles(1)`	Lists profiles assigned to user
`roles(1)`	Lists roles assigned to user
`roleadd(1M)`	Adds a role to the local system
`roledel(1M)`	Deletes a role from the local system
`rolemod(1M)`	Modifies properties of a role on the local system
`useradd(1M)`	Adds a user to the local system
`userdel(1M)`	Deletes a user to the local system
`usermod(1M)`	Modifies properties of a user on the local system

1. Create a local user named `carol`. See the `useradd(1)` man page for an explanation of the available options:

```
# useradd -g staff -s /usr/bin/pfksh -d /home/carol -m carol
64 blocks
# passwd -r files carol
New Password:
Re-enter new Password:
passwd: password successfully changed for carol
```

2. Change the root account from a normal user account to a role:

    # **usermod -K type=role root**

3. Assign the root role to carol:

    # **usermod -R root carol**

From this moment on, `carol` can assume the root role. Other users cannot, even if they know the root password. For example, `bob`'s attempt to assume the root role fails:

```
bob$ su root
Password:
Roles can only be assumed by authorized users
su: Sorry
```

5.3.10 Using Solaris RBAC on a Network

To maintain RBAC databases that are stored in a network repository such as NIS, or LDAP, you must use the Solaris Management Console.

5.4 Privileges for System Services

The Solaris Service Management Facility (SMF) uses authorizations and privileges extensively. With SMF, you can specify which user ID should be used to run a particular service. You can also specify exactly which privileges the process must run with. For example, the Domain Name Service (DNS) is started with an explicit set of privileges:

```
$ svcprop  /network/dns/server:default

...
general/enabled boolean false
general/value_authorization astring solaris.smf.manage.bind

start/user astring root
start/group astring root
start/supp_groups astring :default
start/privileges astring basic,!proc_session,!proc_info,
   !file_link_any,net_privaddr,file_dac_read,file_dac_search,
   sys_resource,proc_chroot
start/limit_privileges astring :default
start/use_profile boolean false

[...]
```

As the svcprop(1) output shows, the DNS server is not enabled by default and requires an authorization to run. The service starts with its UID set to the UID of the root user (start/user property) and its group ID set to the ID of the group named root (start/group property). No supplementary group IDs are specified for this service (start/supp_groups is set to :default).

Also, the DNS server starts with an explicit set of privileges. This set removes the privileges that the daemon does not need, and adds privileges that the daemon needs. For example, the service removes the basic privilege to examine the status of other processes (proc_info) while it adds a privilege to open a reserved network port (net_privaddr).

SMF can also apply a rights profile to a service. In that case, the property profile is set and use_profile is set to true. If use_profile is set, SMF ignores the user, group, privileges and limit_privileges properties.

See smf_method(5) for a detailed description of the properties that can be controlled with SMF.

5.4.1 Authorizations for System Services

The preceding DNS example showed that SMF can assign authorizations to daemons. Several Solaris applications use authorizations internally, like mailq(1M), cron(1), and cdrw(1). The SMF service itself also uses authorizations.

As shown in Table 5.3, five basic authorizations are defined for SMF.

By using rights profiles or by explicitly assigning authorizations to users or roles, you authorize certain roles or users to control the SMF services. Otherwise, only superusers can control the SMF services.

Table 5.3 SMF Service Authorizations

`solaris.smf.modify.method`	Authorized to change values or create, delete, or modify a property group of type method
`solaris.smf.modify.dependency`	Authorized to change values or create, delete, or modify property group of type dependency
`solaris.smf.modify.application`	Authorized to change values, read protected values, and create, delete, or modify a property group of type application
`solaris.smf.modify.framework`	Authorized to change values or create, delete, or modify a property group of type framework
`solaris.smf.modify`	Authorized to add, delete, or modify services, service instances, or their properties, and to read protected property values

Each SMF-managed service has additional authorizations defined. For example, the `svc:/network/smtp:sendmail` service contains the following authorizations:

```
# svcprop sendmail | grep authorization
config/value_authorization astring solaris.smf.value.sendmail
general/action_authorization astring solaris.smf.manage.sendmail
```

These two authorizations specify that

- A user or role that has been granted the `solaris.smf.value.sendmail` authorization can modify the SMF configuration for the `sendmail` service, and

- A user or role that has been granted the `solaris.smf.manage.sendmail` authorization can control (`start/stop/restart`) the `sendmail` service.

These authorizations can be part of a rights profile that is assigned to a user or a role, or can be explicitly assigned to a user, as shown by the following:

```
# usermod -A solaris.smf.manage.sendmail bob
# su - bob
bob$ auths
solaris.smf.manage.sendmail,solaris.device.cdrw,solaris.profmgr.read,
solaris.jobs.users,solaris.mail.mailq,solaris.admin.usermgr.read,
solaris.admin.logsvc.read,solaris.admin.fsmgr.read,
solaris.admin.serialmgr.read,solaris.admin.diskmgr.read,
solaris.admin.procmgr.user,solaris.compsys.read,
solaris.admin.printer.read,solaris.admin.prodreg.read,
solaris.admin.dcmgr.read,solaris.snmp.read,solaris.project.read,
solaris.admin.patchmgr.read,solaris.network.hosts.read,
solaris.admin.volmgr.read

bob$ /usr/sbin/svcadm restart sendmail
bob$
```

Note that the `usermod -A` command *replaces* the authorizations for a particular account. If authorizations need to be *added* to an account, make sure to include the complete list of authorizations. For a similar example using the `rolemod` command, see Section 5.3.5, "Assigning Rights Profiles to Roles."

Further Reading

This chapter has touched the surface of a number of security-related improvements the Solaris OS has made to the traditional UNIX model. For more detailed and complete information, you are advised to read up on these particular subjects. Some suggestions are given below.

The chapter titled "Roles, Rights Profiles, and Privileges" from the *System Administration Guide (Solaris 10 System Administration Collection)*

Sun Blueprints on privileges:
Limiting Services in the Solaris 10 Operating System
(`http://www.sun.com/blueprints/0505/819-2680.pdf`)
Privilege Bracketing in the Solaris 10 Operating System
(`http://www.sun.com/blueprints/0406/819-6320.pdf`)
Privilege Debugging in the Solaris 10 Operating System
(`http://www.sun.com/blueprints/0206/819-5507.pdf`)

Casper Dik's Weblog entry on privileges:
`http://blogs.sun.com/casper/entry/solaris_privileges`

The chapter titled "Developing Privileged Applications" from the *Solaris Security for Developers Guide (Solaris 10 Software Developer Collection)*

Stephen Hahn's Weblog entry on smf(5) authorizations:
`http://blogs.sun.com/sch/entry/smf_5_authorizations_built_in`

Notes

1. We will use the terms "root" and "UID zero" interchangeably.

2. See the intro(2) man page for an explanation of error codes.

3. Privilege assignment to all users of a system can be controlled by setting PRIV_DEFAULT and PRIV_LIMIT in the `policy.conf(4)` file.

4. The `net_bindmlp` privilege is not interpreted unless the system is configured with Trusted Extensions.

5. Not root's processes though, unless the killing process has all privileges; see Section 5.2.3, "Preventing Privilege Escalation."

6

Pluggable Authentication Modules (PAM)

Whenever you want to gain access to a service on a Solaris system, you must provide some credentials that prove you are who you say you are. These credentials can be a user name/password combination, a fingerprint, a token card, a one-time password, or some form of a cryptographic token that only you can possess. Ideally, system administrators, not programmers, define what sort of authentication is needed for each service.

Before the Solaris OS introduced the concept of Pluggable Authentication Modules (PAM), every service hard-coded its access control mechanism. To enforce one-time passwords for the FTP service, for example, an administrator had to change the code of the FTP service. With the introduction of PAM, application code changes are no longer required.

PAM allows the system administrator to define a stack of modules, each performing a small and simple part of the authentication process, for each service. If the company policy changes from user name/password authentication to one-time password authentication, the system administrator can set up the one-time password databases and then change the PAM stack for the impacted service. In effect, PAM de-couples authentication from the service applications.

6.1 The PAM Framework

Even though the name Pluggable Authentication Modules only mentions "Modules," the PAM framework provides more than modules. Four conceptual pieces make up the PAM framework:

- PAM modules—Dynamically loaded executables that implement pieces of an authentication policy. A PAM stack is a collection of modules that together make up the required authentication scheme.
- PAM configuration file—The file for configuring PAM stacks.
- PAM consumers—Applications that use PAM for authentication and account management.
- PAM library—Binds the four pieces together.

Extensive documentation about how to administer PAM on a Solaris host can be found in the *System Administrator Collection* at `http://docs.sun.com/app/docs/doc/816-4557/pam-1`.

6.2 The PAM Modules

The Solaris OS provides a collection of different PAM modules that an administrator can use to build authentication stacks. After installation, some PAM modules are in use. Each module is designed to perform a simple, well-defined task that can easily be understood and combined with other modules into a multitude of different authentication schemes.

The modules are implemented as dynamically loaded executables (the files have a `.so.1` suffix[1]). Modules that are delivered by Sun have filenames that start with `pam_` and are located in the `/usr/lib/security` directory.

6.2.1 Introduction to PAM Modules

Depending on the type of authentication, one or more modules might be needed to implement the required steps. For example, to use regular user name/password authentication, two logical steps are needed: get the user name and password, and then validate the password against the stored password.

Solaris provides two modules that implement these tasks:

- `pam_authtok_get.so.1`
- `pam_unix_auth.so.1`

The users' credentials must be stored in one of the databases ("name services") that the Solaris naming service supports, such as files (/etc/passwd + /etc/shadow), NIS, or NIS+. The pam_authtok_get.so.1 module requests a user name and password, and pam_unix_auth.so.1 verifies that the typed password matches the user's password that is stored in the naming service database.

This simple example hides some complexity. In addition to verifying that the password is accurate, an administrator would also want to check if the account has expired. Perhaps the password is up for renewal. If a new password must be chosen, the administrator would need to ensure that the user has not reused an old password. If the user password does not match, what should the system do? Perhaps the system must lock out the user after a specified number of failed login attempts.

As you can see, a number of variables affect how user access to your system is verified. By putting these tasks into modules and not into the applications themselves, Solaris PAM creates a very flexible system that can be adjusted without touching the applications.

6.2.2 The PAM Stacks for Solaris Login

To complete the PAM stack example with a more realistic set of modules, Table 6.1 is the stack that the Solaris OS uses by default for services like login.

Table 6.1 Default PAM Modules for the Login Service

Module Name	Task Performed by Module
pam_authtok_get.so.1	Get username and password.
pam_dhkeys.so.1	Set network credentials, sometimes needed to access credential database (e.g., NIS+)
pam_unix_cred.so.1	Set user's project, privilege sets, and auditing context.
pam_unix_auth.so.1	Validate user's password. Lock account if too many authentication failures occurred.
pam_roles.so.1	Enforce Solaris "roles" rules.
pam_unix_account.so.1	Verify that the account has not expired and the password is not up for renewal.
pam_unix_session.so.1	Administer this session (/var/adm/lastlog).

This example is among the more complicated PAM stacks. This list of modules handles most of the necessary steps a current Solaris system performs when a user logs in. However, if the user's password has expired, the service that is handling the login needs to call the PAM password management routines. The routines, by default, use the set of modules presented in Table 6.2.

Table 6.2 Default PAM Password Management Modules

Module Name	Task Performed by Module
pam_dhkeys.so.1	Set necessary network credentials.
pam_authtok_get.so1	Read the old and new passwords.
pam_authtok_check.so.1	Check construction of the new password and make sure the old passwords are not reused.
pam_authtok_store.so.1	Store the new password in the password database.

The preceding examples illustrate the kind of PAM modules that the Solaris OS provides. The examples also illustrate the division between the different modules. This division allows you to customize the PAM stack by adding or dropping modules. You can add modules to the stack to implement processes that your environment requires.

Warning

You must not drop part of the authentication process from the stack without a very good reason.

For example, you could add modules to enforce the following kinds of restrictions.

- Specific users cannot log in except at particular times, such as, "Users in group Finance can only log in on weekdays between 9 and 5, except for the last two weeks of a fiscal quarter; then they can log in 24/7."
- Specific users can only log in from a particular system.
- Employees must provide a one-time key when they log in from outside the company's firewall.

You might even want to implement a completely different authentication scheme that is based on identifying objects or colors if your users have trouble remembering or typing UNIX-style passwords.

6.2.3 Available PAM Modules

The Solaris OS provides a set of PAM modules that implement the traditional Solaris authentication mechanism. These mechanisms are augmented with some specialized modules for Kerberos authentication. Because PAM is an open standard, many modules that implement additional restrictions and additional methods of authentication are available on the Internet. Although modules that are written for other UNIX variants might not work "out-of-the-box," they are likely to be easy to deploy on a Solaris system, too.

6.2.4 Standard Solaris PAM Modules

As described earlier, different modules implement different steps of the authentication process. These steps can be grouped into different classes of actions. PAM defines four such classes: authentication, account management, password management, and session management. Each PAM module needs to provide services for one or more of these classes. The modules in Table 6.1 implement authentication, account management, and session management class services, while the modules in Table 6.2 implement password management class services.

Table 6.3 lists the standard Solaris PAM modules, the PAM service-class that the module provides (also called module type), and a brief description of the module's functionality. Each module has its own man page, which is listed in section 5 of the online manual system. These man pages are written for the programmer, but once you have read through this entire chapter, they will be quite informative.

Table 6.3 Standard Solaris 10 PAM Modules

Module Name	Module Type				Description
	Auth	Account	Password	Session	
`pam_authtok_check`(5)			x		Perform password-strength checks on new password that user types
`pam_authtok_get`(5)	x		x		Prompt user for user name and password.
`pam_authtok_store`(5)			x		Store changed password in database

continues

Table 6.3 Standard Solaris 10 PAM Modules (*continued*)

Module Name	Module Type				Description
	Auth	*Account*	*Password*	*Session*	
pam_deny(5)	x	x	x	x	Deny requested operation, regardless of the input. Can be used to deny specific types of services, or to deny all services not explicitly defined by using the other service name together with this module.
pam_dhkeys(5)	x		x		Set or change Diffie-Hellman keys.
pam_dial_auth(5)	x				Simple dial-in authentication
pam_krb5(5)	x	x	x	x	Kerberos authentication management
pam_krb5_migrate(5)	x				Auto-migrate users to local Kerberos realm
pam_ldap(5)	x	x	x	x	Use this module to authenticate users stored in an LDAP server. Account management is also performed by the LDAP server.
pam_passwd_auth(5)	x				A version of pam_unix_auth.so.1 specifically designed for the passwd(1) program
pam_rhosts_auth(5)	x				Implements the authentication scheme for remote shells
pam_roles(5)		x			Verify that a user is allowed to assume a role. It also prevents direct login by a role.
pam_sample(5)	x	x	x	x	Sample PAM module that is not meant for any production environment, but can be used for some PAM debugging
pam_smartcard(5)	x				Reads PIN from user and uses smartcard framework to obtain username and password from a smartcard

Table 6.3 Standard Solaris 10 PAM Modules (*continued*)

Module Name	Module Type				Description
	Auth	*Account*	*Password*	*Session*	
pam_tsol_ account(5)		x			Solaris Trusted Extensions module that performs additional account checks related to labels.
pam_unix_ account(5)		x			Verify that the user's account has not expired, is not locked, and that the password is not up for renewal.
pam_unix_auth(5)	x				Verify the user's password. Lock the account if too many failed login attempts are recorded.
pam_unix_cred(5)	x				Initialize the users' credentials (user's project, privilege sets) and initialize or update the user's audit context.
pam_unix_ session(5)				x	Updates /var/adm/lastlog to record last login time
pam_winbind(7)	x	x	x	x	Authenticate users against the local Windows domain. This module is part of samba(7).

Because Solaris can execute both 32-bit and 64-bit applications, each of the PAM modules is provided in both 32- and 64-bit format. The 32-bit version of the PAM module is located in the /usr/lib/security directory, and the 64-bit version of the same PAM module is located in the /usr/lib/security/64 directory.

6.3 The PAM Configuration File

The previous section showed a number of PAM modules that can be used as building blocks to create the type of authentication and account management that you want to implement. The way to express which building blocks are needed for a particular type of authentication is through a configuration file, /etc/pam.conf(4).

The precise syntax and semantics of this file can be found in the online manual pages. The following section walks you through the basics.

6.3.1 Overview of the `pam.conf`(4) File

Like many UNIX configuration files, the PAM configuration file is a plain text file that you edit with your favorite editor. Blank lines are ignored, so you can use them to make the file more readable. Lines that start with a hash mark, (#), are comments that are ignored by the system. All other lines are configuration lines that conform to the following format:

```
service-name module-type control-flag module-path module-options
```

- `service-name`. Usually application names such as login, ftp, rsh, and so on. `other` is a reserved service name. This reserved name serves as a wildcard or catch-all name for services that are not explicitly specified.
- `module-type`. Holds one of the four module types that were described previously: `auth`, `account`, `password` or `session`.
- `control-flag`. Enables you to define how to combine different modules. Allowed values are `binding`, `include`, `optional`, `required`, `requisite`, and `sufficient`. The use of these flags is the most critical and confusing part of configuring PAM and are discussed in more detail later in this chapter.
- `module-path`. Contains the file system location for the module. If a relative path name is used, the framework prepends `/usr/lib/security/` to the module. If the module is located elsewhere, you must use the full path name.

   When the module name alone is used, the system automatically searches the appropriate architecture directory. For full path names, you must add the token `$ISA` to the path. The system replaces `$ISA` with the correct directory name for the current architecture ("`/`" or "`/64/`").
- `module-options`. Optional. Is used to pass options to the module. Which options are accepted depends on the module. The options that Solaris modules accept are listed on the module's man page.

6.3.2 PAM Stacks and Module Flags

To define a PAM configuration for a particular service, you must build a PAM stack. The stack is a list of modules that is processed in the order in which the modules appear in the `pam.conf`(4) file. Each module performs its specific task and returns a status value to the system. Roughly speaking, this status can be one of three things: success, failure, or ignore. The module flags determine how the system handles these status returns. The six different module flags are used as shown in Table 6.4.

Table 6.4 PAM Module Flags

Flag	Description
`binding`	If the module returned success and no earlier `required` module returned a failure, stop processing the stack and return success to the application.
	If the module returned failure, treat the failure as a `required` failure and continue to process the stack.
`optional`	If the module returned success, record the success and continue down the stack.
	If the module returned failure and no earlier `optional` module has failed, record the failure code as an optional failure and continue down the stack.
`required`	If the module returned success, record the success and continue down the stack.
	If the module returned failure and no earlier `required` module failed, record the failure code as a required failure and continue down the stack.
`requisite`	If this module returned success, record the success and continue down the stack.
	If this module fails, stop processing the stack and return the failure code of the first `required` module, or return the failure code of this module if no earlier `required` module failed.
`sufficient`	If the module returned success and no earlier required module returned a failure, stop processing the stack and immediately return success.
	If the module returned a failure, record the failure as an optional failure and continue down the stack.
`include`	Process the lines from the PAM configuration file specified in the module-path field.

As you can see from the description of these flags, the distinctions between the various flags are subtle. The precise flow of control is detailed in Figure 6.1. When you start to build a PAM stack that codes the exact semantics that your service requires for authentication, you will appreciate the specificity of these flags.

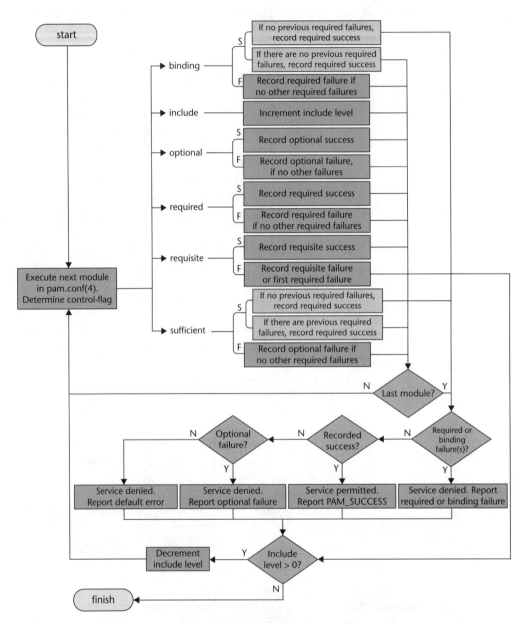

Figure 6.1 PAM Flow Control

6.3.3 The Module Flags for the PAM Stack for Solaris Login

The Solaris OS configures the login service by default. The Solaris `pam.conf` file provides the following stack for login:

```
login   auth requisite       pam_authtok_get.so.1
login   auth required        pam_dhkeys.so.1
login   auth required        pam_unix_cred.so.1
login   auth required        pam_unix_auth.so.1
login   auth required        pam_dial_auth.so.1
```

These login lines define that the login service uses five modules to authenticate users. The stack is executed in the following order:

1. First, the system executes `pam_authtok_get` to obtain the user's user name and password. If this module fails to obtain these two items, the authentication process is aborted by the requisite flag, and the failure code of `pam_authtok_get` is returned to the login service.

2. After the PAM framework has obtained the user name and password, it continues with the `pam_dhkeys` module. This module is needed for certain setups where access to the user database is restricted to processes that have proper Diffie-Hellman keys in place. If the current system configuration does not require these keys, this module returns "ignore." By returning "ignore," this module does not contribute to the overall authentication for this service.

3. `pam_unix_cred` and `pam_unix_auth` are the next modules to be executed. `pam_unix_cred` does not participate in validating the user's password. This module is called by the framework in a later stage. `pam_unix_auth` does the actual password validation. As can be seen from the module flag, this module is required to return success. If it does not, because the passwords do not match, the resulting value of the stack is failure, and failure is then reported to the login service.

4. The last module on the stack is `pam_dial_auth`. This module performs additional verification for users who enter the system through one of the serial dial-up ports. At most installations, this module returns "ignore," and thus does not participate in the decision process.

5. After the authentication has succeeded, the stack is traversed again.
    This time, the stack is used to initialize the users' credentials. This
    implementation detail is not explicitly shown in the PAM configuration
    file, but you must consider this step if you write PAM modules.

The preceding steps illustrate that the login service depends on five modules for
the *authentication* of users.

What about the other module types? Which modules provide account management, password management, and session management to the login service?

The default `pam.conf` file does not explicitly configure these types of management for the login service. Instead, the file contains a number of entries that are
marked with the wildcard service name `other`:

```
other    account    requisite    pam_roles.so.1
other    account    required     pam_unix_account.so.1

other    session    required     pam_unix_session.so.1

other    password   required     pam_dhkeys.so.1
other    password   requisite    pam_authtok_get.so.1
other    password   requisite    pam_authtok_check.so.1
Other    password   required     pam_authtok_store.so.1
```

The preceding configuration lines, together with the authentication lines, make up
the complete PAM specification for the login service.

6.4 PAM Consumers

The preceding discussion examined various parts of the PAM framework: modules
that provide services and a configuration file that allows you to define how
these modules are to be combined to implement a particular authentication
scheme. This section examines some typical services that use PAM, and highlights
some services.

In a default Solaris 10 installation, the services (applications) shown in Table 6.5
are documented PAM consumers. Many of these services are not explicitly configured in `pam.conf`(4), so they use the `other` service name.

For most of these services, the online manual pages explain how the service uses
PAM and what the service name is that should be used in the `/etc/pam.conf` file.
If no service name is explained, and none explicitly listed in the `/etc/pam.conf`
file, the wildcard `other` is used.

Table 6.5 PAM Consumers in the Solaris 10 Release

Service Name	Description	PAM Consumer
login	Terminal login	/usr/bin/login
rlogin	Remote login daemon	/usr/sbin/in.rlogind (executes /usr/bin/login with -r)
rsh	Remote shell daemon	/usr/sbin/in.rshd
rexec	Remote exec daemon	/usr/sbin/in.rexecd
telnet	Telnet daemon	/usr/sbin/in.telnetd (executes /usr/bin/login with -t)
ftp	File Transfer Protocol	/usr/sbin/in.ftpd
krlogin	Kerberos login	/usr/sbin/in.rlogind (with -k)
ktelnet	Kerberos telnet	/usr/sbin/in.telnetd
krsh	Kerberos remote shell	/usr/sbin/in.rshd
passwd	Password maintenance program	/usr/bin/passwd
ppp	Point-to-point protocol	/usr/bin/pppd
xscreensaver	Gnome screen saver	/usr/openwin/bin/xscreensaver
xlock	X11 screen saver	/usr/openwin/bin/xlock
cron	at and cron-jobs	/usr/sbin/cron, /usr/bin/crontab
su	Change user id	/usr/bin/su
ssh-kbdint	Secure Shell	/usr/bin/sshd
gdm	Gnome display manager	/usr/sbin/gdm
dtlogin	CDE login manager	/usr/dt/bin/dtlogin
uucp	UNIX to UNIX copy	/usr/sbin/in.uucpd
samba	Windows File Sharing	/usr/sfw/bin/smbd

The use of PAM by these services is usually straightforward. However, two exceptions must be examined in detail: the remote shell daemon (in.rshd) and the Secure Shell (SunSSH) daemon (sshd).

6.4.1 PAM Configuration for the Remote Shell Daemon, in.rshd

The remote shell daemon is a different type of consumer than most other PAM consumers. As the manual page of in.rshd states, the in.rshd daemon allows for password-less entry to a system if several requirements are met. One such requirement is the presence of a `.rhosts` file in the user's home directory on the remote system. This file must contain a line that explicitly states that the user on the initiating host is allowed entry without providing a password.[2]

This style of authentication is unusual. The user does not need to enter either a user name or a password. This difference is reflected in the `/etc/pam.conf` file:

```
# rsh service (explicit because of pam_rhost_auth)

rsh    auth sufficient          pam_rhosts_auth.so.1
rsh    auth required            pam_unix_cred.so.1
```

For the remote shell service, the module `pam_rhosts_auth.so.1` is marked as `sufficient`. The `pam_rhosts_auth.so.1` module implements the authentication scheme that the remote shell daemon needs. That is, this module checks to see if the target user's `.rhosts` file would allow the remote user access. If the user's `.rhosts` file allows such access, `pam_rhosts_auth.so.1` returns success and the PAM library stops processing the stack. At this point, PAM returns success to the `in.rshd` daemon, because no earlier module on that stack could have set a required error. Therefore, success from the `pam_rhosts_auth.so.1` module returns success immediately.

If the user's `.rhosts` file does not allow entry to the system, `pam_rhosts_auth.so.1` returns failure and the authentication stack at large fails (`pam_unix_cred.so.1` does not perform authentication, only credential management for authenticated users).

Don't forget that if you run the command `rsh` *remote-host command*, the `rsh` command contacts the `in.rshd` daemon on the remote host, and the `rsh` PAM service is used. However, if you run the command `rsh` *remote-host* (without a command argument), the `rsh` command behaves like the `rlogin` command. It contacts the `in.rlogind` daemon on the remote host and uses the `rlogin` PAM stack.

6.4.2 PAM Configuration for `sshd`

Another PAM consumer worth mentioning is the `ssh` service. Just like the remote shell daemon, the `ssh` command allows users to remotely access machines without explicitly providing their user name and password. In fact, `sshd` has several authentication schemes where the user is not required to provide a user name and password. The `sshd_config`(4) file determines what types of authentication schemes are allowed by the `ssh` daemon. For more information on configuring the ssh daemon, see Section 10.3, "Solaris Secure Shell (SunSSH)," in Chapter 10, "Solaris Network Security."

This discussion focuses on how to configure the necessary authentication schemes by using the PAM configuration file.

The online manual page of sshd(1M) explains the different PAM service names for the different ssh authentication schemes as shown in Table 6.6.

Table 6.6 PAM Service Names for the ssh Service

SSHv2 Userauth	PAM Service Name
none	sshd-none
password	sshd-password
keyboard-interactive	sshd-kbdint
pubkey	sshd-pubkey
hostbased	sshd-hostbased
gssapi-with-mic	sshd-gssapi
gssapi-keyex	sshd-gssapi

By default, the ssh daemon does not have explicit entries in the /etc/pam.conf file; therefore, ssh uses the other service name. If you are required to modify the way sshd handles authentication, use the appropriate service name for the specific Userauth setting.

6.5 The PAM Library

The final conceptual piece of the PAM framework is the PAM library. This piece is usually invisible to system administrators. However, the library is the glue that combines all the pieces—consumers, configuration file, and modules—together.

The PAM library is /usr/lib/libpam.so.1. PAM consumers are linked against this file and consumers call routines that this library exports. The PAM library is responsible for reading the configuration file, determining which modules make up the stack that the consumer requested, executing each module listed, and applying the correct module flags to each module. After the PAM library has executed the stack, the library passes the resulting success or failure value back to the PAM consumer.

6.6 PAM Tasks

Sites that need to add or modify a PAM stack also need to debug their code. The following tasks are designed to assist you.

6.6.1 Adding Additional PAM Modules

If access to your system requires an authentication scheme that is not implemented by the Solaris-provided PAM modules, you can write your own PAM module.[3] You can also obtain modules from the Internet that are either written for the Solaris OS or for one of the other UNIX systems that implement PAM. Remember that you might have to include 32-bit and 64-bit versions of these modules if the module's consumers are 32 bit and 64 bit.

Because PAM modules are dynamically loaded executables, the object code must be made "position-independent." The details of position independence are outside the scope of this chapter, but the *Linker and Libraries Guide* that is available from the http://docs.sun.com document Web site explains the details that you need to know.

For the purposes of this chapter, it is enough to know that, in the Solaris OS, position-independent code (PIC) is created by supplying the options -Kpic and -G to the Sun Studio compiler. If you use the GNU compiler to create the module, you supply the options -fpic and -G.

Once the module has been created, it needs to be installed and added to the PAM stack.

To install the module, follow these steps.

1. Store the module in a location where PAM can find it. The standard location is the /usr/lib/security directory. For the 64-bit module, use the /usr/lib/security/64 directory.

2. Install the module with the following UNIX permissions: the owner of the file *must* be root and the file's permissions *must* deny writing to group and other.

3. Verify that your modules have the correct file permissions by running the following commands:

```
# chown root <modulepath-32-bit> <module-path-64-bit>

# chmod 755 <modulepath-32-bit> <module-path-64-bit>
```

Of course, if the applied module is specifically developed for the Solaris OS, these steps are defined in the module's Makefile.

When you add the module to the stack of the intended service in the `/etc/pam.conf` file, do the following.

1. Create a backup copy of the original `pam.conf` file.
2. Modify the `pam.conf` file.
3. Test the new functionality for authentication success.
4. Test the new functionality for authentication failure.
5. Make sure that the new configuration file works. In particular, the file must work for general services that enable you to log in to the system.

   You can easily lock yourself out by making a mistake in the PAM configuration file. In the event that you are locked out of your system, reboot the system in single-user mode: single-user mode login does not use PAM for authentication.

6.6.2 Debugging PAM Stacks

When users are allowed access to a system when they should be denied access, or when users are denied access when they should be allowed access, you need to trace PAM's steps to see where the error occurs. To trace the steps requires a basic understanding of the PAM configuration file and the PAM library.

No dedicated tools currently exist for debugging the PAM stack for a particular service. You must replay the authentication scenario while viewing the log files and tracing the path that the PAM library takes through the PAM stack.

Typically, the PAM framework logs error conditions to the `auth` facility of the system log daemon. Read the comments in the `/etc/syslog.conf` file and read the `syslog.conf`(4) man page to find out which log file contains these error messages, and then search the log file for hints as to why the authentication did not perform as expected.

If the standard logging does not provide enough details, you can enable debug logging in the `pam.conf` file. The Solaris-provided PAM modules implement a `debug` module option. When you specify this option to a module in the PAM configuration file, the module generates debugging output that is directed to the syslog daemon at level `debug`.

By default, the Solaris 10 `syslog.conf` file does not configure the syslog daemon to collect debug messages. To configure your system to collect messages from the debug module option in a PAM stack, perform the following steps.

1. Add `auth.debug` logging to the `/etc/syslog.conf` file. For example, add the following line to the file. Type a TAB between the fields:

   ```
   auth.debug /var/adm/debug
   ```

2. If the /var/adm/debug log file does not yet exist, create it.[4]

   ```
   # mktemp /var/adm/debug
   ```

3. Tell the syslog daemon to reread the configuration file.

   ```
   # svcadm refresh system-log
   ```

4. Use the `tail`(1) command to view the log file for debug messages from the PAM modules.

   ```
   # tail -f /var/adm/debug
   ```

For example, a successful `ssh` login that uses keyboard authentication produces the following messages:

```
pam_authtok_get:pam_sm_authenticate: flags = 0

pam_unix_auth: entering pam_sm_authenticate()
pam_roles:pam_sm_acct_mgmt: service = sshd-kbdint user = bob
        ruser = not set rhost = localhost
pam_unix_account: entering pam_sm_acct_mgmt()
Unix Policy:bob, pw=Unix PW, lstchg=14126, min=-1, max=-1, warn=-1,
        inact=-1, expire=-1
pam_dhkeys: user2netname failed
pam_unix_cred: pam_sm_setcred(flags = 1, argc= 1)
pam_unix_cred: user = bob, rhost = localhost
pam_unix_cred: state = -1, auid = -2
pam_unix_cred: audit already set for -2
pam_unix_session: inside pam_sm_open_session()
pam_unix_session: user = bob, time = Thu Sep  4 16:04:07 2008,
tty = sshd, host = localhost.

Accepted keyboard-interactive for bob from 127.0.0.1 port 32863 ssh2
```

These messages contain useful information for PAM module developers and for administrators who are debugging PAM stacks.

Notes

1. Although the ".1" suffix is technically a version number, all Solaris PAM modules currently are version 1.

2. There are other methods to configure in.rshd. See `in.rshd`(1M) for more information.

3. Information about writing PAM modules can be found at `http://docs.sun.com/app/docs/doc/816-4863/ch3pam-01` and `http://opensolaris.org/os/community/arc/policies/PAM/`.

4. `mktemp`(1) creates the file so that its contents cannot be read by ordinary users. This is a safe creation method for a file that might contain account details that ordinary users must not see.

7

Solaris Cryptographic Framework

The Solaris Cryptographic Framework provides cryptographic services to users and applications through commands, a user-level programming interface, a kernel programming interface, and user-level and kernel-level frameworks. The cryptographic framework provides these services to applications and kernel modules in a manner that is seamless to the end user and brings direct cryptographic services, such as file encryption and decryption, to the end user.

The user-level framework is responsible for providing cryptographic services to consumer applications and the end user commands. The kernel-level framework provides cryptographic services to kernel modules and device drivers. Both frameworks give developers and users access to optimized cryptographic algorithms.

The programming interfaces are a front end to each framework. A library or a kernel module that provides cryptographic services can be plugged into one of the frameworks by the system administrator. This makes the plug-in's cryptographic services available to applications or kernel modules. This design enables the system administrator to plug in different cryptographic algorithm implementations or hardware-accelerated cryptographic providers.

Using the cryptographic framework has many benefits. Applications and kernel services do not need to re-implement complete cryptographic functions but can use existing implementations. This reduces code duplication and therefore reduces the number of bugs. In addition, the cryptographic implementations can be optimized for the available hardware, including hardware accelerators. The resulting performance benefits are directly available to the userland and kernel services. The foundation of the framework is the PKCS #11 library.

7.1 PKCS #11 Standard and Library

PKCS #11 is one of a family of standards that are called Public Key Cryptography Standards, or PKCS.

RSA Laboratories (the research center of RSA, now part of EMC) have developed a family of standards called Public-Key Cryptography Standards (PKCS, `http://www.rsasecurity.com/`). The first standard, PKCS #1, specified the RSA algorithm together with the key formats. Currently, RSA has published 15 standards documents. These standards define several aspects of applied cryptography. Some of the more commonly used standards are given below.

- PKCS #1. Contains recommendations for the implementation of public-key cryptography based on the RSA algorithm.
- PKCS #7. Cryptographic Message Syntax, also used by RFC 2315.
- PKCS #8. Defines Private-Key Information Syntax. Used by Apache.
- PKCS #11. Defines the Cryptographic Token Interface, an API that is used by the Solaris Cryptographic Framework.
- PKCS #12. Defines Personal Information Exchange Syntax. This is used by Java keystore encrypted private keys together with public key certificates.

The PKCS #11 standard defines an API (Cryptoki, pronounced *crypto-key*) that the Solaris Cryptographic Framework offers in RSA's current version, version 2.20. If you are already familiar with the PKCS #11 API, then you can directly use this API in your applications by linking against the Solaris `libpkcs11.so` library.

PKCS #11 is a user-land API, but the Solaris Cryptographic Framework uses much of the same terminology for both the user-land and kernel-level frameworks. The following sections on mechanisms, tokens, and slots apply primarily to the user-land cryptographic framework.

7.1.1 Consumers

An application, library, or kernel module that requests a certain service from the cryptographic framework is called a *consumer*. A consumer only obtains cryptographic services, for example, encryption or decryption services. The Solaris `digest`(1) command is a consumer of the framework by using a user-level library. This command does not itself include the MD5, SHA1, and other algorithms. Rather, the command calls the cryptographic framework to perform these calculations.

7.1.2 Providers and Plug-ins

A userland library or kernel module that offers cryptographic services to consumers is called a *plug-in or provider*. The library or module is plugged into the cryptographic framework and is visible and usable by the consumers. Two examples are the Sun Niagara Crypto Provider (ncp) kernel hardware provider, which uses the Mathematical Arithmetic Unit (MAU) of the UltraSPARC T1 CPU, and the Sun Niagara 2 Crypto Provider (n2cp) kernel hardware provider, which utilizes the Control Word Queue (CWQ) of the UltraSPARC T2 CPU. These plug-ins offer hardware-accelerated cryptographic services.

You might assume that a provider implements one or more cryptographic algorithms such as DES, AES, RSA, SHA1, and so on. This assumption is only partially true. Each algorithm can be used in multiple ways, as explained in the following section.

7.1.3 Mechanism

A *mechanism* is the combination of the use of a specific algorithm, such as triple DES in cipher block chaining mode (3DES in CBC mode), and the way that the algorithm is used. For example, using DES for authentication is different from using DES for encryption. The SHA512_HMAC is a mechanism where the SHA512 algorithm is used as a Hashed Message Authentication Code (HMAC) and the implementation is a keyed hash function to digitally sign something. Another use of an HMAC signature is in authentication protocols, which would be a different mechanism.

Because the term *mechanism* defines the algorithm together with the way it is being used, *mechanism* also specifies the kind of arguments that are required for this usage. For example, compared to a regular hash function, a keyed hash function requires an additional argument, the key.

7.1.4 Tokens

A token is an abstraction of a device that can perform cryptographic operations. A token implements one or more mechanisms and additionally can store information for use in these mechanisms. This information might be a key, an initialization vector, a state, or some other parameter. A token can be a hardware device such as an accelerator board, or a token can be a piece of software. Such a piece of software is called a *soft token*. An example of a soft token in the Solaris OS is the pkcs11_softtoken(5) token. This token is the software implementation of the RSA PKCS #11 v2.20 specification.

7.1.5 Slots

Within the PKCS #11 standard, an application uses a slot to actually connect to a certain cryptographic service. Inside the cryptographic framework, the previously described tokens are plugged into the slots to make implemented mechanisms available to consumers.

Each provider has at least one slot, but can have more slots. The Solaris Cryptographic Framework aggregates all slots from all plug-ins and presents them to the calling application. For an overall view of the framework, see Figure 7.1.

Providers plug in to the cryptographic framework through a PKCS #11 library. Different libraries provide hardware and software support.

7.1.6 PKCS #11 Shared Library and the Software Token

The main library of the user-level framework is `libpkcs11.so`. This Solaris library implements the RSA PKCS #11 API in version 2.20. The library uses installed plug-ins to provide the PKCS #11 slots.

The Solaris OS is shipped with one software token provider (`pkcs11_softtoken`). This provider includes various PKCS #11 mechanisms, including hashes, encryption, decryption, key generation, and so on. The complete list of available mechanisms is documented in the `pkcs11_softtoken`(5) man page, but the list is also visible by using the `cryptoadm list` subcommand. For a discussion and example, see Section 7.3, "Administration of the Solaris Cryptographic Framework," later in the chapter.

Prior to the Solaris 10 8/07 release, Sun shipped a downloadable provider, `pkcs11_softtoken_extra.so`, that included longer key lengths than the base `pkcs11_softtoken.so` provider supported. Starting with the Solaris 10 08/07 release, the `extra` provider is shipped by default. When this provider is present, it is used instead of `pkcs11_softtoken.so`.

7.1.7 Metaslot

Multiple available slots add some complexity to the consumer, who must select a particular slot before using the service. In addition to that, the consumer might not know which slot is the best. Consider a situation where only one slot is using hardware acceleration on a given platform for a particular mechanism, but four slots are shown to the application. The user-level cryptographic framework offers a simple solution for multiple providers: a *metaslot*.

The metaslot is a virtual slot using a union of all available mechanisms. Mechanisms with hardware acceleration are chosen before software implementations. The shared cryptographic library, `libpkcs11.so`, uses the metaslot as a default

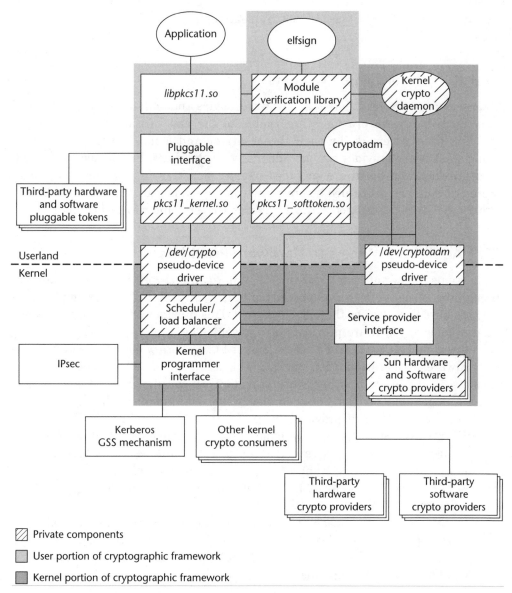

Figure 7.1 Overview of Cryptographic Framework

whenever there are multiple providers present, unless an application selects another specific slot or the metaslot is disabled.

Occasionally, consumers might want to select a specific slot instead of the default metaslot. An example would be a PKCS #11 application, which uses key generation or key storage or both on a hardware device like a smartcard. The application can select a specific slot by searching through the slot information fields.

7.1.8 Kernel Hardware Providers

A kernel hardware provider is a hardware device that offers cryptographic services. Such hardware providers are visible to the rest of the operating system, including the framework, by their device driver and a node in the device tree. A single hardware provider can provide many mechanisms. In contrast to the software provider, the hardware provider usually operates in asynchronous mode. Therefore, a call might return before being completed. For drivers that are shipped with the Solaris OS, see Section 7.4.1, "Solaris Drivers," later in this chapter.

7.1.9 Application Access to Hardware Providers

Applications that want to take advantage of hardware crypto acceleration must go through the kernel. A user-level provider, `pkcs11_kernel.so`, enables applications to access hardware devices through the kernel. This provider is always installed and active whenever hardware providers are present. The `pkcs11_kernel.so` library offers the same PKCS #11 API as the `libpkcs11.so` library does. If the system has no hardware accelerators, then the `pkcs11_kernel.so` library does not offer any slots. In the absence of hardware providers, all consumers use the soft-token plug-in. Depending on the installed hardware, additional mechanisms can be present in slots that are provided by `pkcs11_kernel.so`. External hardware accelerator cards are already available. It is recommended that applications builders use `libpkcs11.so` rather than directly linking to or opening the providers `pkcs11_softtoken.so` or `pkcs11_kernel.so`, since this ensures the best use of hardware when available without the application or developer needing to reconfigure.

Some Sun platforms include hardware crypto acceleration as part of their design. These platforms are described in Section 7.4.1, "Solaris Drivers." Of course, an application can use the metaslot so that the application is not dependent on the presence of any hardware plug-ins.

7.1.10 Kernel Software Providers

A kernel software provider is a loadable kernel module that offers cryptographic services for a single algorithm to other kernel modules and device drivers. The module might offer various implementations, or different modes of those algorithms, and therefore could provide one or more mechanisms. The programming interface is simple. A kernel software provider does not handle scheduling, queueing, and other aspects of the kernel implementation. A software provider is always operating in synchronous mode, so the call to the provider does not return until the request is completed. Asynchronous calling is still available to the kernel cryptographic framework consumers even if only software providers are available; this is done via a pool of threads managed by the framework for its own use.

7.2 User-Level Commands

The Solaris OS ships several user-level programs that by default are consumers of the cryptographic framework. Aside from administrative tools, these programs are digest(1), encrypt(1), elfsign(1), openssl(1), and the Apache Web Server.

7.2.1 digest Command

This program uses the specified algorithm to calculate a message digest of the given files or stdin. If more than one file is given, the program supplies a separate message digest for each file. To list all supported algorithms, use the -l option:

```
% digest -l
sha1
md5
sha256
sha384
sha512
```

To generate an SHA1 digest for the /etc/passwd file, use the digest command:

```
% digest -a sha1 /etc/passwd
4a02fee38d5daf1e56fe1098dde4b3b032999a59
```

For more information, see the digest(1) man page.

7.2.2 encrypt and decrypt Commands

These programs use the specified algorithm to encrypt and decrypt one given file or standard input. The output goes to the standard output unless an output file is specified. The user must provide a key file of the supported length for the specified algorithm:

```
% encrypt -1
Algorithm       Keysize:  Min   Max (bits)
aes                       128   256
arcfour                     8   2048
des                        64    64
3des                      192   192
```

For example, to use AES-192 for encryption, you generate the key file of the specific length, and then encrypt the file. The `pktool` command generates the key file:

```
% pktool genkey keystore=file keytype=aes keylen=192 outkey=key
% encrypt -k key -a aes -i /etc/passwd -o passwd.enc
```

Alternatively, a user can generate a key file by using the dd(1M) command. For more information, see the encrypt(1) and pktool(1) man pages.

7.2.3 `elfsign` Command

The elfsign(1) command is another consumer of the user-level cryptographic framework. This command is used to manually sign Executable and Linkable Format (ELF) objects and to verify the signature, as well as to list various fields from certificates and ELF objects. Most ELF files in the Solaris OS contain an embedded digital signature. This signature can be verified by using the certificate that is shipped with the Solaris OS.

Note

Verification of all encryption modules that plug into the cryptographic framework is a requirement by the U.S. Government for open cryptographic interfaces.

Because of U.S. Government requirements, digital signatures are already used for verification of the user and kernel modules of the cryptographic framework plug-ins. In the Solaris OS, the daemon that performs the verification process is kcfd. For more information, see the kcfd(1M) man page.

In the following example, an administrator uses the elfsign command to verify that the /usr/bin/ssh binary has not been changed since the Solaris OS system was installed or since the ssh binary was last patched by one of the official patches from Sun Microsystems, Inc. The example assumes that the certificates in the `/etc/certs` directory are intact.

First, the administrator determines which certificate to use for the verification:

```
$ elfsign list -e /usr/bin/ssh -f signer
CN=SunOS 5.10, OU=Solaris Signed Execution, O=Sun Microsystems Inc
```

Then, the administrator searches through the certificates in the `/etc/certs` directory:

```
$ elfsign list -c /etc/certs/SUNW_SunOS_5.10 -f subject
CN=SunOS 5.10, OU=Solaris Signed Execution, O=Sun Microsystems Inc
```

The administrator then checks whether the signature is correct:

```
$ elfsign verify -v -c /etc/certs/SUNW_SunOS_5.10 -e /usr/bin/ssh
elfsign: verification of /usr/bin/ssh passed.
format: rsa_md5_sha1.
signer: CN=SunOS 5.10, OU=Solaris Signed Execution, O=Sun Microsystems Inc.
```

Note that you are not required to specify a certificate for the `verify` subcommand. When a certificate is not specified, the command searches for an appropriate certificate in the `/etc/crypto/certs` or `/etc/certs` directory.

You can use the `elfsign` command to sign your own ELF objects. The `sign` subcommand signs an ELF object, and when the corresponding certificate is copied to the `/etc/certs` directory, users can then use the `verify` subcommand to verify the objects.

Cryptographic modules must be signed by a certificate that is issued by Sun Microsystems. You can request a certificate by using the `elfsign request` command. See the `elfsign`(1) man page for more information.

7.2.4 OpenSSL Libraries

The cryptographic framework itself is not aware of the existence of OpenSSL libraries or of the OpenSSL PKCS #11 engine. However, you can use the cryptographic framework from OpenSSL through OpenSSL's PKCS #11 engine. The engine is part of the OpenSSL libraries that are shipped with the Solaris OS. The PKCS #11 engine code serves as a liaison between an application that uses the OpenSSL API and the cryptographic framework. For why you would use

OpenSSL with the cryptographic framework, see Section 7.4.2.1, "Third-Party Applications Use PKCS #11 API through OpenSSL," later in the chapter. OpenSSL is more fully discussed in Chapter 10, "Solaris Network Security."

7.2.5 Apache Web Server

The Apache Web Server that is shipped with the Solaris OS is configured to use the cryptographic framework through the PKCS #11 engine by default. For a description of setting up an Apache Web server, see Section 7.5.5, "Configuring Apache Web server to Use the Cryptographic Framework," later in the chapter.

7.3 Administration of the Solaris Cryptographic Framework

The Solaris OS provides one command, `cryptoadm`, to administer the Solaris Cryptographic Framework. This command controls both the kernel and user parts of the framework. The `cryptoadm` command is used for three sets of administrative tasks:

- Installing and uninstalling cryptographic providers
- Configuring the mechanism policy for each provider
- Displaying information about the framework

For all subcommands aside from `list`, as well as the `--help` option for any subcommands, a privileged user must run the `cryptoadm` command.

7.3.1 `cryptoadm list` Subcommand

The `cryptoadm list` subcommand displays information about available slots, installed providers, and available mechanisms from the installed providers.

7.3.1.1 Listing Providers

With no options, the `cryptoadm list` command displays cryptographic providers:

```
% cryptoadm list
User-level providers:
Provider: /usr/lib/security/$ISA/pkcs11_kernel.so
Provider: /usr/lib/security/$ISA/pkcs11_softtoken_extra.so
```

```
Kernel software providers:
        des
        aes256
        arcfour2048
        blowfish448
        sha1
        sha2
        md5
        rsa
        swrand

Kernel hardware providers:
```

The preceding output displays information about:

- Two libraries that are user-level providers
- Several algorithms that are kernel-level providers

The output includes no hardware providers. Hardware providers are available on systems with hardware accelerators only. On an UltraSPARC T2 machine, the list of kernel hardware providers appears similar to the following:

```
Kernel hardware providers:
        ncp/0
        n2rng/0
        n2cp/0
```

For more information on hardware providers, see Section 7.1.8, "Kernel Hardware Providers," earlier in this chapter.

7.3.1.2 Listing Tokens

The verbose option, -v, displays the tokens that are present in the system. The following output focuses on one part of the output, the metaslot listing:

```
% cryptoadm list -v
Slot #1
Description: Sun Crypto Softtoken
Manufacturer: Sun Microsystems, Inc.
PKCS#11 Version: 2.20
Hardware Version: 0.0
Firmware Version: 0.0
Token Present: True
Slot Flags: CKF_TOKEN_PRESENT
```

continues

```
Token Label: Sun Software PKCS#11 softtoken
Manufacturer ID: Sun Microsystems, Inc.
Model: 1.0
Serial Number:
Hardware Version: 0.0
Firmware Version: 0.0
UTC Time:
PIN Length: 1-256
Flags: CKF_RNG CKF_LOGIN_REQUIRED CKF_USER_PIN_INITIALIZED
CKF_RESTORE_KEY_NOT_NEEDED
CKF_DUAL_CRYPTO_OPERATIONS CKF_TOKEN_INITIALIZED
CKF_USER_PIN_TO_BE_CHANGED
```

Note that the value of the Token Label field, "Sun Software PKCS#11 soft-token," can be used as the value for the `pktool token=` keyword.

7.3.1.3 Listing Mechanisms

The mechanism option, `-m`, displays the capabilities, that is, the mechanisms that are provided in the available tokens. The ncp hardware provider on an Ultra-SPARC T2 machine provides the following mechanisms:

```
% cryptoadm list -m provider=ncp/0
ncp/0:
CKM_DSA,CKM_RSA_X_509,CKM_RSA_PKCS,CKM_RSA_PKCS_KEY_PAIR_GEN,
CKM_DH_PKCS_KEY_PAIR_GEN, CKM_DH_PKCS_DERIVE,CKM_EC_KEY_PAIR_GEN,
CKM_ECDH1_DERIVE,CKM_ECDSA
```

7.3.2 `cryptoadm enable` and `disable` Subcommands

For various reasons, such as during testing or debugging, administrators might want to disable or enable individual mechanisms. The following example uses the `disable` subcommand to demonstrate the difference in encryption speed in hardware and in software.

First, the administrator measures the amount of time the hardware provider spends to encrypt a file. The test is of the AES-CBC mechanism of the n2cp hardware provider.

```
# time dd if=/dev/zero bs=1024k count=500 | encrypt -a aes -k key >/dev/null
500+0 records in
500+0 records out

real    0m13.836s
user    0m2.999s
sys     0m11.868s
```

Then, the administrator disables the AES-CBC mechanism in the n2cp provider:

```
# cryptoadm disable provider=n2cp/0 mechanism=CKM_AES_CBC_PAD
```

After the AES mechanism is disabled in hardware, all cryptographic operations must be performed in the software. When all operations must be performed in the `pkcs11_softtoken.so` library, the time that is required to encrypt the 0.5GB file on the UltraSPARC T2 increases significantly:

```
# time dd if=/dev/zero bs=1024k count=500 | encrypt -a aes -k key >/dev/null
500+0 records in
500+0 records out

real    0m53.961s
user    0m50.986s
sys     0m4.001s
```

7.3.3 `cryptoadm install, uninstall, load,` and `unload` Subcommands

The `install` and `uninstall` subcommands are used for installing and uninstalling both user and kernel-level providers. After a provider is installed, the `load` and `unload` subcommands are used to load and unload specific kernel-module providers.

For more information on the `cryptoadm` command, see the `cryptoadm`(1M) man page.

7.4 Hardware Acceleration

As described in Section 7.1.2, "Providers and Plug-ins," earlier in the chapter, hardware accelerators are reached through kernel-hardware providers. Kernel modules and drivers communicate with hardware providers through the kernel cryptographic framework. User-level applications reach the hardware accelerators through the `pkcs11_kernel.so` plug-in, as explained in Section 7.1.9, "Application Access to Hardware Providers," earlier in the chapter. The `pkcs11_kernel.so` library itself further communicates with the kernel cryptographic framework. For that, the `/dev/crypto` pseudo device is used.

7.4.1 Solaris Drivers

The following drivers are shipped with Solaris systems or with optional products. To detect the drivers, use the `cryptoadm list` command. For examples of listing hardware and the mechanisms that the hardware provides, see Section 7.3.1, "`cryptoadm list` Subcommand," earlier in this chapter.

- Sun Crypto Accelerator 6000 device driver (mca)
  The mca device driver is a multi-threaded, loadable hardware driver that supports cryptographic hardware such as the Sun Crypto Accelerator 6000. This card provides support for asymmetric and symmetric cryptographic operations, plus support for mechanisms such as key generation and storage.

- UltraSPARC T1 server device driver (ncp)
  The ncp device driver is a multi-threaded, loadable hardware driver that supports hardware-assisted acceleration of the following asymmetric cryptographic operations: RSA, DSA, and Diffie-Hellman. This support is built into the UltraSPARC T1 and T2 processors. Machines that include the Ultra-SPARC T1 CPU are the T1000 and the T2000.

- Ultra-SPARC T2 device driver (n2cp)
  The n2cp device driver is a multi-threaded, loadable hardware driver that supports hardware-assisted acceleration of the following cryptographic operations: DES, 3DES, AES, RC4, MD5, SHA1, and SHA256. This support is built into the Ultra-SPARC T2 processor. Note that asymmetric operations in the Ultra-SPARC T2 chipset are supported by the ncp driver. A machine that includes the UltraSPARC T2 CPU is the T5220.

7.4.2 How to Use Existing Hardware Providers in the Solaris OS

This section demonstrates how third-party applications can reach the cryptographic framework hardware providers.

7.4.2.1 Third-Party Applications Use PKCS #11 API through OpenSSL

User-level applications that use the OpenSSL API can use the cryptographic framework through the same OpenSSL API by adding code that loads and initializes the PKCS #11 engine. The applications use the hardware acceleration the same way that they use the mechanisms that are available only in the soft-token library.

Using the cryptographic framework through the OpenSSL API is useful when hardware cryptographic providers are available and you want to speed up an application that already uses the OpenSSL API. Note that the application cannot use the existing OpenSSL API to determine which operations can be off-loaded to the hardware and which operations are performed in the software part of the cryptographic framework. For an example of using OpenSSL and the Cryptographic Framework, see Section 7.5.2, "Determining What Encryption Is Being Handled in Hardware" later in this chapter.

7.4.2.2 Third-Party Applications Use PKCS #11 API through NSS Libraries

Network Security Services (NSS) is an open-source implementation of the cryptographic libraries that are used in a variety of products, including Sun Java Enterprise Web Server, Firefox, Thunderbird, and OpenOffice. NSS libraries provide an internal PKCS #11 module that can be used to access NSS internal cryptographic services. However, NSS can also use shared libraries that provide the PKCS #11 API, and use the slots from the shared libraries through the NSS API. For an example, see Section 7.5.3, "Using the Cryptographic Framework through NSS," later in this chapter.

7.4.2.3 Third-Party Applications Use PKCS #11 API Directly

To make full use of the cryptographic framework, applications can use the PKCS #11 API directly. By using the API directly, applications can explore all available slots and providers and search all available mechanisms. Also, applications can determine which mechanisms are provided in the hardware accelerators and which mechanisms are offloaded to the soft token. For programming examples, see Sun developer documentation at `http://docs.sun.com`.

7.5 Examples of Using the Cryptographic Framework

The following examples demonstrate how to debug the framework, and how to use it from applications that the Solaris OS provides.

7.5.1 Troubleshooting the Cryptographic Framework

The `cryptoadm` command is the first command to use to check whether a certain mechanism is available and active on your system. This command fails if the cryptographic framework daemon, `kcfd`(1M), is not running. In this example, the administrator wants to disable the `des` kernel provider and verify that the kernel is no longer providing `des` mechanisms.

1. Verify that the `cryptosvc` service is online and that the `kcfd` daemon is running:

```
$ svcs -p cryptosvc
STATE           STIME    FMRI
online          10:31:35 svc:/system/cryptosvc:default
                10:31:35     166 kcfd
```

The `cryptosvc` service is usually running, unless an administrator has deliberately disabled it. The following commands disable and enable the service:

```
$ svcadm disable cryptosvc
$ svcadm enable cryptosvc
```

2. List the kernel `des` providers mechanisms:

```
$ cryptoadm list -m provider=des
des: CKM_DES_ECB,CKM_DES_CBC,CKM_DES3_ECB,CKM_DES3_CBC
```

3. Disable the `des` provider, then list which mechanisms are enabled:

```
$ cryptoadm disable provider=des mechanism=all
$ cryptoadm list -p
...

Kernel software providers:
===========================
des: all mechanisms are enabled, except
CKM_DES_ECB,CKM_DES_CBC,CKM_DES3_ECB,CKM_DES3_CBC.
aes: all mechanisms are enabled.
arcfour: all mechanisms are enabled.
...
===========================
```

Section 7.3.1, "`cryptoadm list` Subcommand," earlier in the chapter contains more examples.

7.5.2 Determining What Encryption Is Being Handled in Hardware

To see what is actually offloaded to the hardware providers, you can use the `kstat` command with a specified driver. In this example, an administrator encrypts a file by using an n2cp hardware provider through the OpenSSL PKCS #11 engine.

First, the administrator uses the `kstat` command to determine how many AES blocks the n2cp(7d) driver has already processed:

```
$ kstat -m n2cp
module: n2cp                       instance: 0
name:   n2cp0                      class:    misc

        aes                        1220521
<SOME OUTPUT REMOVED>
```

Then, the administrator encrypts the file:

```
$ openssl enc -aes-128-cbc -engine pkcs11 -in /etc/passwd -out
/tmp/passwd.enc
engine "pkcs11" set.
enter aes-128-cbc encryption password:
Verifying - enter aes-128-cbc encryption password:
```

Finally, the administrator uses the `kstat` command to check the n2cp statistics again:

```
$ kstat -m n2cp | head -10
module: n2cp                       instance: 0
name:   n2cp0                      class:    misc

        aes                        1220523
<SOME OUTPUT REMOVED>
```

Note that the aes output has increased by two. Therefore, the `openssl` command encrypted the `passwd` file in two operations. The `kstat` command can be used in the same way with ncp(7d) and mca(7d) drivers.

7.5.3 Using the Cryptographic Framework Through NSS

As mentioned earlier in the chapter in Section 7.4.2.2, "Third-Party Applications Use PKCS #11 API through NSS Libraries," applications can access the cryptographic framework through the NSS API. In this example, the cryptographic framework makes the soft token accessible through the NSS interface.

1. First, the administrator adds the metaslot `softtoken` as a PKCS #11 module to the NSS database:

```
$ modutil -dbdir ~ -nocertdb -add "softtoken" -libfile
 /usr/lib/libpkcs11.so -mechanisms RSA
```

2. Using the NSS `modutil` command, the administrator lists the available
   slots:

```
$ modutil -dbdir ~ -nocertdb -list
<SOME OUTPUT REMOVED>
  2. softtoken
         library name: /usr/lib/libpkcs11.so
         slots: 1 slot attached
         status: loaded

         slot: Sun Metaslot
         token: Sun Metaslot
```

3. Then, the administrator creates a self-signed certificate. The certificate is created in the soft token of the user who runs the `certutil` command:

```
$ certutil -S -d ~ -n MyCert -s "CN=test.sun.com" -x -t "u,u,u" -h
"Sun Metaslot"
Enter Password or Pin for "Sun Metaslot":
<SOME OUTPUT REMOVED>
Generating key.  This may take a few moments...
```

4. The administrator can use the `pktool` command to verify that a certificate
   and a key were generated in the user's PKCS #11 soft token:

```
$ pktool list objtype=both
Enter PIN for Sun Software PKCS#11 softtoken :
Found 1 asymmetric private keys.
Key #1 - RSA private key:
Found 1 asymmetric public keys.
Key #1 - RSA public key:
Found 1 certificates.
1. (X.509 certificate)
    Label: MyCert
    ID:
a7:d5:5b:42:dd:a9:2e:1e:27:b1:a1:a0:82:e5:fb:1c:2d:6b:e0:65
    Subject: CN=test.sun.com
    Issuer: CN=test.sun.com
    Not Before: Aug  4 15:29:25 2008 GMT
    Not After: Nov  4 15:29:25 2008 GMT
    Serial: 0x8A748005
```

7.5.4 Configuring Java to Use the Solaris Cryptographic Framework

Starting with version 1.5, the JDK/JRE versions have a JCE provider that bridges
to the PKCS #11 C API. The JDK/JRE that is shipped with Solaris releases is pre-
configured to use the cryptographic framework through the `libpkcs11` library.

JDK/JRE does not offload all algorithms by default. This default setting
prevents the expense of making a JNI call and then a PKCS #11 call. Some

algorithms in userland code that access hardware accelerators would suffer from similar performance penalties.

In general, performance penalties apply to hash/digest algorithms such as MD5, SHA1, and SHA256. The default policy for which algorithms are made available from the PKCS #11 provider to the JCE provider is configurable. On a Solaris system, the configuration file is located at:

```
$JAVA_HOME/jre/lib/security/sunpkcs11-solaris.cfg
```

As mentioned previously, the PKCS #11 provider for JDK/JRE on a Solaris system is enabled by default. The configuration file is located at:

```
$JAVA_HOME/jre/lib/security/java.security
```

Because the PKCS #11 provider is listed as provider number one, it is the default. The JDK/JCE also uses the cryptographic framework as the source of random numbers. It does so by using the /dev/urandom module. This default is configured in the java.security policy file.

7.5.5 Configuring Apache Web Server to Use the Cryptographic Framework

The Apache Web server is shipped with the Solaris OS. The Solaris OS includes both the 1.3 and 2.0 versions of the Web server. Each version includes an example configuration file that uses the cryptographic framework by default. This section describes the later version, Apache 2.0.

The directive that is responsible for offloading cryptographic operations to the cryptographic framework is SSLCryptoDevice and its value is pkcs11. For Apache 2.0, these directives are in the /etc/apache2/ssl.conf file that is loaded from the default example configuration file, /etc/apache2/httpd.conf-example.

If a site needs to change the supported cipher suites, the administrator can modify the SSLCipherSuite directive in the configuration file for SSL. Note that the directive SSLEngine has nothing to do with the configuration of OpenSSL engines. Rather, this directive enables the SSL code in the Apache Web server only. SSLEngine is shipped on by default.

To run the Web server in SSL mode, you must generate all the certificates before starting the Web server service. For the location of the certificates, see the /etc/apache2/ssl.conf configuration file.

To start the Apache 2.0 Web server, copy the example configuration file from /etc/apache2/httpd-example.conf to httpd.conf. Then, enable the service:

```
$ svcadm enable svc:/network/http:apache2
```

8

Key Management
Framework (KMF)

The Solaris Operating System supports a unified approach to managing public-key technologies. Reducing the complexity and improving the ease of use will lead to more wide-scale implementation of PKI systems and (hopefully) more secure networks. Often, applications that make use of PKI technologies use different programming interfaces, different key storage mechanisms, different administrative utilities, and different policy enforcement mechanisms. The Key Management Framework (KMF) addresses all of these issues by providing a unified set of administrative tools, a single programming interface, and a policy enforcement system that can enforce PKI policy. Applications must be coded to these interfaces to benefit from the unified approach. The overall design philosophy for KMF is to provide keystore-independence for applications, administrators, and developers of PKI-based software.

KMF provides an administrative tool that allows the user to manipulate keys in any of the supported keystores and to import/export objects from one keystore to another.

KMF also provides a PKI policy system for the Solaris OS. Administrators can configure policies for individual applications at the system level. Then, applications that use the KMF APIs can enforce this policy. PKI policy decisions include operations such as what sort of validation method to apply or limiting certificate use to a particular purpose.

KMF uses a set of programming interfaces that abstract the underlying keystore mechanism so that applications do not have to choose one particular keystore mechanism (NSS, OpenSSL, PKCS#11) and can migrate from one to another. The KMF library supports plug-ins, so that new keystore mechanisms can be added without requiring that the applications themselves be modified.

KMF provides commands and APIs to manage PKI objects for three keystores:

- PKCS#11
- NSS
- File-based keystore for OpenSSL

8.1 Key Management Administrative Utility

KMF manages PKI objects across different keystores with a single utility, `pktool`.

Currently, individual PKI solutions provide their own interfaces. None of these solutions can store certificates in a keystore other than their own. The KMF utility merges these utilities into a single, unified utility. Therefore, administrators must learn one interface for all keystores. Additionally, by unifying the functionality behind a single and interface, more advanced PKI management systems can be built upon the interface provided.

8.1.1 `pktool(1)`

The `pktool(1)` utility provides the user with options for performing a variety of key management functions. It provides multiple keystore support for file-based, NSS, and PKCS#11 keystores.

The following is a list of features that the `pktool` utility provides. This command line utility provides options and an interactive interface.

- X.509 Certificate Operations
  - Create a certificate (self-signed)
  - Import a certificate (DER, PEM, or PKCS#12 format)
  - Export a certificate (DER, PEM, or PKCS#12 format)
  - List certificates
  - Delete certificates
  - Generate a PKCS#10 Certificate Signing Request (CSR)
  - Download a certificate

- Key Operations
  - Create symmetric keys (AES, RC4, 3-DES, DES)
  - Import a key (as part of a PKCS#12 file)

- Export a key (as part of a PKCS#12 file)
- Delete keys
- List keys

- CRL operations
- Import a CRL
- Delete a CRL
- List CRL entries
- Download a CRL

8.1.1.1 Common `pktool`(1) Operations

This section illustrates the use of `pktool` in performing common operations such as importing and exporting certificates or creating self-signed certificates or certificate signing requests.

Importing PKI Objects From a PKCS#12 File to a Keystore   PKI objects are often exported in a standard file format called PKCS#12. PKCS#12 is a portable data format that can include keys and certificates associated with a particular entity. The `pktool` command supports the ability to import the contents of a PKCS#12 file into a supported keystore (PKCS#11 token, NSS database, or filesystem).

```
$ pktool import keystore=pkcs11 infile=/tmp/pktool.test.p12
label=testcert
Enter password to use for accessing the PKCS12 file:
Enter pin for Sun Software PKCS#11 softtoken  :
Found 1 certificate(s) and 1 key(s) in /tmp/pktool.test.p12
```

The following list describes the options that may be used with the `import` subcommand above:

- `keystore:` specifies the type of keystore to store the extracted objects.
- `infile:` is the file name of the PKCS#12 file.
- `label:` identifies the label attribute of the object in the PKCS#11 keystore.

Enter the password for the PKCS#12 file since you are importing private PKI objects in PKCS#12 format when prompted. Next, enter the password for PKCS#11 keystore.

Listing Contents of a Keystore   The contents of a PKCS#11 token keystore, NSS database, or filesystem directory can be viewed with the `pktool list` command. This is useful to determine what is currently stored in the keystore in question.

```
$ pktool list keystore=pkcs11 objtype=both
Enter pin for Sun Software PKCS#11 softtoken  :
Found 1 keys.
Key #1 - RSA private key:  testcert
Found 1 certificates.
1. (X.509 certificate)
        Label: testcert
        ID: 41:cc:4a:60:67:f0:9a:e9:ea:f2:e3:be:6a:8d:78:d4:92:ed:3d:45
        Subject: C=US, ST=CA, L=Menlo Park, O=Sun Microsytems Inc.,
OU=Solaris Security Technologies Group, CN=testuser
        Issuer: C=US, ST=CA, L=Menlo Park, O=Sun Microsytems Inc.,
OU=Solaris Security Technologies Group, CN=testuser
        Serial: 0x01
```

The following list describes the options used with the `list` subcommand above. This is not the complete list of options available for the `list` subcommand, however.

- **`keystore:`** specifies the type of keystore to store the extracted objects.

- **`objtype:`** specifies the class of the objects. The value "both" is to list both the certificates and the keys.

8.1.1.2 Creating a Self-Signed X.509 Certificate

In order to create a self-signed X.509 certificate, `pktool` can be used to quickly generate the keypair and self-signed certificate in a single command. The resulting keys and certificate will be stored in the default PKCS#11 token unless the caller specifies a different keystore using the `keystore` option (ex: `keystore=nss` or `keystore=file`).

```
$ pktool gencert subject="C=US, ST=CA, L=Menlo Park, O=Sun Microsytems Inc., OU=Solaris
Security Technologies Group, CN=testuser" serial=0x0102030405 label=selfsigncert
Enter pin for Sun Software PKCS#11 softtoken  :
```

The following list describes the options used with the `gencert` subcommand above. This is not the complete list of options available for the `gencert` subcommand, however.

- **`subject:`** specifies the distinguished name for the certificate.

- **`serial:`** specifies a unique serial number for the certificate.

8.1.1.3 Verifying the Contents of a Keystore after `gencert`

The previous command generated an RSA keypair and a self-signed X.509 certificate and stored them all in the default PKCS#11 token. Verify their creation by viewing the contents of the keystore with the `pktool list` command.

```
$ pktool list objtype=both
Enter pin for Sun Software PKCS#11 softtoken  :
Found 1 keys.
Key #1 - RSA private key:  selfsigncert
Found 1 certificates.
1. (X.509 certificate)
      Label: selfsigncert
      ID: 64:6c:30:48:f2:4e:9b:70:7c:44:82:75:8c:7c:2e:29:dd:70:4d:61
      Subject: C=US, ST=CA, L=Menlo Park, O=Sun Microsytems Inc.,
OU=Solaris Security Technologies Group, CN=testuser
      Issuer: C=US, ST=CA, L=Menlo Park, O=Sun Microsytems Inc.,
OU=Solaris Security Technologies Group, CN=testuser
      Serial: 0x0102030405
```

8.1.1.4 Generating a Certificate Signing Request

`pktool` provides the ability for the user to create a certificate request that can be submitted to an existing Certificate Authority (CA) to be signed and enrolled in an existing PKI.

Instead of requiring the user to enter the full distinguished name, `pktool` supports the `-i` option, which allows the user to specify the subject-distinguished name interactively for the `gencsr` subcommand as well as the `gencert` subcommand.

```
$ pktool gencsr -i keystore=nss dir=/tmp/nss outcsr=/tmp/testcsr nickname=csrattr
Entering following fields for subject (a DN) ...
        Country Name (2 letter code) [US]:US
        State or Province Name (full name) [Some-State]:CA
        Locality Name (eg, city) []:Menlo Park
        Organization Name (eg, company) []:Sun Microsytems Inc.
        Organizational Unit Name (eg, section) []:Solaris Security
Technologies Group
        Common Name (eg, YOUR name) []:testuser
        Email Address []:testuser@sun.com
Enter pin for internal:
```

The following list describes the options used with the `gencsr` subcommand above. However, this is not the complete list of options available for the `gencsr` subcommand. This example specified the NSS keystore type, but the `gencsr` command also works with PKCS#11 or file type keystores.

- **`keystore:`** specifies the type of keystore to store the extracted objects.
- **`dir:`** specifies the NSS database directory where the objects are to be stored.

- `outcsr:` is the file name of the output CSR.

- `nickname:` specifies the certificate's nickname in the NSS keystore.

Answer the prompts for the subject-DN. Then, if NSS keystore was specified, provide the password for NSS internal database when prompted.

8.1.1.5 Verifying the Existence of the CSR and the Contents of Keystore After `gencsr`

The previous command created a CSR and an RSA keypair in the NSS database. The CSR is a standard file that can be confirmed with the `ls` command and the RSA keypair can be viewed using the `pktool list` command.

```
$ ls -l /tmp/testcsr
-rw-r--r--   1 testuser    staff          499 Jun 26 16:37 /tmp/testcsr
$ pktool list keystore=nss dir=/tmp/nss objtype=key
Enter pin for internal:
Found 1 keys.
Key #1 - RSA private key:  csrattr
Found 1 keys.
Key #1 - RSA public key:  csrattr
```

The following list describes the options used with the `list` subcommand above to view the keys that were created when a CSR is generated. However, this is not the complete list of options available for the `list` subcommand.

- `keystore:` specifies the type of keystore to store the extracted objects.

- `dir:` specifies the NSS database directory where the objects are to be stored.

- `objtype:` specifies the class of the objects. The value `both` is used to list both the certificates and the keys.

8.1.1.6 Generating Symmetric Keys

The `pktool` command also provides tools for generating symmetric keys. Symmetric encryption keys are generally used as a "shared secret" between two parties that wish to maintain a private information link by encrypting an exchange of information between the two parties.

```
$ pktool genkey keystore=file dir=/tmp/openssl outkey=deskey keytype=des
```

The following list describes the options used with the `genkey` subcommand on the previous page. However, this is not the complete list of options available for the `genkey` subcommand.

- **`keystore:`** specifies the type of keystore to store the extracted objects.
- **`dir:`** specifies the NSS database directory where the objects are to be stored.
- **`outkey:`** is the file name of the symmetric key.
- **`keytype:`** specifies the type of the symmetric key.

To verify that the key exists in the file-based keystore after running the `genkey` command:

```
$ ls -l /tmp/openssl/
-r--------   1 testuser    staff        8 Jun 26 17:05 deskey
```

8.2 KMF Policy-Enforcement Mechanism

Popular key-management systems currently lack interfaces or utilities for configuring the policies that govern the use of keys and certificates on the system. X.509v3 certificates are designed to be extensible and potentially contain a great deal of metadata that can be used to dictate how those certificates can be used by PKI-enabled applications. Additionally, the validation algorithms for X.509 certificates as defined in the PKIX specification (RFC 3280) have a set of input parameters that control various decisions in the validation process.

KMF introduces a system-wide PKI policy database. Applications must use the KMF library in order to take advantage of the policy enforcement system. Administrators define policies that the KMF library uses when performing operations that involve certificates.

KMF policies are defined as a set of parameters in XML format. These policies control how the KMF library treats certificates that are being processed while those policies are in effect. The KMF policy rules are applied to all certificate and key objects under KMF control, regardless of keystore. These rules enforce consistency of PKI policy in a keystore-independent manner. Without KMF, PKI policy enforcement is not available when using PKCS#11 or OpenSSL keystores, and very little is available when using certificates that are stored in NSS. With KMF, an application can select the policy that it wants to enforce and can choose different policies for different certificates or operations.

Policies are not bound to specific certificates or applications. In KMF, the applications themselves select the policy to use from the policy database. That policy is in effect until the application exits or until the application changes its policy choice. The system administrator is responsible for managing the policy database. The administrator can create, delete, or modify available policies. The kmfcfg utility is used to manage the policy database. The policy database is delivered with at least one policy that is enforced by default in the absence of any other specific policies.

8.3 Key Management Policy Configuration Utility

KMF provides the kmfcfg(1) utility for defining and managing PKI policy. The administrator requires privileges to write to the policy database. The kmfcfg utility can also be used to write local policy database files that do not necessarily require privileges, depending on the requirements of that application.

8.3.1 kmfcfg(1)

The kmfcfg utility supports multiple operations for listing, importing, exporting, creating, deleting, and modifying key management policy definitions.

To list all policy definitions from the default KMF policy database:

```
% kmfcfg list
Name: default
Ignore Date: true
Ignore Unknown EKUs: false
Ignore TA: true
Validity Adjusted Time: <null>
Trust Anchor Certificate: <null>
Key Usage Bits: 0
Extended Key Usage Values: <null>
Validation Policy Information:
    OCSP:
        Responder URI: <null>
        Proxy: <null>
        Use ResponderURI from Certificate: true
        Response lifetime: <null>
        Ignore Response signature: true
        Responder Certificate: <null>
```

To create a local KMF policy database file with a policy definition:

```
% kmfcfg create dbfile=test.xml policy=testpolicy ta-name="C=US, ST=CA, L=Menlo Park,
O=Sun Microsytems Inc., OU=Solaris Security Technologies Group, CN=testuser"
ta-serial="0x01"
```

The following list describes the options used with the `create` subcommand on the previous page. This is not the complete list of options available, however.

- **dbfile:** specifies the file name of the policy database file.
- **policy:** specifies the policy name.
- **ta-name:** specifies the distinguished name of the trust anchor certificate.
- **ta-serial:** specifies a unique serial number of the trust anchor certificate.

To verify the newly created policy database file:

```
$ kmfcfg list dbfile=test.xml
Name: testpolicy
Ignore Date: false
Ignore Unknown EKUs: false
Ignore TA: false
Validity Adjusted Time: <null>
Trust Anchor Certificate:
        Name: C=US, ST=CA, L=Menlo Park, O=Sun Microsytems Inc.,
OU=Solaris Security Technologies Group, CN=testuser
        Serial Number: 0x01
Key Usage Bits: 0
Extended Key Usage Values: <null>
Validation Policy Information:
```

The following list describes the options used with the `list` subcommand above. This is not the complete list of options available, however.

- **dbfile:** specifies the file name of the policy database file.

To create a policy definition with OCSP revocation method:

```
% kmfcfg create dbfile=test1.xml policy=testpolicy ignore-trust-anchor=true ocsp-
responder=http://ocsp.verisign.com/ocsp/status ocsp-proxy=webcache.sfbay:8080
```

The following list describes the options used with the `create` subcommand above. This is not the complete list of options available, however.

- **dbfile:** specifies the file name of the policy database file.
- **policy:** specifies the policy name.
- **ignore-trust-anchor:** specifies that certificate validation will not verify the signature of the subscriber's certificate.

- **`ocsp-responder:`** is the OCSP responder URL.
- **`ocsp-proxy:`** is the proxy server and port for OCSP.

To verify the newly created policy database file:

```
$ kmfcfg list dbfile=test1.xml policy=testpolicy
Name: testpolicy
Ignore Date: false
Ignore Unknown EKUs: false
Ignore TA: true
Validity Adjusted Time: <null>
Trust Anchor Certificate: <null>
Key Usage Bits: 0
Extended Key Usage Values: <null>
Validation Policy Information:
    OCSP:
        Responder URI: http://ocsp.verisign.com/ocsp/status
        Proxy: webcache.sfbay:8080
        Use ResponderURI from Certificate: false
        Response lifetime: <null>
        Ignore Response signature: false
        Responder Certificate: <null>
```

The following list describes the options used with the `list` subcommand above. This is not the complete list of options available, however.

- **`dbfile:`** specifies the file name of the policy database file.
- **`policy:`** specifies the policy name.

8.4 KMF Programming Interfaces

At the core of KMF is a library of functions that abstract keystore operations and policy enforcement for applications. This API is available to third-party developers who want to implement keystore-independent applications. The interface is delivered as a set of libraries and header files (in the "C" language) that application developers can link into their own projects.

The KMF API provides interfaces that application developers can use to locate, validate, and utilize keys and certificates without having to know all the tedious details of different keystore formats and ASN.1 encoding methods.

A set of modules supports the underlying keystores. Each keystore type has a unique dynamically loaded module that implements the operations on that keystore. KMF is "pluggable," such that additional keystore types can be added. The service provider interface (SPI) is currently not intended to be accessible to third parties, but it is part of the framework.

Note

In the Solaris 10 release, the KMF API is a closed interface. In OpenSolaris distributions, the KMF interfaces are open and exposed for third-party development.

9

Auditing

Auditing is one of the more overlooked security features in the Solaris OS. It gives you the ability to collect data about security-related system events. The data is used for accountability purposes, and is used to assign responsibility for actions that take place on a host.

Auditing has been a security feature since SunOS 3.5e, and the current implementation has been in the Solaris OS since version 2.3. However, recent regulatory requirements, such as SOX (Sarbanes-Oxley Act) and HIPAA (Health Insurance Portability and Accountability Act), which require that all activity on the systems be attributed to the users, have highlighted the necessity of auditing.

9.1 Introduction and Background

The Solaris Audit feature provides the ability to log system activity at a granular level. System activity refers to any auditable Solaris event; for example, system calls on the server machine, packets sent over the network, and a sequence of bits written to disk.

Originally, these auditing capabilities were added to provide the features that were required by the Trusted Computer System Evaluation Criteria (TCSEC)[1] to satisfy a security level referred to as C2. The TCSEC has been superseded by the newer and more internationally recognized Common Criteria[2] security requirements. The Solaris OS has been evaluated under the Controlled Access Protection Profile (CAPP) at Evaluation Assurance Level (EAL) 4. This CAPP includes all functionality that the C2 evaluations required.

9.1.1 Auditing Principles

One of the main principles of security is *accountability*—the ability to trace users' actions that could have security relevance. Two common challenges are associated with accountability:

- Difficulty in determining the security relevance of each user action, and
- Searching through the collected data to find meaningful information

Short of auditing every event exhaustively, there is no way that an administrator can ensure that all attacks will be discovered. An administrator who records selected events in the audit trail, and monitors the audit logs, is more likely to discover suspicious activity and take the action needed to prevent a system from being compromised in the future. Additionally, an administrator can review the audit logs to determine what events transpired during an attack. Solaris auditing is a valuable tool for a security-conscious administrator to counter malicious intent.

An effective audit administrator reviews the audit trail regularly and updates the preselection of audit events. Captured events must cover the latest exploitable weaknesses in the system for which no patches have been delivered.

9.1.2 Goals of Auditing

The goals of auditing are to deter malicious users by observing their actions, attribute actions to users by recording who did what to whom when and from where, and enable after-the-fact analysis of what happened by using forensics. The challenge is to determine which events generate meaningful information and which events are so commonplace that they clutter the audit trail.

9.1.2.1 Satisfying Legal Accountability

Given the world-wide proliferation of regulatory compliance requirements such as Sarbanes-Oxley, full accountability has become even more important. Many sites now have a legal requirement to provide auditors with a complete audit trail of their network and system activity.

9.1.2.2 Tracking System Use

In addition, while administrators can choose to audit events that keep track of currently known intrusion methods, other, currently unknown attack methods might not be covered by the selected audit events. Therefore, an administrator must choose audit events that are sufficiently broad to detect potential mischief, but minimal enough to avoid being overwhelmed with unnecessary information when trying to interpret the audit trail.

9.1.2.3 Avoiding Performance Degradation

A secondary goal of auditing is to avoid performance degradation. In general, the more audit events recorded, the greater the load on the system. Minimizing extraneous audit events therefore reduces the performance impact on the CPU and disk.

9.2 Definitions and Concepts

This section defines Solaris auditing terms and discusses their default values. These terms and concepts provide a baseline understanding of auditing that is essential before you proceed to configure the auditing on your system.

9.2.1 Preselection Mask

The *preselection mask* is a 32-bit field that represents the logical sum of all audit classes being audited for a process. When a user first connects to the system, either on the console or over the network, the `audit_control` file is reviewed to determine the audit classes to be enabled. Any additional audit classes that are set in the `audit_user` file for that user, identified by using the audit ID, are also added to the preselection mask. Unless a process is explicitly assigned a new preselection mask, the process inherits the mask of its parent.

9.2.2 Audit Trail

An *audit trail* is the set of audit log files that have been recorded by the system. The audit trail can be analyzed with the use of the `auditreduce` and `praudit` commands. The `dir:` parameter in the `audit_control` file specifies where these logs are stored.

9.2.3 Audit User ID

When auditing is enabled, a third ID—the audit user ID (or audit ID)—becomes enabled. The audit ID is set during login authentication and does not change for the duration of the session. Actions (such as `su`) that change the real or effective UID do not change the audit ID. The audit ID is recorded in the audit trail with each audit event that is being recorded, thereby tying actions to the user who was authenticated at login, regardless of any `su` or `setuid`(2) actions.

9.2.4 Audit Policy

An audit policy determines characteristics of the audit records or the audit module behavior for the host. The default Solaris audit policy is defined in the

`/etc/security/audit_startup` script, which is run during system startup when auditing is enabled.

9.2.5 Audit Quickstart Guide

To quickly get started with auditing, perform the following five steps. These steps provide a good starting point for developing your own site-specific configuration.

1. Preselect the audit classes in the `/etc/security/audit_control` file:

```
flags:lo,ad,ex,ap
naflags:lo,ad,na
```

2. Update the audit policy by adding the following policies to the `/etc/security/audit_startup` file:

```
/usr/sbin/auditconfig -setpolicy +cnt
/usr/sbin/auditconfig -setpolicy +argv
/usr/sbin/auditconfig -setpolicy +zonename
```

3. Create an email alias for the `audit_warn` script by adding the following to the `/etc/mail/aliases` file:

   `audit_warn:you@company.com`

4. Enable auditing by running the following command, and then reboot the system:

   `# /etc/security/bsmconv`

5. Set up audit file rotation by adding a cron job:

   `0 0 * * * /usr/sbin/audit -n`

The rest of the chapter provides more detail about the steps that you followed and offers further examples of customizing auditing to suit your needs.

9.3 Configuring Auditing

Before you enable auditing on your systems, you should customize the audit configuration files for your site. You can restart the auditing service or reboot the system to read changed configuration files after the auditing service is enabled. However, the recommended practice is to customize your audit configuration as much as possible before you start the auditing service.

The following sections introduce the audit configuration files and provide examples of their use and syntax.

9.3.1 `audit_class` File

An audit class is a group of audit events. Audit classes are defined in the `/etc/security/audit_class` file. Audit events are assigned to audit classes in the `/etc/security/audit_event` file. These audit classes are used by the `audit_control`, `audit_user`, and `audit_event` files, as well as in the preselection mask. Audit classes are recorded in the audit trail if they are enabled globally in the `audit_control` file, or if they are assigned to a specific user in the `audit_user` database.

Entries in the `audit_class` file have the following format:

mask:name:description

where:

- *mask* (class mask) uses an unsigned integer to represent the class mask, providing a total of 32 different classes
- *name* (audit class name) is a two-character mnemonic of the class name used to represent that class in the other audit configuration files
- *description* contains a description of what the class definition represents

In the Solaris 10 release, most audit classes are one bit, but five meta-classes are set up that use more than one bit. The following `audit_class` definitions use only one bit for the preselection mask:

```
0x00010000:ss:change system state
0x00020000:as:system-wide administration
0x00040000:ua:user administration
0x00080000:aa:audit utilization
0x00100000:ps:process start/stop
0x00200000:pm:process modify
```

In the Solaris 10 release, the following classes are set up as meta-classes:

```
0x00070000:am:administrative (meta-class)
0x000f0000:ad:old administrative (meta-class)
0x00300000:pc:process (meta-class)
0x01c00000:xx:X - all X events (meta-class)
0xffffffff:all:all classes (meta-class)
```

9.3.2 `audit_event` File

Audit events are assigned to specific actions in the Solaris OS. Some events are low level and are associated with calls to the kernel. Some events are high level and are associated with specific programs, such as `login`. Audit events can be assigned to more than one audit class.

There are two categories of audit events.

- Kernel-level events are numbered from 1 to 2047.
- User-level events are numbered from 2048 to 65535.
- Events defined by a third party are assigned to the upper range of user-level audit events, that is, from 32768 to 65535.

> **Note**
>
> The action of reviewing an audit log can also be an auditable event.

If an audit event is in an audit class that is in the process preselection mask, that audit event is recorded in the audit trail.

The `/etc/security/audit_event` file defines the `audit events` and assigns each event to one or more audit classes. Software developers can define new audit events in the `audit_event` file. These events must also be defined in either:

- `/usr/include/bsm/audit_uevents.h` or
- `/usr/include/bsm/audit_kevents.h`.

As a general rule, software developers do not add kernel events.

For more information about the `audit_event` file, see the `audit_event`(4) man page.

9.3.3 `audit_control` File

The `/etc/security/audit_control` file describes system parameters for auditing, such as the audit trail storage directories, the minimum free space warning value, and the audit flags that are assigned to user processes and system processes.

Administrators can choose to audit only failed or only successful audit events. For example, you might record a successful attempt to allocate memory, but not record a failed attempt. The audit classes that you specify in the `audit_control` file record the events for all users of the system. The classes that you specify in the `audit_user` file record the events for only the users that you list in the `audit_user` file.

The default Solaris 10 `audit_control` file contains the following settings:

```
dir:/var/audit
flags:
minfree:20
naflags:lo
```

You can specify five kinds of information in the `audit_control` file. Each line begins with a keyword.

- `dir` keyword—Begins the directory definition lines. Each line defines an audit-file system and directory that the system uses to store its audit files. You can define one or more directory definition lines. The order of the `dir` lines is significant, because the `auditd` daemon creates audit files in the directories in the specified order.

- `flags` keyword—Begins the entry that preselects which classes of events are audited for all users on the system.

- `minfree` keyword—Begins the entry that defines the minimum free space level for all audit file systems. The `minfree` percentage must be between 0 and 100. The default is 20 percent. When an audit file system is 80 percent full, the audit data is then stored in the next listed audit directory and an email warning is sent to the `audit_warn` alias.

- `naflags` keyword—Begins the entry that preselects which classes of events are audited when an action cannot be attributed to a specific user. These events include login programs (such as `dtlogin`) and other programs that are launched during system boot, such as `mountd` and `inetd`. Only the `lo` and `am` classes should be specified in the `naflags` field. Programs that have not set their audit context do not generate audit events.

- `plugin` keyword—Specifies the plug-in path and options for the plug-in module. One of the modules provides instant conversion of Solaris audit records to text and sends them to `syslog` (see Section 9.6.2, "Using the `audit_syslog` Plug-in," later in this chapter). The audit classes in the `plugin` line must be a subset of the audit classes in the `flags` line and `naflags` line.

Note

When the `audit_binfile.so` is defined with the `plugin` keyword, the `dir` and `minfree` keywords are not used. The values for these keywords are set as options on the `plugin` line (`p_dir` and `p_minfree`).

9.3.4 `audit_user` File

The `/etc/security/audit_user` file provides the ability to configure additional auditing for individual users. You can configure

- Audit classes that always are to be audited for the user
- Audit classes that never are to be audited for the user

Each line in the `audit_user` file contains three fields:

username:always-audit-classes:never-audit-classes

The *preselection mask* is generated by combining a user's `audit_user` *always* audit entry, if any, with the host-specific audit flags contained in `/etc/security/audit_control` and, finally, subtract the user's *never* audit entry.

Access to this database follows the rules for the password database that is specified in the `/etc/nsswitch.conf` file. For example, LDAP can be used to simplify administration of per-user entries for all your servers.

9.3.5 Audit Policy

An audit policy determines characteristics of the audit records or the audit-module behavior for the host. The default Solaris audit policy is defined in the `/etc/security/audit_startup` script, which is run during system startup when auditing is enabled.

You can inspect, enable, and disable the current audit policy with the `auditconfig` command. To make the changes permanent, you add the audit policies to the `audit_startup` file. Table 9.1 describes some of the most important polices. For the full list, see the `auditconfig`(1M) man page.

Table 9.1 Some of the Most Important Audit Policies

Policy	Description
`argv`	Include the `execv`(2) system call parameter arguments to the audit record. This information is not included by default. This policy should be enabled when you need to see the arguments the user supplied, which you almost always want.
`cnt`	Do not suspend processes when audit resources are exhausted. Instead, drop audit records and keep a count of the number of records dropped. By default, processes are suspended until audit resources become available. When this policy is disabled, you need to keep track of the free space in the audit directory (`/var/audit` by default).

Table 9.1 Some of the Most Important Audit Policies (*continued*)

Policy	Description
group	Include the supplementary group token in audit records. By default, the group token is not included.
perzone	Maintain separate configuration, queues, and logs for each zone, and execute a separate instance of auditd(1M) for each zone. This policy can only be enabled in the global zone.
public	Audit public files. By default, read-type operations (which are included in the fr, fa, and cl audit classes) are not audited for files that are public:owned by root, readable by all, and not writable by all.
zone-name	Include the zone name token as part of every audit record. By default, the zone-name token is not included. The zonename token gives the name of the zone from which the audit record was generated.

Note

You almost always want to use the +argv audit policy, because when the policy is not used, the exec() audit records show only the executed command and not the command's arguments. Therefore, you see who used /usr/bin/vi to edit a file, but not which file was edited.

The following listing shows the default contents of the audit_start script:

```
#!/bin/sh
/usr/bin/echo "Starting BSM services."
/usr/sbin/auditconfig -setpolicy +cnt
/usr/sbin/auditconfig -conf
/usr/sbin/auditconfig -aconf
```

By specifying setpolicy +cnt, the audit_startup script forces auditable events to be dropped if, for instance, audit partitions are full. The kernel keeps a count of the total number of dropped events.

If the goal is to suspend all processes when the audit partitions are full, then modify the cnt policy by changing the following line:

```
auditconfig -setpolicy +cnt
```

to

```
auditconfig -setpolicy -cnt
```

Once you have modified the script, you must reboot the system or run the following command:

auditconfig -setpolicy -cnt

To verify that the audit policy is in effect on the system, use the -getpolicy option:

```
# auditconfig -getpolicy
audit policies = none
```

The output displays none instead of -cnt because -cnt is the default value, and thus is not shown.

To determine if audit records have been dropped, use the auditstat command. The output includes other information. In the following example, the auditstat command is run with an output interval of 60 seconds for a total number of 3 times.

```
# auditstat -i 60 -c 3
   gen nona  kern  aud  ctl   enq  wrtn wblk rblk drop  tot  mem
 14823    1 14128  694    0 14823 14822    0 3916    0 2586    0
 14824    1 14129  694    0 14824 14824    0 3917    0 2586    0
 14926    1 14231  694    0 14926 14926    0 3935    0 2793    0
```

Table 9.2 describes some of the columns from the preceding output. For a full list of column descriptions, see the auditstat(1M) man page.

Table 9.2 Some of the Columns of Output from Auditstat

Value	Description
gen	The total number of audit records that have been constructed (not the number written).
kern	The total number of audit records produced by user processes (as a result of system calls).
enq	The total number of audit records put on the kernel audit queue.
wrtn	The total number of audit records that were written. The difference between enq and wrtn is the number of outstanding audit records on the audit queue that have not been written.
drop	The total number of audit records that have been dropped. Records are dropped according to the kernel audit policy.

It is important to archive and remove old audit trail data to avoid filling up audit storage. A denial-of-service (DoS) attack could attempt to deliberately fill all available audit log storage space. Similarly, auditing network events should be scrutinized routinely because an intruder could generate an enormous amount of audit data in a DoS attack.

Note

When a root compromise occurs, the audit trail should no longer be trusted. Audit logs are stored in a binary format, but this format provides no protection against modification by unauthorized individuals.

9.3.6 Enabling Auditing

By default, auditing is not enabled when you install Solaris 10 from CD or Jump-Start. As `root`, after configuring the audit files, use the `bsmconv` command to enable Solaris auditing, then reboot the system.

```
# /etc/security/bsmconv
This script is used to enable the Basic Security Module (BSM).
Shall we continue with the conversion now? [y/n] y
bsmconv: INFO: checking startup file.
bsmconv: INFO: turning on audit module.
bsmconv: INFO: initializing device allocation.

The Basic Security Module is ready.
If there were any errors, please fix them now.
Configure BSM by editing files located in /etc/security.
Reboot this system now to come up with BSM enabled.
```

To verify whether the system is currently auditing, use the `auditconfig` command with the `-getcond` option:

```
# auditconfig -getcond
audit condition = auditing
```

When auditing is enabled, a log file is written to the `/var/audit` directory, or to the directory that is defined by using the `dir` or `p_dir` keywords in the `audit_control` file. The listing is similar to the following:

```
# ls -l /var/audit
-rw------- 1 root root 27947 Nov 30 16:15
20081030153253.not_terminated.vaccine
```

If auditing is no longer required, you can disable it by using the bsmunconv(1M) command.

9.3.7 Verifying `audit_control` and `audit_user` Changes

To verify that the changes you have made to the audit_control and audit_user files produce the desired effect, you can use the auditconfig -getpinfo command to inspect the preselection mask of a running process. In the following example, the current process is inspected:

```
# auditconfig -getpinfo $$
audit id = martin(1000)
process preselection mask = ex,aa,ua,as,ss,ap,lo,na(0x400f5400,0x400f5400)
terminal id (maj,min,host) = 622,202240,airlock(192.168.10.20)
audit session id = 2401943795
```

Note

A user's preselection mask is set when the user logs in. Therefore, to set a user's new mask after an update, the user must log out and log back in again.

9.3.8 `audit_warn` Script

The Solaris auditing system is designed to alert the administrator of a number of different conditions. For example, the audit_warn script sends email to the audit_warn email alias when log directories are full. You set up this alias when you enable auditing.

The following is an example of an email that was sent by the auditing system when the /var/audit directory exceeded the minfree limit that the administrator specified in the audit_control file:

```
From: root@x2200
Subject: AUDIT DAEMON WARNING (soft)
Date:       Tuesday 30 Sep 2008 05:30:00 GMT+02:00
To: audit_warn@localhost
/etc/security/audit_warn: Soft limit exceeded in file /var/audit.
```

The audit_warn script contains several warnings. The most common warnings are presented in Table 9.3.

Table 9.3 Some of the `audit_warn` Script Warnings

Name	Description
`allsoft`	All audit file systems have exceeded the minfree limit.
`hard`	An audit file system is completely full.
`allhard`	All audit file systems are completely full; the audit daemon will remain in a loop sleeping and checking for space until some is freed.

9.4 Analyzing the Audit Trail

The audit trail is stored in a binary format. This format saves space, but cannot be read without an application that understands the file format. To analyze the audit trail, you use the `praudit` command. By default, this command converts the audit records to a plain text format, but the command can also generate XML format. XML output is useful input to other programs.

Because the audit records are ordered in the audit trail by time of creation, the actions of multiple users are mingled. To follow the actions of a single user, you must filter the audit trail. The `auditreduce` command is a filtering command. This command enables you to select specific records from the audit trail based on a number of criteria, such as audit ID, user ID, session ID, audit event, and audit class.

The process of reviewing the audit trail itself generates a significant quantity of audit data. You can reduce this extra audit data by creating a special role with the Audit Review profile assigned to it, and not audit events from the `aa` class for that role. For an example, see Section 9.6.1, "Configuring an Audit Review Role That Is Not Audited."

9.4.1 Details of an Audit Record

To view the details of an audit record, you must first convert the record to text. The `praudit` command prints numerical representations of things like user IDs, group IDs, and IP addresses in text format. The following command converts a specific audit file to text:

```
# praudit 20081003194007.20081005220000.x2200 > audit.txt
```

> **Note**
>
> The conversion of numerical information assumes that you have a single system image; that is, that the user name and user ID is consistent across all systems. If the UID is not consistent across all systems and across time, you must run the `praudit` command on the system that generated the audit record.

In the following example, the record is the result of an `ssh` login. This login record contains five audit tokens. The token names are the first item on every line:

```
header,86,2,login - ssh,,x2200,2008-07-19 20:43:41.628 +02:00
subject,me3x,me3x,staff,me3x,staff,6553,2442234132,13733 71168 u40
group,staff,rails
return,success,0
zone,global
```

- The `header` token records what kind of event this is (`login - ssh`), which system the event was generated on (`x2200`), and when the event occurred (`2008-07-19 20:43:41.628 +02:00`).

- The subject token records *who* generated this record. The record consists of the following fields: audit ID (`me3x`), user ID (`me3x`), group ID (`staff`), effective user ID (`me3x`), effective group ID (`staff`), process ID (`6553`), session ID (`2442234132`), and terminal ID, where the terminal consists of port ID (`1373371168`) and host name or IP address (`u40`).

- The group token lists every group that the user belongs to. The subject token contains only the group ID. This token is present only when the `group` audit policy is used.

- The return token records the status of the event; that is, if the event succeeded or failed, and the error value. See the `errno(3C)` man page for more information.

- The zone token records the name of the zone in which the record was generated (`global`). This token is present only when the `zonename` audit policy is used.

The next example records a `chmod` event:

```
header,190,2,chmod(2),,x2200,2008-07-19 20:44:32.576 +02:00
argument,2,0x1ed,new file mode
path,/home/rails/prod/start.sh
attribute,100644,rails,rails,65557,20099,18446744073709551615
subject,me3x,rails,rails,rail,rails,6586,2442234132,13733 71168 u40
group,rails
return,success,0
zone,prod
```

- The header, subject, group, return, and zone tokens are recorded. In addition, this audit record for `chmod` contains an argument, path, and attribute token.

- The argument token records arguments to the audit event, and in this case, the new file mode in hex (`0x1ed`) for the file, and a text description of the change. You need to convert the hex value of the file mode to octal to read the value more easily (`755`).

- The path token records which file got changed.
- The attribute token records the file access mode (`100644`), the user (`rails`), the group (`rails`), the file system ID (`65557`), the node ID (`20099`), and the device (`18446744073709551615`).

Instead of generating plain text output, as in the preceding examples, you can generate XML output by passing the `-x` option to the `praudit` command. The following is an `ssh` login audit record in plain text format:

```
header,86,2,role login,,x2200,2008-07-19 20:43:49.957 +02:00
subject,me3x,root,root,root,root,6561,2442234132,13733 71168 u40
group,me3x
return,success,0
zone,global
```

Some reviewers might find the XML format of the same record easier to read than plain text format because the field names are displayed in the tokens.

```
<record version="2" event="login - ssh" host="x2200" iso8601="2008-07-19 20:43:41.628
+02:00">
<subject audit-uid="me3x" uid="me3x" gid="me3x" ruid="e3x" rgid="me3x" pid="6553"
sid="2442234132" tid="13733 71168 u40"/>
<group><gid>me3x</gid></group>
<return errval="success" retval="0"/>
<zone name="global"/>
</record>
```

To view the output in HTML, you can use the `xsltproc(1)` command. This command translates XML to HTML.

```
# praudit -x 20081003194007.20081005220000.x2200 > audit.xml
# xsltproc audit.xml > audit.html
# firefox audit.html
```

The display in the Firefox browser is similar to the following:

```
Event: login - ssh
time: 2008-07-19 20:43:41.628 +02:00 vers: 2 mod: host: x2200
SUBJECT
audit-uid: me3x uid: me3x gid: me3x ruid: me3x rgid: me3x pid: 6553
sid: 2442234132 tid: 13733 71168 u40
GROUP
gid: me3x
RETURN errval: success retval: 0
ZONE name: global
```

9.4.2 Examining Parts of the Audit Trail

When you examine the audit trail, you are doing one of three things.

- You are reviewing what a particular user did.
- You are looking for who caused something to happen on the system.
- Or, you are looking for suspicious activity.

The first case is the easiest. To review what a particular user did, you first extract all records from the `lo` class (logins and logouts) for that user:

```
# auditreduce -u martin -c lo | praudit
header,86,2,login - ssh,,x2200,2008-10-03 21:41:27.779 +02:00
subject,martin,martin,staff,martin,staff,17141,1792435243,16058 136704 u40
group,staff,hg
return,success,0
zone,global
header,86,2,login - ssh,,x2200,2008-10-03 21:56:53.351 +02:00
subject,martin,martin,staff,martin,staff,18544,1795425262,16058 136704 airlock
group,staff,hg
return,success,0
zone,global
```

Then, select the session that interests you and extract all audit records for that session ID:

```
# auditreduce -s 1792435243 | praudit > audit.txt
```

Now you have the full audit trail for that particular user's session, and you can review what that user did.

To find audit records for the second case, when you are looking for who caused a specific event, is slightly more complicated. Typically, you are looking for a changed file or for a specific command that a user ran. For example, if you want to know who removed the file `/tmp/dummy`, you use the `auditreduce` command with the `-m` option to select the event. Use the `audit_event` file to determine the event name. Event `AUE_UNLINK` is `unlink(2)`, the system call that the `rm` command uses to remove a file.

```
# auditreduce -o file=/tmp/dummy -m AUE_UNLINK | praudit
header,152,2,unlink(2),,x2200,2008-10-05 22:35:19.278 +02:00
path,/tmp/dummy
attribute,100666,me3x,staff,7,3690920589,18446744073709551615
subject,me3x,me3x,staff,me3x,staff,6596,2442234132,13733 71168 u40
group,staff
return,success,0
zone,prod
```

Based on this, you can see that the user `me3x` removed the file. Note that the `AUE_UNLINK` event requires that you have preselected the `fd` class to audit.

If you instead are trying to determine who ran a particular command, you use the `-o` option to select the command by its full pathname and the `-m` option to select the `execve` system call.

```
# auditreduce -o file=/usr/bin/cat -m AUE_EXECVE | praudit
header,444,2,execve(2),,x2200,2008-10-03 21:41:27.876 +02:00
path,/usr/bin/cat
attribute,100555,root,bin,2,295,0
subject,martin,martin,staff,martin,staff,17147,1792435243,16058 136704 u40
group,staff
return,success,0
zone,global
```

To determine which file the `/usr/bin/cat` command operated on, you must have enabled the `argv` audit policy. The following entry in the `audit_startup` file enables the `argv` policy:

`/usr/sbin/auditconfig -setpolicy +argv`

This policy adds the following output to the preceding audit record:

`exec_args,2,/usr/bin/cat,/etc/motd`

In this case, the user `martin` ran the `/usr/bin/cat` command on the `/etc/motd` (message of the day) file.

To find audit records of suspicious activity is a much harder problem than the first two cases, as there is no exact formula for determining what is suspicious. However, the following five criteria provide a good starting point. Be aware that the following events all occur during normal operations.

9.4.2.1 Finding Records Where the Audit ID Differs from the Real or Effective UID

The audit ID differs from the user's real or effective ID due to a `setuid(2)` execution or through the use of `su` to a role or another user. This case is interesting because the user is now able to modify objects outside the user's normal scope of influence.

```
header,158,2,open(2) - write,,x2200,2008-11-17 03:53:35.510 +01:00
path,/home/rails/.bash_history
attribute,100600,rails,rails,65557,4,18446744073709551615
subject,me3x,rails,rails,rails,rails,14370,3092986400,8372 136704 u40
group,rails
return,success,4
zone,prod
```

9.4.2.2 Finding Records That Include the `use_of_privilege` Token

Successful `use_of_privilege` events happen during normal operations as part of the *principle of least privilege*. The reason that the use of privilege is interesting is because the user has been able to affect objects outside the user's normal scope of influence.

```
header,133,2,open(2) - read,write,sp,x2200,2008-07-19 20:43:41.592 +02:00
path,/db/mysql/.my.cnf
attribute,100644,mysql,mysql,2,2062,0
subject,me3x,me3x,rails,me3x,rails,6553,2442234132,13733 71168 airlock
group,rails
use of privilege,successful use of priv,file_dac_write
return,success
```

Here, the user `me3x` used the the `file_dac_write` privilege to open the file `/db/mysql/.my.cnf`, which is owned by the `mysql` user. Failed `use_of_privilege` events can indicate an attack that failed to affect objects outside the user's normal scope of influence.

9.4.2.3 Finding Records Where the User Modifies Files That the User Does Not Own

A user can modify another user's files when that user has, intentionally or unintentionally, granted other users (explicit or implicit) access to the file. For example, if a file has mode `666`, anyone can modify it, which might not be the intention of the owner of the file.

```
header,158,2,open(2) - write,,x2200,2008-11-17 05:43:05.310 +01:00
path,/home/rails/README
attribute,100664,rails,rails,65557,4,18446744073709551615
subject,me3x,me3x,rails,me3x,rails,14370,3092986400,8372 136704 u40
group,rails
return,success,4
zone,prod
```

Here, the user `me3x` opened the file `/home/rails/README` for writing. The file is owned by the `rails` user. The `me3x` user can open the file because the mode is `664` and the `me3x` user is a member of the `rails` group. The mode is recorded in the `attribute` token.

9.4.2.4 The AUE_prof_cmd Records

The three preceding types of audit records are generated when users use the `pfexec` command, or a profile shell such as `pfksh`, to execute commands that are in an RBAC profile the user is assigned.

```
header,149,2,profile command,,localhost,2009-02-07 13:41:38.825 +01:00
subject,martin,root,staff,martin,staff,837,184833447,0 0 localhost
path,/tmp
path,/usr/bin/vi
cmd,argcnt,1,/etc/shadow,envcnt,0,
process,martin,root,root,root,root,837,184833447,0 0 localhost
return,success,0
```

Here, the user `martin` with current working directory in `/tmp` is authorized to use `/usr/bin/vi` to edit `/etc/shadow` by being assigned an RBAC profile, Primary Administrator. In addition to the preceding audit record, the following `exec()` audit record is generated for the actual execution of `/usr/bin/vi`.

```
header,134,2,execve(2),,localhost,2009-02-07 13:41:38.827 +01:00
path,/usr/bin/vi
attribute,100755,root,bin,47775746,14846,4294967295
exec_args,2,vi,/etc/shadow
subject,martin,root,root,root,root,837,184833447,0 0 localhost
return,success,0
```

9.4.2.5 Finding Records That Show Failures due to EPERM or EACCES

EPERM or EACCES failures happen when a user tries to do something that violates the Solaris security policy. One example would be to `rm` (that is, `unlink(2)`) a file that the user does not have permission to remove.

```
header,584,2,unlink(2),fp:fe,x2200,2008-11-22 22:10:36.481 +01:00
path,/etc/passwd
attribute,100644,root,sys,65553,52868,18446744073709551615
subject,martin,martin,martin,martin,martin,22405,765996641,894 136704 u40
group,martin,10001,10002
use of privilege,failed use of priv,file_link_any,proc_exec,proc_fork,proc_session
return,failure: Permission denied,-1
zone,public
```

In this case, the user `martin` tried to remove the `/etc/passwd` file. This last category of events is the one most likely to show malicious intent.

9.5 Managing the Audit Trail

Configuring a system to generate audit information is easy—the hard part is dealing with the resulting data.

9.5.1 Log Rotation

The audit files can grow very quickly on a busy system, and it is not uncommon to generate gigabytes of audit data per day. To keep the audit files in manageable sizes, you must periodically rotate them. The frequency of rotation depends on the activity on the system; that is, how large you want the files to get. The easiest way to rotate the audit files is to add a cron job that rotates the logs weekly, daily, or hourly, depending on your requirements. The following cron job rotates the logs once a day at one minute to midnight:

```
59 23 * * * /usr/sbin/audit -n
```

If you are going to send a copy of the logs to a remote system for secure storage, you might want to rotate the files more frequently. Smaller files transmit more quickly.

You can also use the `logadm` command to rotate the logs. However, because the name of the audit file changes each time that the log is rotated, this command is not as straightforward to use.

9.5.2 Remote Storage

One of the issues with the audit trail is that it is written to local disk. So, if the system is compromised, the intruder can just stop auditing and delete the audit trail, and you'll never figure out what happened.

You can mitigate some of this risk by using the `audit_syslog`(5) plug-in, which writes a truncated plain-text version of Solaris audit data to `syslog` messages. By using syslog to write the audit records to a different system, you can protect the audit trail on a remote system where the attacker cannot modify or delete them, at least not without compromising that system, too. For an example of configuring syslog for remote storage, see Section 9.6.2, "Using the `audit_syslog` Plug-in."

While syslog is neither a secure nor safe transport method, and audit records can be lost unintentionally or though a DoS attack, syslog is nevertheless a good complement to storing the binary audit trail on the local system.

The best way to mitigate the risk is to rotate audit logs frequently, and immediately copy rotated logs to a secure remote system. One method is to set up an account on the remote system that is used as a "drop box." A drop box is a location where audit files can be deposited through the `scp`(1) command, but the files cannot be modified or deleted. This method creates a chain of trust between the systems. One important feature is that a compromise of the audited system cannot lead to a compromise of the system with the drop box.

A second method is provided by an open source tool called ALF (Audit Log Fetcher)[3]. ALF uses the pull method instead of the push method that the preceding paragraph describes. The pull method is better suited for large environments where hundreds of systems could try to copy audit files to the same server at the same time.

ALF uses an "outbox" directory on each system. The outbox directory contains the audit files that are ready to be transferred. The remote storage system uses the sftp command to retrieve the files that are ready for pickup in the outbox.

9.5.3 Compression

The audit files can consume a considerable amount of disk space, especially when the argv audit policy is used. Luckily, the audit files compress well, so it is advisable to configure automatic compression of the audit files once they are rotated. However, compressed files require extra work when you want to analyze the files. The work is especially difficult when you are looking for an event, but you do not know which audit file contains it. Then, you must uncompress the files before you can use the auditreduce command to look for the event. You can also try the gzcat command.

A more efficient method of compression uses a ZFS file system. You can set up a ZFS file system with compression enabled and rotate the audit files to that file system. With this setup, you do not have to compress the files or uncompress them when you want to analyze them.

To create a ZFS file system with maximum compression for your audit files, use the following command:

```
# zfs create -o compression=gzip-9 -o mountpoint=/audit z0/audit
```

Then, set up your audit file rotation to copy the files to the /audit directory and the files will be automatically compressed and uncompressed.

9.6 Common Auditing Customizations

Some typical site customizations of auditing include creating a role to review the audit records, sending syslog output to a remote system, and configuring site-specific audit classes. This section provides examples of these customizations.

9.6.1 Configuring an Audit Review Role That Is Not Audited

The Audit Review role is designed for the user who is to review the audit records. The actions of this role are not audited, so do not fill up the audit trail with unnecessary events.

1. Add the role by using the `roleadd` command, and set a password for the role:

```
# roleadd -P "Audit Review" -d /var/audit -c "audit review role" audit
# passwd audit
Enter password:
Retype password:
```

This command creates a role named `audit` that is assigned the Audit Review rights profile.

2. Then, edit the `audit_user` database to add the following line:
    `audit:lo:aa`

    This entry specifies that the `audit` user is always audited for logins, and never audited for events in the `aa` class.

3. Finally, you assign the role to the user who is going to review the audit trail:
    `# usermod -r audit martin`

Now, the audit trail will not be filled with audit records that are generated when the audit records are reviewed.

> **Note**
>
> The default directory that is used by the `auditreduce` command to combine audit trails is `/etc/security/audit/localhost/files`. This directory is a symbolic link to `/var/audit`. If you store rotated audit files somewhere else, you can specify the directory by using the `-R` option to `auditreduce`.

9.6.2 Using the `audit_syslog` Plug-in

You can mitigate some of the risk of locally stored audit records by using the `audit_syslog`(5) plug-in. This plug-in writes Solaris audit data to `syslog` messages. By this means, you can send the audit trail to a remote system where the attacker cannot reach the logs, at least not at once.

1. Add the following line to your `audit_control` file to send all login and logout events and all failed file modifications to `syslog`:

    `plugin: name=audit_syslog.so;p_flags=lo,-fm`

2. To send the syslog output to your secure syslog server (called `remoteloghost`), configure your local `syslogd` to forward the log entries with the facility code of

LOG_AUDIT and severity of LOG_NOTICE, by adding the following to the `/etc/syslog.conf` file:

```
audit.notice                    @remoteloghost
```

> **Note**
>
> syslog messages have a maximum length of 1024 bytes because they are delivered by UDP datagrams. Therefore, the log entries can be truncated. The `audit_syslog` plug-in retains as much information as possible by truncating paths from the left and other text from the right. Truncation might be an issue if you want to use the syslog messages as legal evidence, because the record could be incomplete.

9.6.3 Creating Your Own Audit Class

Using the default audit classes can sometimes give you too much audit information. For example, to record when processes open server sockets, you must enable auditing of the `nt` class. However, auditing `nt` has the side effect of recording every network-related event. As a result, the audit trail can be flooded with records of the very *chatty* `sendto`(2) and `sendmsg`(2) system calls.

The best way to reduce an unwanted flood of audit information is to create a custom audit class that includes only the audit events you want. Another benefit of adding your own audit class is that you retain the original Solaris audit event-audit class mappings. Retaining the original mappings makes it easier to migrate to newer versions of the Solaris OS.

In the following example, you create a custom class that includes events that directly manipulate security attributes of files and processes, like the `chown`(2) and `setuid`(2) system calls. Your custom class includes events from both the `fm` and `pm` audit classes.

1. First, edit the `audit_class` file and pick a bit that is not used, like `0x08000000`. Give the new class a short name and a description.

   `0x08000000:ms:manipulate security attributes`

2. Add the new ms audit class to the audit events that you want. In the `audit_event` file, add ms to the following events. Use a comma as the separator:

```
10:AUE_CHMOD:chmod(2):fm,ms
11:AUE_CHOWN:chown(2):fm,ms
24:AUE_CHROOT:chroot(2):pm,ms
31:AUE_SETPRIORITY:setpriority(2):ms
```

continues

```
38:AUE_FCHOWN:fchown(2):fm,ms
39:AUE_FCHMOD:fchmod(2):fm,ms
40:AUE_SETREUID:setreuid(2):pm,ms
69:AUE_FCHROOT:fchroot(2):pm,ms
200:AUE_OSETUID:old setuid(2):pm,ms
203:AUE_NICE:old nice(2):pm,ms
212:AUE_PRIOCNTLSYS:priocntlsys(2):pm,ms
215:AUE_SETEUID:seteuid(2):pm,ms
237:AUE_LCHOWN:lchown(2):fm,ms
251:AUE_ACLSET:acl(2) - SETACL command:fm,ms
252:AUE_FACLSET:facl(2) - SETACL command:fm,ms
289:AUE_SETPPRIV:setppriv(2):pm,ms
```

These events note changes to file and process attributes that might or might not require privilege. Frequently, an *intruder* would need to change file attributes in order to abuse the system, while *users* do not normally change file permissions. Note that a recursive chmod(1) can generate a large amount of audit information.

3. After you update the audit_event file, run the following command to load your changes in the kernel:

   # **auditconfig -conf**

Notes

1. For more information, see http://nsi.org/Library/Compsec/orangebo.txt.

2. For more information, see http://www.commoncriteriaportal.org/.

3. http://projects.codenursery.com/projects/show/alf/

Solaris Network Security

The Solaris OS includes several features that enable you to protect a single system, systems on local and wide area networks, and traffic across the Internet. IP layer filtering is used to create firewalls to protect networks and hosts from intrusion. IPsec provides encryption and authentication at the IP layer. Solaris Secure Shell (SunSSH) provides a suite of tools that enable remote systems to be accessed in a secure manner. It can be used in place of older, insecure methods such as ftp, telnet, rlogin, and rsh. At the transport layer, the Solaris OS provides OpenSSL as a cryptography toolkit.

The Solaris OS also includes Kerberos. Kerberos is the foundation of many single sign on solutions. Kerberos provides a flexible, dynamic, robust, and secure mechanism for applications or users to authenticate and function over the network. The chapter concludes with extended examples of how to administer Kerberos with a variety of applications, including Microsoft Active Directory.

10.1 IP Filter

Solaris IP Filter provides packet filtering functionality, which enables a Solaris system to be used as either a firewall, when the system is configured as a router, or to simply provide security for the local host. In addition, Solaris IP Filter provides Network Address Translation (NAT) capabilities for systems that border different networks. Solaris IP Filter can be used with all of the existing networking technologies in the Solaris OS to provide additional security at the network layer. Solaris

IP Filter provides the user with the option of using stateful packet filtering or stateless packet filtering.

Use of IP Filter to enforce a host security policy enables the system administrator to implement fine-grained access control to applications. The filter can control who can access applications over the network. The control is independent of how each application is configured. Thus, the access control policy for network services is stated in one location, not per application.

NAT is most often used when connecting a private network that is using one of the networking address spaces set aside in RFC1918[1], to a larger network, such as the Internet. NAT can also be used to join two networks together where the address space of the two networks overlaps and full connectivity is required.

10.1.1 IP Filter Configuration

In the Solaris 10 release, IP Filter is enabled and disabled through the use of SMF. The service identifier for IP Filter is `svc://network/ipfilter`. The IP Filter configuration files on a Solaris system are in the `/etc/ipf` directory. The following commands enable and disable IP Filter:

```
# svcadm enable ipfilter
# svcadm disable ipfilter
```

Like all SMF services, once the IP Filter service is enabled, the service is active and is enabled when the system reboots. When IP Filter is enabled, a booting system looks in the `/etc/ipf` directory for two files: `/etc/ipf/ipf.conf` and `/etc/ipf/ipnat.conf`. These files contain the configuration rules for creating a firewall and for NAT, respectively. To modify these files, use an editor such as `vi`. For detailed documentation on the file formats for the `ipf.conf` and `ipnat.conf` files, see the `ipf`(5) and `ipnat`(5) man pages.

10.1.1.1 Last Match Versus First Match

When designing a filter policy for use with IP Filter, it is worth remembering that it is possible to write the firewall packet matching rules to be *either first* or *last* match. By default, the filter matching on the firewall will be *last* match. To change the behavior of a rule to be *first* match, the keyword **quick** is added to the filter rule.

The combination of first match filter and last match filter rules enables the writer of the configuration file to start out with a few statements that match all packets and to then use the **quick** keyword to progressively implement the security policy for the network.

An example of the combination of first and last match is shown in the sample configuration in the next section.

10.1.2 Starting Out

To begin using IP Filter, you can start with an empty configuration file for both `ipf.conf` and `ipnat.conf` and then enable the service.

```
##################################################
# Simple IPFilter configuration file
#
# By default, all traffic is blocked.
# The rules that define the default blocking actions are all
# last match rules. Thus, for example, every inbound packet starts
# off being blocked but can then be allowed depending on the
# policy for the machine/services.
#
block in all
block out all
#
# For TCP packets that attempt to establish a connection, send
# them back a reset
#
block return-rst in proto tcp all
#
# For UDP packets, sending back ICMP errors returns a quicker
# error than just a simple timeout.
#
block return-icmp in proto udp all
#
# We're running a web server on this host, so we allow in
# connections to ports 80 (http) and 443 (https)
# Here "quick" is used to implement "first match". A packet that
# matches these rules finishes matching rules here. Stateful
# filtering is used for access to the web server.
#
pass in quick on bge0 proto tcp from any to any port = 80 flags S keep state
pass in quick on bge0 proto tcp from any to any port = 443 flags S keep state
#
```

10.1.3 Stateful Versus Stateless Filtering

Many firewall products make a point of mentioning whether they can perform stateful packet filtering or not. IP Filter supports both styles of filtering and allows the administrator to decide which style of filtering best supports their security policy.

In stateful filtering, IP Filter remembers some of the details from packets it has seen in the past and uses this information to help in deciding whether or not to allow future packets through. Stateful filtering is most often used with TCP to reduce the risk of TCP connections, where the concept of a virtual connection exists. For other protocols, such as UDP and ICMP, stateful filtering assumes that most applications expect a response to packets that they send. For example, the `ping` program sends out an ICMP ECHO packet, and expects an ECHO-REPLY packet back. With stateful filtering, both of these packets are allowed with one rule.

With stateless filtering, you need to create an explicit rule for each type of packet. However, stateless filtering cannot distinguish an ECHO-REPLY packet that is actually a reply to an ECHO, from an ECHO-REPLY packet that was generated by a hacker or rogue system on the Internet. Thus, a stateless filtering policy is more open in the packets that it allows through.

To illustrate the difference between stateful and stateless filtering and their effects on configuration, see the following sample configuration file for a Web server that is protected by a firewall using IP Filter. The example assumes the following:

- Access to the Web server is to be provided to hosts both on the Internet and on the local LAN.

- Content can be uploaded to the Web server by using ssh, so local LAN access to the Web server for this service is also required.

- The Web traffic is all unauthenticated and accesses no confidential data, thus so long as packets go to and from the Web server's ports, there is little concern for the traffic.

```
##################################################
# Simple IPFilter configuration file
#
# Internet is connected to bge0, internal network is via bge2 and
# a DMZ for the web server is connected via bge1.
#
# Default deny all policy
#
block in all
block out all
#
# Allow access to the web server ports 80 and 443.
#
pass in quick on bge0 proto tcp from any to 1.1.1.1 port = 80
pass out quick on bge1 proto tcp from any to 1.1.1.1 port = 80
pass in quick on bge1 proto tcp from 1.1.1.1 port = 80 to any
pass out quick on bge0 proto tcp from 1.1.1.1 port = 80 to any
pass in quick on bge0 proto tcp from any to 1.1.1.1 port = 443
pass out quick on bge1 proto tcp from any to 1.1.1.1 port = 443
pass in quick on bge1 proto tcp from 1.1.1.1 port = 443 to any
pass out quick on bge0 proto tcp from 1.1.1.1 port = 443 to any
#
# Allow internal hosts to access the web server too.
#
pass in quick on bge2 proto tcp from any to 1.1.1.1 port = 80
pass out quick on bge2 proto tcp from 1.1.1.1 port = 80 to any
pass in quick on bge2 proto tcp from any to 1.1.1.1 port = 443
pass out quick on bge2 proto tcp from 1.1.1.1 port = 443 to any
#
# Allow internal hosts to ssh to the web server
#
pass in on bge2,bge1 out-via bge1,bge2 proto tcp from any to 1.1.1.1 port = 22 flags S
keep state
```

The single stateful filtering rule is able to define the network interfaces upon which traffic should arrive for each of the four directions relative to the firewall host:

- Forward in—in on bge2, from the internal network to the Web server
- Forward out—out on bge1, from the internal network to the Web server
- Reverse in—in on bge1 from the Web server to the internal network
- Reverse out—out on bge2, from the Web server to the internal network

10.1.4 Troubleshooting IP Filter

Because IP Filter is enabled or disabled by using SMF, the correct first step in determining if IP Filter is functioning is to query the status of the SMF service:

```
# svcs -x ipfilter
```

To verify that the kernel module is loaded and running, use the `ipf` command:

```
# ipf -V
```

To verify the rules have been loaded and are active, use the `ipfstat` command:

```
# ipfstat -io
```

To augment the output of the rules loaded in the kernel with the number of times each one has been successfully matched, add the `-h` option to the `ipfstat` command:

```
# ipfstat -hio
```

The number that is printed at the start of each line is the number of times each rule has been matched. To reset these numbers back to zero, use the `ipf` command:

```
# ipf -zf /etc/ipf.conf
```

which prints out the count for each line as it was in the kernel prior to being reset to zero.

To view the overall statistics for IP Filter, use the `ipfstat` command without any command line options:

```
# ipfstat
```

When stateful filtering is being used, the counter for rule matches is only incremented each time a packet arrives that matches the rule but for which there is no existing state.

10.1.5 IP Filter in Zones

On systems that are configured to support local zones, IP Filter is available to the local zone system administrator if the zone has been configured with an exclusive IP instance. If the zone has not been explicitly configured with an exclusive IP instance, the local zone is subject to the IP Filter policy in the global zone's configuration files.

From the global zone, it is not possible to configure rules in the `ipnat.conf` or `ipf.conf` files that affect packets that are received by zones with exclusive IP instances.

To enable, disable, or otherwise administer IP Filter in a local zone that has an exclusive IP instance, the global zone system administrator must log in to the local zone and run commands within the domain of the local zone. For example:

```
# zlogin test_zone1 svcadm enable ipfilter
# zlogin test_zone1 ipfstat
```

10.1.6 Filtering Inter-Zone Packets—Loopback Packet Filtering

By default, on systems with more than one local zone using the shared IP instance model, it is not possible to filter on the packets that are exchanged by the zones. To enable IP Filter to control the packets between these zones, you need to enable filtering of *loopback* packets; that is, packets that are local to the machine. To enable filtering of loopback packets, the following statement needs to be added to the top of the IP Filter configuration file, `/etc/ipf/ipf.conf`. This statement must precede any policy rules in that file. The line to add is:

```
set intercept_loopback true;
```

Packets that are from or to a local zone that is using a shared instance of IP are considered to be part of the loopback packets for the system.

It is important to recognize that once loopback filtering has been enabled, you *must* review which services on the system make use of loopback traffic. Often local applications use TCP/IP over the loopback interface for IPC (Inter Process Communication). Rather than surveying all of the local applications, you can explicitly

allow all communication that uses the loopback interfaces with rules such as
these:

```
#
# Enable interception of loopback packets for local zone filtering
#
set intercept_loopback true;
#
# We trust all packets on the loopback interface as they are only
# to/from local applications
#
pass in quick on lo0 all
pass out quick on lo0 all
```

Of course, if security policy requires you to filter on TCP/IP traffic local to the
host, then you could also filter the local TCP/IP traffic rather than just allowing all
loopback traffic.

For local zones with a shared IP instance, the network interfaces that are
assigned to the zones, such as bge0:1 or xge2:3, define the name of the network
interface with which the local traffic is associated.

So, for example, if there are two zones that are using a shared instance of IP
(the current default configuration) and the zones have been assigned IP addresses
on the network interfaces bge0:2 and bge0:3, then the traffic between the zones
will appear leaving the first zone as going *out* on bge0 and entering the second
zone as coming *in* on bge0. The appearance of bge0 as both *out* and *in* can compli-
cate the construction of anti-spoofing rules.

Thus, the safest way to permit inter-zone IP traffic is to use stateful filtering on
the packets that leave the zone that is making the connection, and to not filter
packets as they arrive from another zone. In the following example, all communication between the two zones is prohibited except for the Web server zone to connect to the MySQL database, which is running in another zone:

```
#
# Enable interception of loopback packets for local zone filtering
#
set intercept_loopback true;
#
# The web server is running in a zone that is using IP address
# 10.10.1.2 and we're running a MySQL server in the zone using
# IP address 10.10.1.3. Some of the web applications need access
# to MySQL.
#
block in on bge0 from 10.10.1.3 to 10.10.1.2
block in on bge0 from 10.10.1.2 to 10.10.1.3
pass out on bge0 in-via bge0 proto tcp from 10.10.1.2 to 10.10.1.3 port = mysql flags S
keep state
```

10.1.7 IP Filter and Anti-Spoofing

It is not unusual, when given a raw connection to the Internet from an ISP, to receive packets that you should not. For example, packets arrive at your firewall that, by virtue of the source address on the packets, claim to be from systems on your network. Packets that have obviously forged IP addresses are considered to have their source address "spoofed." Therefore, a firewall commonly has a set of rules early in the configuration that drops all such packets. For example:

```
#################################################
# Simple IPFilter configuration file
#
# Internet is connected to bge0, internal network is via bge2 and
# a DMZ for the web server is connected via bge1.
#
# Default deny all policy
#
block in all
block out all
#
# RFC1918 networks are private and should not appear from the
# Internet, so drop them as they must be spoofed.
#
block in quick on bge0 from 10.0.0.0/8 to any
block in quick on bge0 from 192.168.0.0/16 to any
block in quick on bge0 from 172.xxx.0.0/Y to any
```

Anti-spoofing rules are useful even when the system is providing services, such as a Web server, where everyone, everywhere is permitted to access the system. The rules make the log files and the Web server's security configuration make sense. For example, if the internal network is using the subnet `10` internally, then dropping all spoofed packets ensures that all entries in the Web server's logs from `10.1.0.0/16` record activity from internal networks.

10.1.8 Using NAT with IP Filter

When connecting a small private network to the Internet, often only a single IP address for the Internet has been assigned by the Internet Service Provide (ISP), but the private network has more than one host. With respect to RFC ABCD, IP Filter's NAT can be said to provide restricted-cone NAT, the most secure variation of NAT. IP Filter's NAT provides the following features:

- ▪ SNAT (Static NAT)—Fixed address assignment
- ▪ DNAT (Dynamic NAT)—Where the new address used is non-deterministic

- PAT (Port Address Translation)—Changes source and destination ports for TCP/UDP. PAT is often also referred to as PNAT, Port Network Address Translation.

Solaris IP Filter NAT allows for the source address to be changed on packets leaving the machine, using *map* rules, or for the destination address to be changed on packets coming in, using *rdr* rules. Both styles of rules must be placed in the NAT configuration file, `/etc/ipf/ipnat.conf`.

10.1.8.1 Source Network Address Translation (SNAT)

When NAT is used, the number of addresses that are available in the new network address space is often less than those in the original address space. For the two most common protocols that support Internet applications, TCP and UDP, IP Filter allows the port number to be changed through the use of the portmap keyword with *map* rules.

The following example, although simple, is all that is required for most systems that attach to the Internet.

```
#
# Rewrite all packets exiting the host to have the source address
# assigned to bge0.
#
map bge0 0/0 -> 0/32 portmap 10000:65500 tcp/udp
map bge0 0/0 -> 0/32
#
```

10.1.8.2 Destination Network Address Translation (DNAT)

In situations where limited Internet-accessible addresses are available, Web servers that are providing content to the Internet can be assigned *private* addresses from RFC1918. If IP Filter is being used as the firewall between the Internet and the Web server, IP Filter can change the destination address of incoming connection requests from the external address to an internal, private address.

```
#
# All incoming packets to port 80 are to be sent to the server
# providing web content.
#
rdr bge0 0/0 port = 80 -> 10.1.1.2 port 80 tcp
#
```

10.1.8.3 NAT Proxies

Most services used on the Internet today are relatively simple and involve the client making connections to the server on a small number of well-known ports that can be configured in the `ipf.conf` file. Some services are more complicated and require additional protocol inspection. The most common application that requires additional inspection is File Transfer Protocol (FTP). FTP is complex to handle on firewalls because FTP embeds IP addresses in the commands sent to and from the client and the server. Thus, for the proper, safe use of FTP with IP Filter, you need to use the inbuilt kernel proxy. NAT is used to achieve this, although it is not necessary for address translation to happen.

The FTP proxy can be used to assist in accessing external FTP servers or internal servers. To aid in accessing FTP servers outside your network, you construct a NAT rule that is applied on the interface where packets leave the firewall. To aid in accessing FTP servers inside the network, the best approach is to use a NAT rule on the network interface where the FTP sessions first enter the firewall. In the following example, no actual address translation happens. The proxies are merely being associated with TCP connections.

```
#
# Simple NAT configuration to use the FTP proxy. bge0 is our
# connection to the Internet and is where all the FTP servers are
# that we wish to interact with.
#
map bge0 0/0 -> 0/0 proxy port ftp ftp/tcp
#
# Allow external parties to contact our FTP server
#
rdr bge0 0/0 port 21 -> 0.0.0.0 port 21 proxy ftp
#
```

10.1.9 Logging with IP Filter

By default, Solaris IP Filter does not log any packet information. Packets are dropped or passed, quietly, with the appropriate counter ticking over. Logging of packets can happen in one of two ways when configuring the `ipf.conf` file:

- As an explicit action to be taken, or
- As part of the result of matching a rule

The first option is achieved with a "log" rule. A log rule is constructed in the same manner as one might construct a "pass" or "block" rule. These log rules are actions—they do *not* have any impact on the end result of applying the policy. This can result in a packet being logged twice: once for matching the log rule and again for matching the rule that blocks the packet.

When using the "log" keyword with stateful filtering, you might want to log only the *first* packet that causes the state to be created. Otherwise, every packet for the connection is logged. To log only the first packet that creates the state, the word "first" must be added to the syntax. The security policy that is being applied and enforced by IP Filter determines whether the word "first" is required.

```
#
# Log all ICMP packets from the Internet
#
log in on bge0 proto icmp all
#
# log any blocked packets that have been spoofed and look like
# they are from an internal network.
#
block in log quick on bge0 from 10.0.0.0/8 to any
#
# Log only the packet that attempts to connect to the SSH server
# running on the web server, not every packet for the session
# that follows.
#
pass in log first quick on bge2,bge1 out-via bge1,bge2 proto tcp from any to 1.1.1.1
port = 22 flags S keep state
#
```

10.2 What Is IPsec?

IP Security (IPsec) is IP network layer encryption and authentication. IPsec encryption protects the contents of IP packets in the network so that they can only be read by the intended recipient. IPsec authentication ensures that the data on the wire has not been tampered with in transit.

IPsec on public or otherwise potentially hostile networks ensures safe transit of sensitive data to the intended recipients only. It may also be used by secure facilities or for sensitive financial data within an otherwise open network. Virtual Private Networks (VPNs) typically use IPsec to offer secure remote access to a private network over the public Internet.

IPsec offers choices of encryption and authentication algorithms, as well as key sizes. These choices give the administrator various levels of assurance on the difficulty of cracking the keys and exposing the data. In general, the larger the key size and the stronger the algorithm, the harder it is for an adversary to mount a successful brute force attack. This higher level of assurance comes with a computational price for the systems doing the encryption. Therefore, CPU speeds and the type of data might dictate trade-offs.

10.2.1 What Do IPsec Packets Look Like?

Some background terminology is necessary in order to understand IPsec configuration. This section defines AH, ESP, SA, SADB, SPI, IKE, SPD, tunnel mode, and transport mode.

Packets that are protected with IPsec have one or more IPsec headers on them. Someone who is sniffing the network sees these headers instead of the actual data. Note that the following discussion is about IP protocols, which are not to be confused with ports. For example, TCP is IP protocol 6 and UDP is IP protocol 17. ESP and AH are their own IP protocols as well:

- **AH:** Authentication Header, IP Protocol 51
  - Authenticates packet for integrity checking. Does not provide encryption.
  - Ensures that the packet has not been tampered with in transit.
  - Uses a hash algorithm such as MD5 or SHA1.
  - Authentication includes the packet payload and part of the IP header. This includes the IP addresses in the outer header and some routing headers.
  - Is incompatible with Network Address Translation (NAT) because the hash is invalidated when the IP address changes.
- **ESP:** Encapsulating Security Payload, IP Protocol 50
  - Encrypts packet by using an algorithm such as AES, 3DES, DES, Blowfish.
  - Optionally authenticates encrypted payload with a hash algorithm.
  - ESP authentication covers packet data only, so it can be used with NAT.

Users can use AH or ESP or both. If both are used, the AH header in an IPsec packet that is generated by the Solaris OS always appears as the outside header. The AH-only mode of IPsec is seldom used, but it has some applications. Examples include systems with slower CPUs or sites that ban secretive data for auditing purposes, but the site wants to ensure that the auditing data is not tampered with. Typical deployments use ESP with encryption and authentication.

The term SA is worthy of a special note. SA means "Security Association," which means a group of parameters, including encryption keys, that are associated with a particular session between two hosts in a particular direction. SAs are unidirectional and are typically used in pairs. A "shared" SA means that sessions between the same two addresses in the same direction use the same SA. The alternative is a "unique" SA, which tracks a separate SA for each pair of source and destination ports. An SA is indexed by a number called an SPI (Security Parameters Index), which is a hexadecimal number either assigned manually or by a key management daemon such as IKE.

SA data is stored in memory in the SADB, the security association database. The SADB tracks AH and ESP SAs separately.

The term SPD refers to the security policy database. The SPD is the location in memory where security policy, that is, to allow or disallow packets and how to protect them, is stored. In the Solaris OS, security policy is handled separately from keys and key management.

IPsec can also be used in transport mode or tunnel mode. Transport mode protects the data only, while tunnel mode encapsulates and protects the entire original IP packet. The following explanation and examples concern transport mode.

10.2.2 How Is IPsec Configured?

To use IPsec, you must have keying material and an IPsec policy. The IPsec policy is configured by editing the `/etc/inet/ipsecinit.conf` file. Keying material can be provided by using Internet Key Management (IKE) or by providing keys manually. IKE is the preferred method because it is simpler to set up and replaces keying material at regular intervals.

10.2.2.1 Assigning IPsec Policy

An IPsec policy tells the system how to protect traffic, as well as what not to protect. It can also be used as a rudimentary firewall for blocking or allowing certain IP addresses or simple port-based services. For transport mode, policy is applied by using the `ipsecconf(1m)` command:

```
# ipsecconf -a /etc/inet/ipsecinit.conf
```

The file `ipsecinit.conf` is the default location for a security policy to be read on boot. The following is a sample `ipsecinit.conf` file:

```
##################################################
# Simple IPsec policy example

# Note that IP addresses are acceptable and preferable in most environs
# though hostnames will work.  Use of hostnames implies trusting that
# naming services are secure, therefore is highly discouraged.
#
# In this example, we use the following hosts:
#
# 1.1.1.1 spiderweb (local host)
# 2.2.2.2 arachnid (remote)
# 3.3.3.3 spiderwoman (remote)
# 4.4.4.4 tarantula (remote)
```

continues

```
#
# Allow all outgoing (local-address to remote-address )
# web traffic (rport 80
# to go to arachnid (2.2.2.2)
# in the clear (bypass)
#
{ laddr 1.1.1.1 raddr 2.2.2.2 ulp tcp rport 80 dir both } bypass {}


#
# Encrypt from local address spiderweb to remote address arachnid
# using IPsec with ESP encryption algorithm AES and ESP auth algorithm sha1
#
{ laddr 1.1.1.1 raddr 2.2.2.2 } ipsec { encr_algs aes encr_auth_algs
   sha1 sa shared}


#
# Use AH authentication only to spiderwoman. Note "auth_algs" specifies
# AH algorithms while "encr_auth_algs" specifies ESP authentication
#
{ laddr 1.1.1.1 raddr 3.3.3.3 } ipsec { auth_algs md5 sa shared}


#
# Use ESP with encryption and authentication and AH authentication to
# tarantula. Note that encr_auth_algs refers to ESP authentication
# while auth_algs refers to AH authentication. Confusing these keywords
# is a very common mistake.
#
{ laddr 1.1.1.1 raddr 4.4.4.4 } ipsec { encr_algs 3des encr_auth_algs
   md5 auth_algs sha1 sa shared }


#
# Block incoming web traffic from arachnid. Note that we use local
# port 80 here, as opposed to remote port in the outgoing pass example
#
{ laddr 1.1.1.1 raddr 2.2.2.2 ulp tcp lport 80 dir both } drop {}
#################################################
```

10.2.2.2 Commands for Viewing and Debugging Your IPsec Configuration

When configuring IPsec, the following commands are used frequently.

To verify that the IPsec policy file syntax is correct, run the following command:

```
# ipsecconf -c -f filename
```

To view the current policy, run the `ipsecconf` command with no options:

```
# ipsecconf
```

To view the complete internal representation, add the `-ln` option:

```
# ipsecconf -ln
```

For more information, see the `ipsecconf`(1m) man page.

10.2.2.3 Assigning IPsec Keys Manually

The IPsec policy configures the system to drop, encrypt, or authenticate traffic. However, encryption and authentication require SAs that match the policy entries. The SAs can be added manually by using the `ipseckey(1m)` command or automatically by using a keying daemon such as `in.iked(1m)`. The SA contains the keys actually used to encrypt/authenticate the traffic.

To assign keys and create SAs manually, use the `ipseckey` command:

```
# ipseckey -f file
```

The default file that contains the SAs and keys for the system to read on boot is `/etc/inet/secret/ipseckeys`.

The syntax for this file is described in the `ipseckey(1m)` man page. However, to discourage its use, we do not provide an example. The `ipseckeys` file contains the actual keys. Because sensitive keying material is left on the disk and not changed periodically, manual setup is not typically recommended. If the keying material is lost, then an attacker can use your keys and eavesdrop and decrypt all traffic, including traffic that was collected earlier. The alternative is IKE, which changes keying material periodically. If you do opt to use manual keys, you must guard and update the `ipseckeys` file with the utmost care to protect the keys.

10.2.2.4 Using IKE for Automated Key Management

The Internet Key Exchange (IKE) provides a better way to manage keys for IPsec. The IKE daemon, `in.iked`, communicates over UDP port 500. The IKE daemon and its peer on the other system authenticate each other and then establish an encrypted channel between them. The two peers negotiate common protocols and authentication methods during this phase. This is called "Phase 1" in the IKE exchange. It is sometimes called "Main Mode."

Once the two systems establish an encrypted channel, they communicate and negotiate algorithms and keys for the actual network traffic that is to be encrypted. This is called "Phase 2," also referred to as "Quick Mode." At this stage, the IPSec SAs are created. The advantage of IKE is that the SAs expire periodically and are replaced automatically by subsequent exchanges. Occasionally, the Phase 1 session rekeys itself as well. IKE is also much better at choosing random values for SPIs and keys, which makes them harder to crack. This rekeying and randomization greatly reduce the risk of people having their private keys stolen and then having all of their historical data be able to be decrypted offline.

10.2.2.5 IKE Setup

The simplest form of system authentication when using IKE is preshared keys. These keys are used in Phase 1. This form of system authentication involves setting up a preshared secret, which is usually an ASCII passphrase, between two peers. The Solaris OS expects ASCII character equivalents, so the secret abc in the preshared keys file would be 616263. Keep in mind that other operating systems vary, so for example on Microsoft Windows, the preshared key would be abc, not 616263. Of course, you use a much longer passphrase than abc when doing your deployment.

The preshared key file is located here:

```
/etc/inet/secret/ike.preshared
```

The syntax is described in the ike.preshared(4) man page. The following is a sample preshared keys file for IKE:

```
###########################################
# Simple example ike.preshared file

#
{
    # The localid/remoteid addresses are the IP addresses
    # of the systems running in.iked (the IKE daemon)
    localidtype IP
    localid 1.1.1.1
    remoteidtype IP
    remoteid 2.2.2.2
    key 616263
}
```

10.2.2.6 IKE Daemon Configuration

The behavior of the IKE daemon, in.iked, is controlled by its own configuration file, /etc/inet/ike/config. The syntax is described on the ike.config(4) man page. The IKE daemon is located at /usr/lib/inet/in.iked.

The configuration file controls Phase 1 behavior. A simple example for our preshared example would be the following:

```
########################################

{
  #
  # The label is an ASCII string used to identify each "rule"
  # in the in.iked configuration file. The label needs to be
  # unique and, ideally, is meaningful to your setup.
  #
  label "spiderwalker"
```

continues

```
#
# These are the addresses of the systems running in.iked or some
# other IKE daemon. They might possibly be different from the
# addresses used in your policy, such as some cases of tunnel mode.
# When using preshared keys, the IP addresses  for
# local_addr/remote_addr must match those in the ike.preshared file
#
local_addr 1.1.1.1
remote_addr 2.2.2.2

#
# Phase 1 parameters acceptable to this system are described
# in a phase 1 transform. Each rule must have one or more
# phase 1 transforms (p1_xform).
# The IKE daemon (in.iked) will negotiate with its peer to
# find a transform they both find acceptable. This transform is
# used to provide the phase 1 SA, and is used to protect later
# phase 2 exchanges.
#
 p1_xform
  { auth_method preshared oakley_group 2 encr_alg 3des auth_alg sha1 }
}

#########################################
```

The peer must be configured similarly. On the peer, the label would be unique, and the value of local address and remote address would be reversed. Note that this is only the Phase 1 configuration.

You must also set up Phase 2 configuration; that is, your IPsec security policy. The following example shows a suitable policy entry for transport mode. You type the entry in the `etc/inet/ipsecinit.conf` file and the policy is read in with the `ipsecconf` command.

```
{laddr 1.1.1.1 raddr 2.2.2.2} ipsec
    {encr_algs aes encr_auth_algs sha1 sa shared}
```

To force the `in.iked` daemon to re-read its configuration file after the file is changed, you can run the following command:

pkill -HUP in.iked

This command does not kill the daemon. Rather, it sends a signal for the daemon to read its configuration file.

10.2.2.7 Commands for Viewing and Debugging Your IKE Configuration

When configuring IKE, the following commands are used frequently.

To verify that the IKE configuration file syntax is correct, run the following command:

```
 # /usr/lib/inet/in.iked -c [-f filename]
```

To observe what the `in.iked` daemon is doing, you run the daemon in debug mode. Readability and completeness of the debug output improves with each incremental release of Solaris 10. For testing purposes, you can run in debug mode by using the `-d` option to the daemon:

```
# pkill in.iked
# /usr/lib/inet/in.iked -d
```

Much more suitable for a production site, you can turn on debugging on the fly:

```
# ikeadm set debug all /path/to/some/file
# tail -f /path/to/some/file
```

You sometimes do not want to use old keys until they expire. For example, if the peer has rebooted, lost its configuration, or changed its configuration, you would need new keys. To flush all of your SAs and force IKE to renegotiate the session from scratch, you can flush the keys and then restart traffic:

```
# ipseckey flush
```

If you want to see if you have an active SA and Phase 1 keys between you and your peer, you can dump the Phase 1 keys. The output also displays when the keys expire and how that peer is authenticated. For example, you can view the X.509 DN to see who is associated with the other connection.

To dump your SAs and derived—that is, Phase 2 keys—run the following command:

```
# ipseckey -n dump
```

To see the Phase 1 SAs, which are between the IKE daemons and different from the Phase 2 SAs, run the following command:

```
# ikeadm -n dump p1
```

10.2.2.8 Certificates for IKE

An alternative to using preshared keys is to use certificates. The `in.iked` daemon can use X.509 certificates to authenticate each peer and establish the Phase 1 session. Certificates are a much stronger authentication method for IKE and are preferred over preshared keys. IKE accepts self-signed certificates and CA-signed certificates. The examples in this chapter use self-signed certificates. Section 10.2.2.8.2, "Notes on Self-Signed and CA Certificates," discusses the differences.

Besides stronger authentication, another advantage to certificates is that you can identify a system by its certificate identity rather than by its IP address. For users of nomadic systems or systems with DHCP, a certificate-based setup is essential.

Creating Certificates with `ikecert(1m)`   The way to create a private key and matching certificate, and to import peer certificates, is with the `ikecert` command.

To create a private key and public certificate, use the `ikecert  certlocal` command, as in the following example:

```
# ikecert certlocal -ks -t rsa-sha1 -m 2048 \
    -D "C=US, O=Sun, OU=Service Division, CN=arachnid"
Creating private key.
Certificate added to database.
-----BEGIN X509 CERTIFICATE-----
MIIDHzCCAgegAwIBAgIFAMIUzsgwDQYJKoZIhvcNAQEFBQAwRzELMAkGA1UEBhMC
VVMxDDAKBgNVBAoTA1N1bjEZMBcGA1UECxMQU2Vydml jZSBEaXZpc2lvbjEPMA0G
--[SNIP]--
cyBnD9doGUMM25DyTtEk9ZrZj1YWE+oyqKKGWAyABbskWW8MqFtKYn6eYK3NoEjR
KGMRgAAM3eTLXuaMAGw7W6bnbHrVFl8a5pKwS5RtU7+kc9uwweU6bVWsGxlivcCH
zBmAEVvqB1NCr8LA6o6P6ry+w0SkWHCK7rg6PaCkZTQ1UHg=
-----END X509 CERTIFICATE-----
```

The `-D` option specifies your X.509 Distinguished Name. This name describes the entity by location and organization and ends with Common Name (CN). The Common Name is where you put the unique identifier, such as a system name or a person's name. You must use unique Distinguished Names when generating keys and certificates.

You can view the contents of your certificate database with the `ikecert certdb` command:

```
# ikecert certdb -1
Certificate Slot Name: 9   Key Type: rsa
        (Private key in certlocal slot 7)
        Subject Name: <C=US, O=Sun, OU=Service Division, CN=arachnid>
        Key Size: 2048
        Public key hash: 25741FE24684FF65AE2B477E38629532
```

The `Private key in certlocal slot` line indicates that you have a private key on this system that is associated with your public key. The Subject Name line is your identifier.

The peer that you want to communicate with ran a similar command, but with its Distinguished Name:

```
# ikecert certlocal -ks -t rsa-sha1 -m 2048 \
    -D "C=US, O=Sun, OU=Service Division, CN=spiderwoman"
```

Before you can communicate, each of you must have your peer's *public* certificate. Unlike the private key, the public key is not sensitive material because it is used to encrypt data that only the owner of the private key can read. To extract your public key, run the `ikecert certdb` command with the `-e` option:

```
# ikecert certdb -e "C=US, O=Sun, OU=Service Division,
CN=arachnid"
```

The output is a blob of ASCII-armored text. This output is your certificate in PEM format, an industry-standard text-based encoding format. You transfer the blob to the peer as a file. The peer would import your output by reading the transferred file into the peer's certificate database:

peer# **ikecert certdb -a < filename**

The import command does not generate any output. To verify that the certificate was imported properly, list the contents of the certificate database with the `ikecert certdb -1` command. For the imported certificate, the `private key in slot` line is not present because only the public certificate was imported.

Both peers must export their public certificate(s) and import their peer's public certificate(s). After the certificates are imported by both peers, you set up the IKE configuration file to use them.

```
##################################################
# Example ike config file for self-signed certificates

# Must list self-signed certificates as explicitly trusted
# This establishes trust by saying that you verified
# the sender of the certificate by some out-of-band method
# before blindly trusting the peer's certificate.
#
# Trust my own certificate
cert_trust "C=US, O=Sun, OU=Service Division, CN=arachnid"
# Trust my peer
cert_trust "C=US, O=Sun, OU=Service Division, CN=spiderwoman"
```

```
# This example lets any IP talk to any other, provided that the
# identity listed in the distinguished name checks out
{
    label "arachnidlink"
    local_id_type DN
    local_id "C=US, O=Sun, OU=Service Division, CN=arachnid"
    local_addr 0.0.0.0/0
    remote_id "C=US, O=Sun, OU=Service Division, CN=spiderwoman"
    remote_addr 0.0.0.0/0

    p1_xform {auth_method rsa_sig oakley_group 5
        auth_alg md5 encr_alg 3des}
}

###########################################
```

Notes on Self-Signed and CA Certificates   For large scale deployments, the best approach is to use X.509 certificates that are signed by a Certificate Authority (CA). CA-signed certificates eliminate the need to exchange public certificates with each potential peer. The `ikecert(1m)` command can be used to generate a Certificate Signing Request (CSR), which you send to the CA for signing. You can create your own CA by using the `openssl(5)` toolkit that is bundled with the Solaris OS. You can also use a commercial product, third-party software, or a Web-based commercial CA. When using a CA-signed certificate, keep the following information in mind.

First, you must have imported the certificate authority's certificate and have a `cert_root` line in your IKE configuration file to indicate that this CA is a trusted CA. This `cert_root` listing is similar to the Root CA lists that you see in a Web browser.

Second, the `in.iked` daemon tries to download the certificate revocation list (CRL) unless the daemon is configured to ignore CRLs. If you are using a CA certificate on a network where CRL traffic is blocked by a firewall, you can add `ignore_crls` to bypass that check.

Solaris IKE has its own CRL database, which can be manipulated with the `ikecert certrldb` command. Because CRLs are generally handled by a company's PKI infrastructure, Solaris's CRL functionality is not used very much.

10.2.2.9 IPsec Tunnels

The discussion so far used transport mode to illustrate IPsec policies. The Solaris OS also supports IPsec in *tunnel mode*. In transport mode, the original IP packet payload is encrypted and/or authenticated, the original IP header is retained, and a new ESP or AH header is inserted into the packet, after the IP header.

In tunnel mode, the entire original packet is protected with ESP or AH, and a new IP header is created. The new IP header might well have different IP addresses from the original. Different addresses in the header allow packets from private networks to be routed across the Internet. Tunnel mode is commonly used with encrypting gateways, sometimes called VPN gateways.

In many operating systems, tunneling is done by security policy. In the Solaris OS, tunneling and security policy are independent. All tunnels on a Solaris system are created by using the ifconfig command, and traffic is routed over those tunnel interfaces. To encrypt the tunneled traffic, IPsec policy is applied to that tunnel instance.

Though most of the transport mode concepts apply to tunnel mode, some tunnel mode concepts are important to note.

Tunnel mode configures an ip.tunN interface, and uses the keywords tsrc and tdst to indicate the tunnel addresses to be used in the new IP header. The ip.tunN interface can also have the Phase 2 security parameters associated with it, rather than specifying those parameters with an ipsecconf command. So, you create a Phase 1 IKE configuration entry, as before, between the peers' outer addresses. But to create the tunnel itself, you use the ifconfig command:

```
# ifconfig ip.tun0 plumb 192.168.6.106 192.168.6.2 tsrc 1.1.1.1
tdst 2.2.2.2 up
```

Tunnel-mode policy can and should be specified with the ipsecconf command. In the ipsecinit.conf file, use the tunnel keyword, as the following example illustrates:

```
{tunnel ip.tun0 negotiate tunnel laddr 192.168.6.106/32 raddr 192.168.6.2}
ipsec {encr_algs des encr_auth_algs md5 sa shared}
```

This ipsecinit.conf file entry, together with the ifconfig command, set up the following tunnel configuration:

```
# ifconfig ip.tun0
  ip.tun0: flags=10028d1<UP,POINTOPOINT,RUNNING,NOARP,MULTICAST,UNNUMBERED,IPv4> mtu
1419 index 10
        inet tunnel src 1.1.1.1 tunnel dst 2.2.2.2
        tunnel security settings  --> use 'ipsecconf -ln -i ip.tun0'
        tunnel hop limit 60
        inet 192.168.6.106 --> 192.168.6.2 netmask ffffff00
```

This syntax is important to use if your peer is a non-Solaris host. The `ipsecconf` input just shown is cumulative, so you could have many lines with the inner addresses of multiple hosts and networks behind the tunnel.

When configuring tunnels for a VPN, you must have IP forwarding turned on for the tunnel interface and make sure that routing is correct.

Although you can completely define tunnel policy with the `ifconfig` command, that method is deprecated. The `ifconfig` command does not allow you to specify inner addresses. It assumes that every address behind the tunnel is to be assigned the same IPsec policy. The following example is provided for completeness:

```
# ifconfig ip.tun0 plumb 192.168.6.106 192.168.6.2 \
 tsrc 1.1.1.1 tdst 2.2.2.2 encr_algs des encr_auth_algs md5 up
# ifconfig ip.tun0
 ip.tun0: flags=10028d1<UP,POINTOPOINT,RUNNING,NOARP,MULTICAST,UNNUMBERED,IPv4> mtu
1419 index 10
        inet tunnel src 1.1.1.1 tunnel dst 2.2.2.2
        tunnel security settings  esp (des-cbc/hmac-md5)
        tunnel hop limit 60
        inet 192.168.6.106 --> 192.168.6.2 netmask ffffff00
```

Equivalently, you could specify this sort of policy with the `negotiate transport` keywords for the `ipsecconf` command. The only reason to use this syntax is to communicate with an older Solaris system in tunnel mode.

10.2.2.10 Other IPsec Considerations

The following considerations are useful to know when deploying IPsec at your site.

NAT Traversal   Sometimes two peers try to talk to each other and an intervening gateway performs Network Address Translation on their session. In the Solaris 10 release, IKE automatically detects this condition and uses NAT-Traversal (NAT-T). NAT-T is an Internet standard used by all compliant operating systems. The IKE negotiation on UDP port 500 "jumps" to UDP port 4500. For the duration of the session, all encrypted traffic is encapsulated in UDP port 4500. This behavior applies to both tunnel and transport mode. If you are using policy with IP addresses, you must use the address that you see on the wire. The peers figure out the rest.

PKCS #11 Hardware Devices   You can create and store private keys/public certificates on PKCS #11 devices by using the `-T` flag with the `ikecert` command. PKCS #11 devices are devices such as smartcards, hardware accelerators, and so on. The PKCS #11 library also has a software implementation. Enhancements in the Solaris 10 code enable you to more easily migrate material on and off devices that support PKCS #11 migration operations, though many devices purposely do not allow the private key to ever leave the hardware device.

Per-Socket Policy   Much like tunnel policy, where policy is associated with the tunnel itself, per-socket policy is possible, where IPsec policy is different on the socket than the global policy that is specified in the IPsec policy file. Per-socket policy is used when writing and compiling custom programs that want to enforce IPsec on themselves in some way that might be different from the rest of the system. Per-socket policy can use different algorithms or bypass policy altogether, with the proper privilege, by using the setsockopt(3SOCKET) library call with the IP_SEC_OPT option. This option is documented in the ipsec(7p) man page. Per-socket policy overrides global policy unless specifically forbidden with the ndd(1m) parameter ipsec_override_persocket_policy.

Interoperability   In transport mode, the Solaris OS interoperates very well with other implementations of IPsec. In tunnel mode, use the Solaris 10 8/07 release or later with the tunnel keyword to the ipsecconf command in order to interoperate. This configuration has been tested very thoroughly against many other implementations.

Technical Notes   Policy is pushed down from user space to the kernel by using a special socket called PF_POLICY. SAs, including keys, are transferred from user space key management (ipseckey(1m)/in.iked(1m)) using a special socket called PF_KEY (see the pf_key(7p) man page). The IKE daemon, in.iked, has an administrative interface called ikeadm(1m), which communicates with in.iked through a door interface. Debug messages that include PF_POLICY or PF_KEY are about IPsec and refer to the PF_POLICY socket and the PF_KEY interface.

10.3 Solaris Secure Shell (SunSSH)

The Solaris Secure Shell (SunSSH) is a program for logging in to a remote system and for executing commands on that system. SunSSH is based on the open source OpenSSH project. It is intended to replace the insecure rlogin and rsh commands, and to provide secure encrypted communications between two untrusted systems over an insecure network. X11 connections and arbitrary TCP/IP ports can also be forwarded over the secure channel. SunSSH is a collection of commands that do the following:

- Listen for incoming connections
- Log in to a remote system

- Work with public and private keys
- Simplify and secure file transfer between systems
- Secure access when working with remote files and directories

The current implementation of SunSSH supports both versions 1 and 2 of the Secure Shell protocol. However, because of inherent security weaknesses in the version 1 protocol, sites are encouraged to use only version 2. This section considers version 2 only.

10.3.1 Versions of SunSSH

SunSSH was integrated into Solaris 9 in 2001. The Solaris OS has delivered the following versions:

- Version 1.0: Is the initial version that was based on OpenSSH 2.3 and integrated into Solaris 9.
- Version 1.0.1: Is a backport of the `SSH_BUG_EXTEOF` compatibility flag from OpenSSH and is part of Solaris 9 only.
- Version 1.1: Contains Solaris-specific changes and fixes plus some new code. OpenSSH 3.5p1 is the base version. Version 1.1 was shipped with the first release of Solaris 10.
- Version 1.2: Resyncs the `SSH_OLD_FORWARD_ADDR` compatibility flag from OpenSSH. As of July 2008, this version is part of OpenSolaris only, and is not in the Solaris 10 release.

Solaris engineering resyncs individual OpenSSH features when a business case is made for the resync, and also does an independent development. Engineering contributes bug fixes back to the OpenSSH project.

To determine the version of SunSSH on your system, run the `ssh -V` command:

```
$ ssh -V
Sun_SSH_1.1, SSH protocols 1.5/2.0, OpenSSL 0x0090704f
```

10.3.2 Notable SunSSH Differences from OpenSSH

SunSSH made several notable changes to the code after the project forked from OpenSSH. These changes better integrate Secure Shell with Solaris features.

- PAM: The code for interaction with PAM was changed, and SunSSH must use Solaris's implementation of PAM. The original OpenSSH UsePAM configuration option is not supported.

- Privilege separation: SunSSH does not use OpenSSH's privilege separation code. SunSSH takes a simpler approach that does not apply the privilege separation concept to the version negotiation, initial key exchange, or user authentication phases of the SSH protocol.

  Instead, SunSSH separates the processing of auditing, record keeping, and rekeying from the processing of the session protocols. By taking this approach, SunSSH provides a very simple monitor protocol.[2] SunSSH privilege-separation code is always on and cannot be switched off. The UsePrivilegeSeparation option is not supported.

- Locale: SunSSH fully supports language negotiation as defined in the Secure Shell Transfer Protocol (RFC 4253). After the user logs in, the user's shell profile can override the SunSSH negotiated locale settings.

- Auditing: SunSSH is fully integrated into the Solaris Auditing subsystem. See Chapter 9, "Auditing," for more information.

- GSS-API support: GSS-API can be used for user authentication *and* for initial key exchange. The GSS-API is defined in RFC4462, *Generic Security Service Application Program Interface*.

- Proxy commands: SunSSH provides proxy commands for SOCKS5 and HTTP protocols. For an example, see Section 10.4.3.7, "`ssh-socks5-proxy-connect`, `ssh-http-proxy-connect`—Proxy Commands," later in this chapter.

10.3.3 Starting and Stopping SunSSH

By default, SunSSH is enabled. You do not need to do anything to make SunSSH work on your system. You use the Solaris Management Framework (SMF) to start, stop, or restart the daemon.

For example, to notify the master SSH daemon to reread its configuration files, you use the following command:

```
$ svcadm restart svc:/network/ssh:default
```

10.4 Configuring SunSSH

As in OpenSSH, you configure SunSSH by editing configuration files. The system-wide configuration files, `sshd_config` and `ssh_config`, are in the `/etc/ssh` directory. A configuration file for every user is `$HOME/.ssh/config`. For more information, see the `sshd_config`(4) and `ssh_config`(4) manual pages.

Note that Solaris is shipped with some default settings that might be different from various OpenSSH installations. By default, the following defaults are installed.

- Protocol version 2 only is in effect.
- Port forwarding is disabled on both the server and client side.
- X11 forwarding is disabled on the server side, but is enabled on the client side.
- All authentication methods are enabled, including GSS-API.
- GSS-API is the preferred authentication method. Therefore, if Kerberos is configured then SunSSH will use it out of box.

10.4.1 How the SSH Protocol Version 2 Works

SSH protocol version 2 has three major parts.

- SSH Transfer Protocol: Is used for server authentication, algorithm negotiation, and the key exchange. When this part of the SSH protocol completes, an encrypted communication channel is established between the server and the client.
- SSH Authentication Protocol: Is used for user authentication; that is, to verify the identity of the user that runs the SSH client. This protocol uses the established transfer protocol.
- SSH Channel Protocol: Multiplexes the encrypted channel into logical connections. These connections can be used, for example, for user shell sessions, port forwarding, or X11 forwarding. This protocol uses the authentication protocol that the user established.

Note that SSH protocol involves two different types of authentication. The first one is the server authenticating to the client. The second one authenticates the user, on whose behalf the SSH client is run, to the SSH server in order to log in remotely. See RFC 4251, *The Secure Shell Protocol Architecture*, for more information.

10.4.2 Authentication Methods

SunSSH supports six different user authentication methods for SSH protocol version 2. These methods are defined in RFC 4252, *The Secure Shell Authentication Protocol*, unless a method is defined in its own RFC.

- **none** method: Is reserved, is not offered by the server, and can be sent by the client. The server rejects this method unless the user is granted access without any authentication. Typically, the client uses the none method to get the list of methods that the server supports.

- **gssapi-with-mic** and **gssapi-keyex** methods: Are methods that use the Generic Security Service Application Program Interface (GSS-API). This API provides security services to callers in a mechanism independent fashion.[3] The gssapi-keyex method is available only if the initial key exchange used GSS-API.

- **publickey** method: Relies on the public/private key pair that the ssh-keygen command generates. The user is expected to obtain the server's public key in advance. However, unknown host keys can be accepted during the host authentication phase.

- **password** method: Authenticates the user by the user's password.

- **keyboard-interactive** method: Is a general purpose authentication method[4] for the SSH protocol. This method is suitable for interactive authentications where the authentication data is entered by using a keyboard or an equivalent input device. This authentication method allows for a wide class of interactive authentication types.

- **hostbased** method: This authentication type is based on the knowledge of the host that the user is coming from and the user name on the remote host. The trust is based on the server owning the client host machine's public key before the client tries to establish the connection. This method is not suitable for high security environments.

For additional information on the authentication methods in SunSSH, see the sshd(1M) manual page.

10.4.3 SunSSH Commands

The following section describes the most frequently used SunSSH commands.

10.4.3.1 sshd—Secure Shell Daemon

The sshd daemon listens for connections from clients. For each incoming connection, sshd forks a new daemon. The forked daemons handle key exchange, encryption, authentication, command execution, and data exchange. Typically, you do not run sshd manually. As described in the section "Configuring SunSSH," SMF is used to enable and disable the daemon. However, situations occur when running `sshd` from command line is necessary.

For example, the following command debugs an `sshd` process:

```
$ /usr/lib/ssh/sshd -p 2222 -d
debug1: sshd version Sun_SSH_1.1
debug1: read PEM private key done: type RSA
debug1: private host key: #0 type 1 RSA
debug1: read PEM private key done: type DSA
debug1: private host key: #1 type 2 DSA
debug1: Bind to port 2222 on ::.
Server listening on :: port 2222.
```

For information about the options to the `sshd` command, see the `sshd`(1M) manual page.

10.4.3.2 `ssh`—Secure Shell Client

The `ssh` command is for logging in to a remote system and for executing commands on that system. This program provides secure encrypted communications between two untrusted systems over an insecure network. X11 connections and arbitrary TCP/IP ports can also be forwarded over this secure channel. The `ssh` command connects to the specified system name and logs the user in. The user must authenticate to the remote system by using one of several methods mentioned in Section 10.4.2, "Authentication Methods," earlier in this chapter.

To log in to a remote system, run the `ssh` command:

```
$ ssh user@machine
Password:
```

For information about the options to the `ssh` command, see the `ssh`(1) manual page.

10.4.3.3 `ssh-keygen`—Authentication Key Generation

The `ssh-keygen` command generates, manages, and converts authentication keys. Other SunSSH commands use these keys. Typically, each user who wants to use SSH with RSA or DSA authentication runs this command once to create the authentication in their `$HOME/.ssh` directory. The system administrator or the system itself, upon the first boot, runs this command to generate host keys.

To generate an RSA public/private key pair for SunSSH, run the `ssh-keygen` command:

```
$ ssh-keygen -t rsa
Generating public/private rsa key pair.
Enter file in which to save the key (/home/user/.ssh/id_rsa):
```

For information about the options to the `ssh-keygen` command, see the `ssh-keygen`(1) manual page.

10.4.3.4 `ssh-agent`—Authentication Agent

The `ssh-agent` command holds private keys used for public key authentication; that is, for RSA or DSA. The `ssh-agent` command is often run at the beginning of a login session. Then, later windows or programs start as clients of the `ssh-agent` program. Through the use of environment variables, the agent can be located and automatically used for authentication when the user logs in to other systems as an SSH client. Typically, the `ssh-agent` command is run automatically when users log in to the Java Desktop System (JDS). Therefore, Solaris users normally do not run the command directly. For more information about the `ssh-agent` command, see the `ssh-agent`(1) manual page.

10.4.3.5 `ssh-add`—Add RSA or DSA Identities to the Authentication Agent

The `ssh-add` command adds RSA or DSA identities to the authentication agent, `ssh-agent`(1). When the command is run without arguments, it attempts to add every default key file from `$HOME/.ssh`. The passphrase for decrypting stored identities is read from the user's terminal or by running the program that is defined in `SSH_ASKPASS` environment variable. The `ssh-agent` command must be running before you can use this command.

For example, to list the identities that are stored in the agent, type the following command:

```
$ ssh-add -l
1024 58:ef:6a:5d:16:c7:e3:22:a2:1d:da:ac:90:0f:2e:33 /home/jp161948/.ssh/id_rsa (RSA)
```

For information about the options to the `ssh-add` command, see the `ssh-add`(1) manual page.

10.4.3.6 `scp`, `sftp`, `sftp-server`—**Programs for Secure File Transfer**

The `scp` command copies files between hosts on a network. This command uses `ssh` for data transfer and uses the same simple protocol that was used for the `rcp` command.

The `sftp` command is an interactive file transfer program. Its user interface is similar to `ftp(1)`, but unlike the `ftp` command, `sftp` uses the `ssh` command to create a secure connection to the server. `sftp-server` is the server that `sftp` connects to. According to the IETF draft from October 2001, `draft-ietf-secsh-filexfer-02.txt`, `sftp` and `sftp-server` implement protocol version 3. As of July 2008, no RFC defines the SSH file transfer protocol. The SSH file transfer protocol for `sftp` is completely different from the protocol for `scp`.

The file transfer commands work by default. For more information, see the manual pages for `scp(1)`, `sftp(1)`, and `sftp-server(1M)`.

10.4.3.7 `ssh-socks5-proxy-connect`, `ssh-http-proxy-connect`— **Proxy Commands**

These SunSSH commands are not part of OpenSSH. These commands can be used as proxy commands using SOCKS5 and HTTP protocols, respectively. Users use those commands through ProxyCommand configuration option. See manual pages for `ssh-socks5-proxy-connect(1)` and `ssh-http-proxy-connect(1)` for more information.

For example, the following entry in the user's `$HOME/.ssh/config`, file enables the user to use a SOCKS5 proxy to reach the outside network from the internal network:

```
Host outside.domain.com
ProxyCommand /usr/lib/ssh/ssh-socks5-proxy-connect proxy.in.company.com %h %p
```

10.5 OpenSSL

OpenSSL is a cryptography toolkit that implements the Secure Sockets Layer (SSLv2/v3) and Transport Layer Security (TLS v1) network protocols. In addition, a general purpose cryptography library is shipped as part of OpenSSL.

OpenSSL 0.9.7d is shipped with the Solaris 10 OS, and patches are released when security vulnerabilities are discovered.

To determine the OpenSSL version number, run the following command:

```
$ openssl version
OpenSSL 0.9.7d 17 Mar 2004 (+ security patches to 2006-09-29)
```

The date corresponds to the date of the last patched vulnerability that the Common Vulnerability Database reported.[5]

The OpenSSL code in the Solaris OS is not a fork of the open source OpenSSL project. The Solaris OS adds support for two Solaris features to the OpenSSL code:

- The Solaris WAN boot installation method can use a standalone OpenSSL library. WAN boot enables administrators to boot and install software over a wide area network (WAN) by using HTTP or HTTPS. By using WAN boot, you can securely install the Solaris OS on SPARC systems over a large public network where the network infrastructure might be untrustworthy.

- A PKCS #11 engine enables cryptographic operations to be offloaded to the Solaris Cryptographic Framework through the OpenSSL API.

This section focuses on the PKCS #11 engine.

10.5.1 PKCS #11 Engine

OpenSSL provides an engine API.[6] This API enables the creation, manipulation, and use of cryptographic modules in the form of engine objects. Engine objects act as containers for implementations of cryptographic algorithms (called "mechanisms" by the Solaris Cryptographic Framework). With the open source OpenSSL distribution, users can write their own engine implementations and use the dynamic loading capability of OpenSSL to load and use those engines on the fly. Engine support determines which operations can be offloaded to the engine. Operations include, but are not limited to, RSA, DSA, DH, symmetric ciphers, digests, and random number generation. For operations that are not available in the engine, native OpenSSL code is used.[7]

OpenSSL in Solaris OS is shipped with a Sun-developed PKCS #11 engine. This engine enables cryptographic operations to be offloaded to the Solaris Cryptographic Framework, (see Chapter 7, "Solaris Cryptographic Framework"). Due to U.S. export laws, OpenSSL in the Solaris OS does not support dynamic engine loading. Also, Sun does not ship other engines, because any hardware cryptographic provider must be plugged into the Solaris Cryptographic Framework and used through the PKCS #11 engine.

The main reason the PKCS #11 engine was developed was to offload RSA/DSA operations to the Niagara cryptographic provider (ncp) on the UltraSPARC T1[8] platform when the platform is configured with the Apache Web server. However, with the introduction of the next version of the ncp driver (n2cp) for UltraSPARC T2[9], because this version of the driver is capable of hardware-accelerated symmetric cryptographic and digest mechanisms, many more applications can make use of the PKCS #11 engine on that platform.

The PKCS #11 engine in Solaris 10 update 5 relies on the PKCS #11 API from the `libpkcs11` library. This library provides a special slot[10] called the metaslot. The metaslot provides a virtual union of capabilities of all other slots. When available, the metaslot is always the first slot provided by `libpkcs11`. The metaslot is optimized to choose the best implementation of the requested mechanism available.

To determine the list of supported mechanisms that can be offloaded to the Solaris Cryptographic Framework from OpenSSL through the PKCS #11 engine, run the following command:

```
$ openssl engine -vvv -t -c
(pkcs11) PKCS #11 engine support
 [RSA, DSA, DH, RAND, DES-CBC, DES-EDE3-CBC, AES-128-CBC, RC4, MD5, SHA1]
```

In Solaris 10 update 5 (5/08), the Apache Web server and the OpenSSL command are the only applications that use the PKCS #11 engine by default. On systems with hardware-accelerated RSA/DSA operations, such as the UltraSPARC T1, OpenSSL significantly accelerates the initial TLS/SSL handshakes. For more information, see Section 7.5.5, "Configuring Apache Web Server to Use the Cryptographic Framework," in Chapter 7, "Solaris Cryptographic Framework." The OpenSSL command line tool uses the engine through the `-engine` option.

For example, to encrypt a file and offload the cryptographic operations to the available hardware, run the following command:

```
$ openssl enc -aes-128-cbc -in data -out data.enc -engine pkcs11
     engine "pkcs11" set.
     enter aes-128-cbc encryption password:
Verifying - enter aes-128-cbc encryption password:
```

10.6 Kerberos

Kerberos is a network authentication protocol designed to provide strong authentication for client/server applications by using secret-key cryptography. Originally developed at the Massachusetts Institute of Technology, it has been included as part of Solaris to provide strong authentication for Solaris network applications. Because of its widespread acceptance and implementation in other operating systems, including Windows, Linux, and OS/X, the Kerberos authentication protocol can interoperate in a heterogeneous environment, allowing users on machines running one OS to securely authenticate themselves on hosts of a different OS.

10.6.1 Why Use Kerberos?

Kerberos allows administrators and users to secure their networks by using secure authentication protocols for users and services. Instead of users transmitting passwords over the network in the clear, Kerberos enables the user to type a password just once per work session (work day), and yet still access network services with secure authentication methods that protect the passwords. Kerberos is a Single Sign-On (SSO) system.

10.6.2 Introduction to Kerberos

Kerberos technology provides a central database for managing user authentication instead of maintaining separate password files on many different client systems. Kerberos technology is also compatible and interoperable with other operating systems such as Windows, Linux, and Mac OS/X. Solaris users can use Kerberos authentication to access services on those other operating systems as long as they are participating in the same Kerberos realm (explained below).

10.6.2.1 Secret Keys and Insecure Networks

For any two users or services to communicate in a secure fashion over a potentially insecure network using symmetric key cryptography, they must share a secret key. Because the number of potential users and services on a network can be large, it would be impractical to generate, distribute, and manage keys for all possible combinations of users and services. Indeed, the majority of such keys would never be used.

Instead of statically generating keys for all possible pairs of users or services, a third-party service instead could be used to generate keys as they are needed. The third party would have to know the secret keys of every entity in the system so it could securely deliver the keys to requesters. The keys could then be used to secure a communications channel between users and services. It would be desirable for the third-party generated keys to have a limited lifetime, because they would be exposed on the network and would be vulnerable to brute-force attacks.

Kerberos implements this model by providing a pair of services known collectively as a Key Distribution Center (KDC). The first of these services is the Authentication Service (AS). The AS provides a means for a user to obtain a session key. With this session key, the user or client can communicate securely with the second service provided by the KDC—the Ticket Granting Service (TGS). This session key is delivered to the client along with a special Kerberos *ticket* known as a Ticket Granting Ticket (TGT).

10.6.2.2 Tickets

A Kerberos ticket for a given service consists of the session key plus the client's identity. These items are encrypted with the service's long-term secret key. A ticket generally has a lifetime of eight hours.

The client authenticates to the service by forwarding the ticket along with an authenticator to the service during authentication. The ticket is used as a means to securely distribute session keys to users and services. For example, when an ssh(1) client wishes to authenticate to sshd(1M), it first obtains a ticket for the sshd service from the KDC and then uses that ticket when authenticating to sshd(1M).

The service decrypts the ticket by using the service's long-term secret key. The service uses the enclosed session key to securely communicate with the user. Note that the service and the KDC do not directly communicate—the service obtains the session key from the user via the ticket.

The KDC Ticket Granting Service (TGS) is a network service similar to other Kerberos services such as sshd(1M) or Kerberized rlogin (in.rlogind(1M)). A service ticket is required to authenticate users. The enclosed session key provides security and integrity for any subsequent communication. The Ticket Granting Ticket (TGT) obtained during the initial authentication with the KDC Authentication Service (AS) is used when communicating with the KDC TGS. The KDC, as the name suggests, generates session keys, bundles them in Kerberos tickets, and distributes the tickets to users. Whenever a user needs to communicate for the first time with a Kerberos-enabled server, a ticket for that service is requested by using the TGT from the KDC AS.

AS tickets, also called service tickets, are used to authenticate to services. These tickets can be automatically obtained by using the TGT. After the user obtains the TGT (signs on), no further interaction is required for the user to authenticate to other kerberized services.

10.6.2.3 Realms

A Kerberos *realm* is a administrative domain. A realm contains a single authoritative database of Kerberos principals and policies. Typically there is a single master KDC and a number of slave KDCs. The convention when choosing a realm name is to derive it from a DNS domain name by taking the DNS domain name and making it all-caps. Unlike DNS domain names, realm names are case-sensitive. Multiple realms may be deployed in a single organization and may be completely independent or may have a *trust relationship* (http://docs.sun.com/app/docs/doc/816-4557/planning-29?a=view).

10.6.2.4 Principals

Every user or service in Kerberos has an associated *principal*. For users this is generally in the form <username>@<realm> and for services normally service/<FQDN>@<realm>. Kerberos cannot be used as an account authority for Solaris, but normally Kerberos principals are derived from their UNIX username counterparts. For example:

- Solaris user name and DNS domain: jdoe, abc.com
- Kerberos principal name (realm = ABC.COM): jdoe@ABC.COM

10.7 Kerberos in the Solaris OS

The Solaris Kerberos service is based on the Kerberos v5 network authentication protocol that was developed at the Massachusetts Institute of Technology (MIT). The Kerberos protocol is documented in RFC 4120 (`http://www.ietf.org/rfc/rfc4120.txt`). Kerberos has emerged as a de facto industry standard for network security.

The version of Kerberos in Solaris 10 5/08 is based on MIT Kerberos 1.4.3 (`http://web.mit.edu/Kerberos/`). Solaris Kerberos backported some features from later MIT releases such as LDAP support and limited client-side referral support.

Solaris Kerberos also includes enhancements not found in the MIT code base such as:

- Incremental propagation (see Section 10.8.3, "Slave KDCs," later in this chapter)
- Configurable replay cache
- A kernel GSS-API mechanism used by NFS for increased performance (see Section 10.9.3, "Example 2: Encrypted NFS," in this chapter)
- A client configuration utility—kclient (see Section 10.8.4, "Configuring Kerberos Clients," in this chapter)
- Kerberos support in `ssh` by using the GSS-API authentication method (see Section 10.9, "Application Servers," in this chapter)
- Leverages the Solaris Cryptographic Framework
- Automatic ticket renewal and ticket expiration warning (`ktkt_warnd`(**1M**))

- PAM integration (`pam_krb5`(5), `pam_krb5_migrate`(5))

- Kerberos daemons are run as SMF services (see Chapter 3, "System Protection with SMF" and use least privilege

- Client zero-conf support

- Internationalization support

- Solaris audit support (see Chapter 9, "Auditing")

10.7.1 Configuring a KDC

Before a KDC can be run, DNS must be configured. Kerberos on the Solaris OS does not use the name service switch, `nsswitch.conf`(4). Rather, Kerberos makes calls directly to the `libresolv`(3LIB) library.

After configuring DNS, the DNS client SMF service must be enabled:

```
# svcadm enable svc:/network/dns/client:default
```

The KDC requires the following site-specific information:

- The default realm. Normally an upper-cased DNS domain name.

- The Kerberos realm to KDC mapping for the default realm.

- The DNS domain name to realm mapping.

The main configuration file for Kerberos is `/etc/krb5/krb5.conf`(4). The following sample `krb5.conf` file is configured for the ACME.COM realm:

```
[libdefaults]
default_realm = ACME.COM

  [realms]
     ACME.COM = {
          kdc = kdc.acme.com
     }

  [domain_realm]
acme.com = ACME.COM
```

Realm-specific information is located in the `/etc/krb5/kdc.conf`(4) file. Information such as the location of the Kerberos principal and policy database and the

KDC listening ports are included here. The following is a sample realm section for the ACME.COM realm:

```
[realms]
ACME.COM  = {
        profile = /etc/krb5/krb5.conf
        database_name = /var/krb5/principal
        admin_keytab = /etc/krb5/kadm5.keytab
        acl_file = /etc/krb5/kadm5.acl
        kadmind_port = 749
        max_life = 8h 0m 0s
        max_renewable_life = 7d 0h 0m 0s
        default_principal_flags = +preauth
    }
```

Note

Typically, for a realm with a single KDC, the default values are sufficient.

10.7.2 Create the Kerberos Database

By default, Kerberos uses a db2 file-based database to store principal and policy records. This database must be created and initialized.

```
# kdb5_util create -s
Initializing database '/var/krb5/principal' for realm 'ACME.COM',
master key name 'K/M@ACME.COM'
You will be prompted for the database Master Password.
It is important that you NOT FORGET this password.
Enter KDC database master key:
Re-enter KDC database master key to verify:
#
```

The database data is encrypted with a key derived from the typed passphrase. When you specify the -s option, that password is stored in a root-owned file known as a stash file. The KDC uses this file on startup to decrypt the Kerberos database records.

10.7.3 Kerberos and LDAP

Kerberos also has support for storing the principal and policy database in a Directory Server such as Sun Java Enterprise Directory Server 6 (http://www.sun.com/software/products/directory_srvr_ee/index.jsp). A separate utility, kdb5_ldap_util(1M), creates the Kerberos database on the Directory Server.

10.7.3.1 Start the KDC

Once the database is initialized, the KDC service can be started. The KDC, like other Solaris network services, is managed by SMF. Administrators use the `svcadm` command to start, stop, or restart the KDC service:

```
# svcadm enable svc:/network/security/krb5kdc:default
```

10.8 Kerberos Administration

For Kerberos to be useful, principals must be created, passwords must be changed, keytab files must be created, and policies must be applied. An administrative daemon that runs on the same host as the KDC and directly accesses the Kerberos principal and policy database provides this functionality. This daemon is `kadmind`(1M). It is a regular Kerberos service, `svc:/network/security/kadmin`, and requires Kerberos authentication to access.

The `kadmin`(1M) command acts as a client to the `kadmin` service. This command is used to administer the Kerberos database, so is used to add, delete, and modify principals and policies and manage keytabs (see Section 10.8.2, "Keytabs and Passwords," later in this chapter). The command can be run in both an interactive and a non-interative mode.

10.8.1 Configure `kadmind` Daemon

To configure the `kadmin` service, add the following line to the `/etc/krb5/krb5.conf` file in the [realms] section for the realm. The realms section should look similar to the following:

```
[realms]
    ACME.COM = {
        kdc = kdc.acme.com
        admin_server = kdc.acme.com
    }
```

By default, regular users cannot create new principals, new policies, or administer the Kerberos database. Regular users can only change their own passwords. An administrator principal must be created to administer the Kerberos database. To create the initial administrator principal, `kadmin.local` is used.

The `kadmin.local`(1M) command is used to directly access the Kerberos database without using the `kadmind()` daemon. This command is used to create the first principal. The `kadmin.local` command requires the "Kerberos Server

Management" profile (see Section 5.3, "Solaris Role-Based Access Control," in Chapter 5, "Privileges and Role-Based Access Control").

```
# kadmin.local -q "addprinc jdoe/admin"
```

The conventional form for administrator principals is <username>/admin@<realm>.

After the administrator principal has been created, that principal is assigned full access rights to administer the Kerberos database. These rights are defined in the `kadm5.acl`(4) file. The following entry allows any principal of the form <username>/admin@ACME.COM to perform any action on the Kerberos database.

```
*/admin@ACME.COM *
```

10.8.2 Keytabs and Passwords

When Kerberos requires a user's long-term secret key, it simply prompts the user for his/her password. The password is then used to derive the user's long-term secret key. Kerberos requires a user password when a user's long-term secret key is required to decrypt the session key associated with the TGT. A Kerberos service requires its long-term secret key whenever a user presents it with a ticket. To lessen the requirement for user prompts, Kerberos stores a service's long-term secret key in a special file known as a `keytab`. The default system-wide keytab file is `/etc/krb5/krb5.keytab`. This file contains any long-term keys that services on that system require. The `ktadd` subcommand of kadmin generates new random keys for the given principal, stores the new keys in the Kerberos database, and then copies them to the keytab file. The location of the keytab file is configurable.

10.8.2.1 `kadm5.keytab` File

The `kadmind`(1M) daemon, like any other Kerberos service, requires access to its long-term secret keys before it can decrypt tickets that are sent by Kerberos clients. Traditionally, kadmind uses its own keytab file, `/etc/krb5/kadm5.keytab`, instead of using the system-wide keytab file.

The `kadmin.local` command can be used to create the correct principals and store their keys in the `kadmin` keytab. When the the Kerberos database was created (see Section 10.7.1, "Configuring a KDC," and Section 10.7.2, "Create the

Kerberos Database"), a number of principals were automatically created. Two of these principals are used by the `kadmin` service:

```
# kadmin.local -q "ktadd -k /etc/krb5/kadm5.keytab kadmin/kdc.acme.com"
# kadmin.local -q "ktadd -k /etc/krb5/kadm5.keytab changepw/kdc.acme.com"
```

After the keytab is populated with keys for the `kadmin` service, `kadmind` is started by enabling the `kadmin` service:

```
# svcadm enable svc:/network/security/kadmin:default
```

After the `kadmin` service starts, the `kadmin`(1M) client program is used to connect to the service.

```
# kadmin -p jdoe/admin -q "addprinc testuser"
```

10.8.2.2 `gkadmin`(1M) GUI

Solaris Kerberos provides a GUI, `gkadmin`(1M), to administer the `kadmin` service. See Figure 10.1.

10.8.3 Slave KDCs

To provide load-balancing and availability, *slave KDCs* can be deployed. Slave KDCs can issue tickets to Kerberos clients, but they cannot administer the Kerberos principal and policy database. Periodically, the Kerberos database is propagated from the master KDC to the slave KDCs. Then, the slave KDCs use that copy when issuing tickets.

The master copy of the database is directly accessible from the master KDC only. The Kerberos database on the master KDC is propagated by one of two methods:

1. Incremental propagation
2. Traditional propagation

10.8.3.1 Incremental Propagation

When incremental propagation is enabled, the slaves periodically poll for new updates from the master KDC. New updates are sent by the master KDC to the clients. The `kadmin` service on the master KDC implements this service. To enable

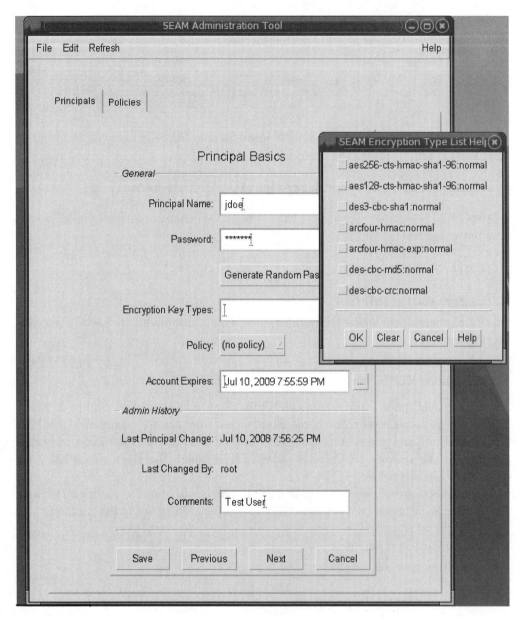

Figure 10.1 Creation of a New Principal with `gkadmin`(1)

the service on the master KDC, the default keytab must have the keys for the
kiprop/<fqdn>@<realm> principal. This principal is automatically created when
the Kerberos database is created. Also, the `kdc.conf`(4) file must be updated to

set the "sunw_dbprop_enable" configuration value to "true." New entries must also be added to the `kadm5.acl`(4) file to allow access to the Kerberos database.

A new daemon, `kpropd`(1M), is automatically run on the slave KDCs when `krb5kdc`(1M) is started via SMF. The slaves also require changes to `kdc.conf`(4): `sun_dbprop_enable` must be set to "true" and `sunw_dbprop_slave_poll` should be set to control how often the slave KDC polls for new updates. The slave KDCs use the kadmin/<fqdn>@<realm> principal when authenticating to the master KDC. This principal must be added to the default keytab on the slave.

Incremental propagation is a unique feature of Solaris Kerberos. This feature greatly reduces the amount of network traffic that is required to keep the KDC databases synchronized. It is best practice to use incremental propagation rather than traditional propagation, which is described in the next section.

10.8.3.2 Traditional Propagation

Slave KDCs can be configured to listen for the master KDC to supply an updated Kerberos database. The `kpropd`(1M) daemon can listen for these requests. Upon receipt of the updated Kerberos database, `kdb5_util`(1M) is called to update the local copy. When operating in this mode, `kpropd`(1M) uses the host/<fqdn>@<realm> principal. The host/<fqdn>@<realm> principal must be available in the slave's default keytab. A special `acl` file, `kpropd.acl`, on the slave KDC must be updated with an entry for the host/<fqdn of master KDC>@<realm>.

To propagate an updated Kerberos database, the `kprop`(1M) command is used. This command is always run from the master KDC.

10.8.4 Configuring Kerberos Clients

Just as for the KDC, DNS must be configured on the clients. A Kerberos client requires the same information that a KDC does.

- Identify the default realm.
- Map the Kerberos realm to KDC.
- Map the DNS domain name to the Kerberos realm.

In addition to this configuration, it is best practice for the client machine to have a keytab with keys for host/<fqdn-of-client-machine>@REALM if `pam_krb5` is used to log in to the client machine. The keytab is used by the `pam_krb5` module to verify that the TGT that was issued to the client came from the same KDC as the keys in the keytab. This extra verification step prevents a certain type of DNS spoofing attack. This verification step is controlled by the `verify_ap_req_nofail` configuration variable in the `/etc/krb5/krb5.conf` file.

10.8.4.1 Zero-Configuration Clients

In a suitably configured environment, Kerberos clients might need no explicit Kerberos configuration. A zero-configuration (`zero-conf`) Kerberos client uses a simple heuristic to perform the DNS domain name to Kerberos realm mapping. Both the default realm and the realm of any given host are derived from the DNS domain name of that host (or the local host in the case of the default realm).

The heuristic works as follows: The DNS domain name of the host (or local host) is converted to an all-caps format and Kerberos then tries to find a KDC for that realm. If a KDC cannot be found for that realm, then a component of the DNS domain name is removed and the search for a KDC begins again. This procedure is repeated until there are only two components left in the potential realm name, or a KDC is found. This heuristic exploits the convention of using an all-caps DNS domain name as the realm name.

By default, Kerberos will query DNS server records when trying to find a KDC for a given realm. This query is equivalent to having the `dns_lookup_kdc` configuration variable set to true.

By default, all Ticket Granting Service (TGS) requests ask for tickets with the referral bit turned on. The referral bit allows for the KDC to inform the client what realm the host is in. Microsoft's Active Directory product supports referrals.

Therefore, in an environment where KDC information is in DNS, realm names match the DNS names, and DNS is configured on the client; no further configuration is necessary.

> **Note**
>
> `zero-conf` is not suitable when the system uses the `pam_krb5` module for authentication. See Section 10.8.4, "Configuring Kerberos Clients," earlier in this chapter.

10.8.4.2 `kclient`

In a Kerberos environment where `zero-conf` Kerberos clients are not possible, or where more control over the client configuration is desired, the `kclient`(1M) command can be used. This command generates a valid `krb5.conf` configuration file and populates the default keytab file with the host principal and NFS principals, if requested. The `kclient` command can be run in both an interactive and a non-interactive mode.

The following is an example of running the `kclient` command in interactive mode:

```
# kclient
Starting client setup


-------------------------------------------------------
Do you want to use DNS for kerberos lookups ? [y/n]: n
        No action performed.
Enter the Kerberos realm: ACME.COM
Specify the KDC hostname for the above realm: kdc.acme.com
kdc.acme.com

Note, this system and the KDC's time must be within 5 minutes of each other for Kerberos
to function. Both systems should run some form of time synchronization system like Net-
work Time Protocol (NTP).

Setting up /etc/krb5/krb5.conf.
Enter the krb5 administrative principal to be used: jdoe/admin
Setting up /etc/krb5/krb5.conf.
Enter the krb5 administrative principal to be used: jdoe/admin
Obtaining TGT for jdoe/admin ...
Password for jdoe/admin@ACME.COM:

Do you have multiple DNS domains spanning the Kerberos realm ACME.COM ? [y/n]: n
No action performed.

Do you plan on doing Kerberized nfs ? [y/n]: y

nfs/kdc.sun.com entry ADDED to KDC database.
nfs/kdc.sun.com entry ADDED to keytab.

host/kdc.sun.com entry ADDED to KDC database.
host/kdc.sun.com entry ADDED to keytab.

Do you want to copy over the master krb5.conf file ? [y/n]: n
        No action performed.


-------------------------------------------------------
Setup COMPLETE.
#
```

Kerberos clients can also be configured by directly editing the `/etc/krb5/krb5.conf` file.

10.8.4.3 `kinit` Command

A UNIX user who is logged in to a Kerberos client system can obtain a TGT by typing the `kinit` command. If the UNIX username of the user is not the same as the principal name, or if the principal is in a non-default realm, the user must specify the full principal name.

```
% kinit
Password for jdoe@ACME.COM:
%
```

10.8.4.4 Automatic Credential Renewal

Although a TGT typically has a lifetime of eight hours, the TGT can be renewed without requiring the users to re-type their passwords.

```
% klist
Ticket cache: FILE:/tmp/krb5cc_101
Default principal: jdoe@ACME.COM

Valid starting             Expires                Service principal
07/10/08 17:24:36  07/11/08 01:24:36  krbtgt/ACME.COM@ACME.COM
       renew until 07/17/08 17:20:13
% kinit -R
% klist
Ticket cache: FILE:/tmp/krb5cc_101
Default principal: jdoe@ACME.COM

Valid starting             Expires                Service principal
07/10/08 17:24:52  07/11/08 01:24:52  krbtgt/ACME.COM@ACME.COM
       renew until 07/17/08 17:20:13
%
```

The ability to renew a TGT is useful for long-running sessions. The Solaris OS ships with a daemon, ktkt_warnd(1M). This daemon automatically renews TGTs for users. When a user obtains an initial ticket (TGT), the ktkt_warnd daemon is notified and automatically renews the TGT before the TGT expires. The daemon continues to renew the TGT until the maximum renew lifetime is reached. The default renew lifetime is one week. The KDC issues the renewed ticket.

The ktkt_warnd daemon is an SMF service, so you enable the service to start the daemon:

```
# svcadm enable svc:/network/security/ktkt_warn:default
```

The ktkt_warnd daemon is configured by modifying warn.conf(4). The daemon can be configured to warn users that their TGT is about to expire or to automatically renew user credentials. Warning notifications can be sent to syslog, to the console, and to email.

10.8.4.5 Kerberos and PAM

Two Kerberos PAM modules are shipped with the Solaris OS, pam_krb5 and pam_krb5_migrate. For a better understanding of PAM, see Chapter 8, "Key Management Framework (KMF)."

The pam_krb5 module handles authentication, account management, session management and password management. The authentication module provides a means to authenticate a user through the Kerberos authentication service. When authentication is successful, a TGT is stored for the user (see Section 10.8.4, "Configuring Kerberos Clients," earlier in this chapter). For a more comprehensive overview of `pam_krb5` functionality, see the `pam_krb`(5) man page.

The `pam_krb5_migrate` module is used to automatically create a Kerberos principal for a user at login. An authentication module is provided. The principal is created in the default realm. The module uses the host keys in the default keytab to authenticate to the `kadmin` service on the KDC and create the user. The `kadmin` service must be configured to allow the host principal to access and modify the Kerberos principal records. For more information, see the `pam_krb5_migrate`(5) man page.

10.9 Application Servers

A number of daemons and client applications that are shipped with the Solaris OS support Kerberos (or GSS-API). Applications such as `samba`(7), `postgresql`, SunSSH, and NFS can all use Kerberos.

10.9.1 Example 1: SunSSH

By default, both the SSH client and the SSH server support Kerberos out of the box. See Section 10.4.2, "Authentication Methods," for more information on authentication methods. When using Kerberos with SunSSH, the `sshd`(1M) daemon uses the host/<fqdn>@<realm> principal's long-term secret keys from the default keytab file. This principal must be created and its keys added to the default keytab file.

```
# kadmin -p jdoe/admin -q "addprinc -randkey host/kdc.acme.com"
Authenticating as principal jdoe/admin with password.
Password for jdoe/admin@ACME.COM:
WARNING: no policy specified for host/kdc.acme.com@ACME.COM; defaulting to no policy
Principal "host/kdc.acme.com@ACME.COM" created.
unknown# kadmin -p jdoe/admin -q "ktadd host/kdc.acme.com"
Authenticating as principal jdoe/admin with password.
Password for jdoe/admin@ACME.COM:
Entry for principal host/kdc.acme.com with kvno 3, encryption type AES-256 CTS mode
with 96-bit SHA-1 HMAC added to keytab WRFILE:/etc/krb5/krb5.keytab.
Entry for principal host/kdc.acme.com with kvno 3, encryption type AES-128 CTS mode
with 96-bit SHA-1 HMAC added to keytab WRFILE:/etc/krb5/krb5.keytab.
Entry for principal host/kdc.acme.com with kvno 3, encryption type Triple DES cbc mode
with HMAC/sha1 added to keytab WRFILE:/etc/krb5/krb5.keytab.
Entry for principal host/kdc.acme.com with kvno 3, encryption type ArcFour with HMAC/
md5 added to keytab WRFILE:/etc/krb5/krb5.keytab.
Entry for principal host/kdc.acme.com with kvno 3, encryption type DES cbc mode with
RSA-MD5 added to keytab WRFILE:/etc/krb5/krb5.keytab.
#
```

If the user has an account on the system where the `sshd` daemon is running and has a valid TGT, the user can log in to the remote host without being prompted for a password:

```
% kinit
Password for jdoe@ACME.COM:
% ssh kdc.acme.com hostname
kdc.acme.com
%
```

If the ticket cache is displayed, the ticket for host/<fqdn>@REALM can be seen.

```
% klist
Ticket cache: FILE:/tmp/krb5cc_101
Default principal: jdoe@ACME.COM

Valid starting        Expires              Service principal
07/10/08 17:42:25  07/11/08 01:42:25  krbtgt/ACME.COM@ACME.COM
        renew until 07/17/08 17:42:25
07/10/08 17:42:48  07/11/08 01:42:25  host/kdc.acme.com@ACME.COM
        renew until 07/17/08 17:42:25
```

10.9.2 Kerberos Authorization

Kerberos uses a number of methods to authorize a principal that originates from a remote system.

1. First, an entry for the principal is searched for in the `$HOME/.k5login` file. This plain-text file lists the Kerberos principals that are authorized to access the account of that user.

2. If no match for the principal is found in the `.k5login` file, the `gsscred` table is checked. The `gsscred` table maintains a mapping between principal names and local UNIX user ids. It can be modified and displayed by using the `gsscred`(1M) command.

3. If no match is found in the `gsscred` table, the default GSS/Kerberos authentication rules are used. Access is granted if the following conditions are satisfied:

   - The user part of the authenticated principal name matches the UNIX account name

   - The realm of the principal matches the realm of the service

   - The UNIX user exists on the server

The default rules can be modified by using the following configuration variables in the `krb5.conf` file:

- *auth_to_local_realm* Non-default realms are mapped to the default realm for authorization purposes.

- *auth_to_local_names* Explicit mappings of principals to UNIX user names can be listed.

- *auth_to_local* A general rule for mapping principal names to UNIX user-names can be defined. The rule is used only if the principal is not explicitly matched to the UNIX username. The rule can contain regular expressions. Use this rule with caution.

These variables are documented in the man page for `krb5.conf`(4). For more information on Kerberos authorization, see `krb5_auth_rules`(5).

10.9.3 Example 2: Encrypted NFS

The NFS server fully supports Kerberos authentication and can further use Kerberos for both integrity and privacy. The NFS server requires a keytab entry for nfs/<fqdn>@REALM in the default keytab. To configure an NFS server for secure NFS, you must remove the comments from the Kerberos security modes in the `nfssec.conf`(4) file.

To create an NFS share with authentication (sec=krb5), integrity checking (sec=krb5i), and privacy protection (sec=krb5p), the following command is used:

```
# share -o sec=krb5p <name of share>
```

When a user with a valid TGT browses the shared directory, the automounter ensures that the share is mounted correctly. The share can also be explicitly mounted. The `gsscred`(1M) command and the `krb5.conf`(4) file are used to control the authorization of Kerberos principals.

10.10 Interoperability with Microsoft Active Directory

Active Directory (AD) from Microsoft (`http://www.microsoft.com/windows server2008/en/us/active-directory.aspx`) can be used to authenticate Solaris clients using the Kerberos protocol. Authentication may happen at login time to the Solaris server or later by explicitly running `kinit`(1). Using AD to authenticate might be desirable when users in AD must authenticate to applications that run on a Solaris client, such as when accessing an ssh(1) server. AD acts as a KDC and can service ticket requests. In this configuration, the "kdc" variable in the "realms" section of the krb5.conf(4) file must be set to the DNS name of the AD server.

The password-changing protocol that is used by AD is different from the protocol that a Solaris client uses by default. To enable Solaris clients to use the password-changing service provided by AD, the kpassword_protocol in the krb5.conf file must be updated:

```
[realms]
    ACME.COM = {
            kdc = microsoft.acme.com
            admin_server = microsoft.acme.com
            kpasswd_protocol = SET_CHANGE
    }
```

If keytab entries for the host principal are required on the Solaris client, the host principal and the keytab for that principal must be created on the AD server. For example, the pam_krb5 module requires those keytab entries.

10.10.1 Example: Generate a Keytab That Contains a Host Principal's Key on a Windows 2003 Server

Create the principal in the GUI.

1. Start->Administrative Tools.

2. Select Active Directory Users and Computers.

3. Select the domain for the targeted host.

4. Right-click on User.

5. Select New->User.

6. In the Full Name text box, enter the short name of the host, for example, "solarisclient".

7. In the User logon name text box, enter the same string.

8. Select Next.

9. Type a password, such as "xyzABC123".

10. Check the "Password never expire" box.

11. Select Next, then Finish.

Generate the keytab by running the following command from the command line:

```
ktpass -princ host/solarisclient.acme.com@ACME.COM -mapuser
    solarisclient -pass xyzABC123 -out solarisclient.keytab
```

Securely transfer[11] the `solarisclient.keytab` file to the Solaris client system. Use the `ktutil` command to merge the keys into the default keytab.

```
# ktutil
    ktutil: rkt /var/tmp/keytabdir/solarisclient.keytab
    ktutil: list
    slot KVNO Principal
    ---- ----
    ------------------------------------------------------------------
       1     4  .host/solarisclient.acme.com@ACME.COM
    ktutil: wkt /etc/krb5/krb5.keytab
    ktutil: quit
```

Users should now be able to log in to a properly configured Solaris server and obtain a TGT from `pam_krb5` or connect to the server via `ssh(1)` using their existing Kerberos credentials.

Notes

1. The Internet Engineering Task Force (IETF) publishes Requests for Comment (RFCs) to build standards for Internet architecture. For a link to the RFCs, see `http://ietf.org/`.

2. For more information about this topic, see `README.altprivsep` file in SunSSH source code directory in source code browser on OpenSolaris.Org.

3. RFC 4462, Generic Security Service Application Program Interface (GSS-API) Authentication and Key Exchange for the Secure Shell (SSH) Protocol

4. RFC 4256, Generic Message Exchange Authentication for the Secure Shell Protocol

5. `http://nvd.nist.gov`

6. For more information, see the `engine(3)` manual page.

7. During the initialization of the engine, a set of mechanisms that the engine supports is returned to OpenSSL through the engine-initialization function. OpenSSL then offloads only mechanisms that are part of the set.

8. Also known as Niagara-1.

9. Also known as Niagara-2.

10. For a definition of a *slot,* see the PKCS #11 standard on `http://www.rsa.com.`

11. There are numerous SSH clients available on Windows.

11

Zones Virtualization Security

The Solaris operating system employs an operating system virtualization technology called zones. This chapter focuses on security aspects of this technology. For example, the zones abstraction has significant security advantages because applications or servers run in a protected environment, isolated from all other applications on the system.

The applications that execute inside zones are also restricted in their ability to interact with privileged system processes or resources, because only a limited set of privileges are available to them. With the use of exclusive IP stack instances, different IPsec, packet filtering, and VLAN access policies can be employed for applications in different zones on the same machine. Zones are the primary mechanism used to implement data separation in Solaris Trusted Extensions. Finally, virtual machine-based introspection is enabled from the administrative global zone. This chapter not only explains these technologies and benefits, but also provides detailed examples about how to configure and explore them.

11.1 The Concept of OS Virtualization: Introduction and Motivation

In operating system-level virtualization (short OS virtualization), the single kernel of an operating system provides multiple isolated user-space instances. In the Solaris operating system such instances are called *zones*. Zones look and feel to their users and administrators just like separate operating system instances. The technology has significant security advantages and includes fine-grained resource management to keep the applications that are inside zones within the limits of the resources that they are allowed to consume.

A zone is therefore a virtual operating system abstraction that provides a protected environment in which applications run isolated from all other applications on the system. Such containment of applications has a number of advantages with respect to security goals. For example, damage that is caused by an application that is isolated inside a zone remains contained within that zone, as if the application had run on its own dedicated machine. In other words, applications are protected from each other to provide software fault isolation.

11.2 The Architecture of Solaris Zones

OS-level virtualization can be thought of as an advanced extension of the UNIX chroot mechanism. It provides an isolated operating-system environment, where each zone supplies the security, name space, and fault isolation, supplemented by resource management to prevent processes in one zone from using too much of a system resource, or to guarantee processes a certain service level.

To ease the labor of managing multiple applications and their environments, zones coexist within one operating system instance and are usually managed as one entity. Most software that runs on the Solaris OS runs unmodified in a zone. Because zones do not change the Solaris Application Programming Interface (API) or Application Binary Interface (ABI), recompiling an application is not necessary in order to run it inside a zone. A small number of applications that are normally run as *root* or with certain privileges may not run inside a zone if they rely on being able to access or change some global resource. An example might be the ability to change the system's time-of-day clock.

The following are features of zones.

- Applications that access the network and files, and perform no other I/O run unmodified within zones.

- A superuser in a zone cannot affect or obtain privileges in other zones. This feature provides users with a safe sandbox in which to experiment even with software that requires traditional root privileges.

- Zones are useful for testing different versions of applications on the same OS.

- Zones can be used as an instructional tool or infrastructure component. For example, one can allocate each student an IP address and a zone and allow him/her to safely share one machine.

The following are examples of applications that might need to be modified to run in zones.

- Applications that require direct access to certain devices, for example, a disk partition, will usually work if the zone is configured correctly. However, in some cases this may increase security risks.

- Applications that require direct access to, for example, `/dev/kmem` or a network device may need to be modified to work correctly. Applications should instead use one of the many IP services.

11.2.1 Branded Zones (BrandZ)

Zones provide protected environments for Solaris applications. Separate and protected run-time environments are available through a Solaris feature commonly referred to as BrandZ.

BrandZ is a framework that extends the zone's infrastructure to create branded zones, which are zones that contain non-native operating environments. A branded zone can be as simple as an environment where the standard Solaris utilities are replaced with their GNU equivalents, or as complex as a complete Linux user space environment.

BrandZ extends the zone's infrastructure in the user space in the following ways.

- A brand is an attribute of a zone, set at zone-configuration time.
- Each brand provides its own installation routine, which enables the installation of an arbitrary collection of software in the branded zone.
- Each brand may include pre-boot and post-boot scripts that provide any final boot-time setup or configuration.
- The `zonecfg` and `zoneadm` tools can set and report a zone's brand type.

BrandZ provides a set of interposition points in the kernel.

- These points are found in the system call path, process loading path, thread creation path, etc.
- At these interposition points, code is executed that is only applied to processes in a branded zone.
- At each of these points, a brand can choose to supplement or replace the standard behavior of the Solaris OS.
- Fundamentally different brands might require new interposition points.

The linux (lx) brand enables Linux binary applications to run unmodified on a Solaris system, within zones that are running a complete Linux user space. In other words, user-level Linux software runs on a machine with a Solaris kernel. Solaris includes the tools necessary to install a CentOS or Red Hat Enterprise Linux distribution inside a zone on a Solaris system. The linux brand runs on x86/x64 systems booted with either a 32-bit or 64-bit kernel. Regardless of the underlying kernel, only 32-bit Linux applications are able to run. The linux brand is available only for x86 and AMD x64 architectures at this time.

Note that the linux brand does not work with Solaris Trusted Extensions. This is because the linux brand requires a kernel-loadable module that violates Trusted Extensions' ability to enforce its mandatory security policies.

11.2.2 Labeled Zones

Solaris zones are also the primary mechanism used to implement data separation in Solaris Trusted Extensions. Solaris Trusted Extensions is a feature of the operating system that enforces multilevel security (MLS) policies. It is the latest in a series of MLS workstation and server operating systems that have been under development at Sun since 1988. Each zone is assigned a unique sensitivity label.

11.2.3 Zones and Networking

A Solaris zone can be designated as one of the following:

- Exclusive-IP zone
  Exclusive-IP zones each have their own IP stack and can have their own dedicated physical interfaces. An exclusive-IP zone can also have its own VLAN interfaces. The configuration of exclusive-IP zones is the same as that of a physical machine.

- Shared-IP zone
  Shared-IP zones share the IP stack with the global zone, so shared-IP zones are shielded from the configuration details for devices, routing, and so on. Each shared-IP zone can be assigned IPv4/IPv6 addresses. Each shared-IP zone also has its own port space. Applications can bind to INADDR_ANY and then receive traffic only for that zone.

Neither types of zone can see the traffic of other zones. Packets coming from one zone have a source address belonging to that zone. A shared-IP zone can only send packets on an interface on which it has an address. A shared-IP zone can only use a default router if the router is directly reachable from the zone. The default router has to be in the same IP subnet as the zone.

Shared-IP zones cannot change their network configuration or routing table and cannot see the configuration of other zones. The device file `/dev/ip` is not present in shared-IP zones. SNMP agents must open `/dev/arp` instead. Multiple shared-IP zones can share a broadcast address and can join the same multicast group.
Shared-IP zones have the following networking limitations.

- They cannot put a physical interface inside a zone.
- IPfilter does not work between zones.
- DHCP does not work for a zone's IP address.
- Dynamic routing is not possible.

Exclusive-IP zones do not have the aforementioned limitations and can change their network configuration or routing table inside the zone. The device file `/dev/ip` is present in exclusive-IP zones.

11.2.4 Zone Identity, CPU Visibility, and Packaging

Each zone controls its node name, time zone, and naming services like LDAP and NIS. The `sysidtool` can be used to configure these attributes. The ability to maintain separate and different `/etc/passwd` files is the mechanism to delegate `root` privileges to a zone. User IDs can map to different names when domains differ.
By default, all zones see all CPUs. A restricted view automatically happens when resource pools are enabled. Zones can add their own packages. Those packages can be patched. System patches are applied in the global zone. Then, in non-global zones the zone will automatically boot into superuser mode (`boot -s`) to apply the patch. The `SUNW_PKG_ALLZONES` package must be kept consistent between the global zone and all non-global zones. The `SUNW_PKG_HOLLOW` package parameter causes the package name to appear in non-global zones (NGZ) for dependency purposes, but the contents are not installed.

11.2.5 Zones and Devices

Each zone has its own devices. Zones see a subset of *safe* pseudo devices in their device directory `/dev`.
Applications reference the logical path to a device that is listed in `/dev`. The `/dev` directory exists in non-global zones; the `/devices` directory does not. Devices like `random`, `console`, and `null` are safe, but other devices such as `/dev/kmem` are not.

Zones can modify the permissions of their devices but cannot issue the mknod(2) system call. Physical device files, like those for raw disks, can be put in a zone with caution. Devices can be shared among zones, but need careful security evaluation before doing so.

For example, you might have devices that you want to assign to specific zones. Allowing unprivileged users to access block devices could permit those devices to be used to cause a system panic, bus resets, or other untoward events. Placing a physical device into more than one zone can create a covert channel between zones. Global zone applications that use such a device risk the possibility of compromised data or data corruption by a non-global zone.

11.2.6 Resource Control in Zones

Controlling which resources are available to which parts of the system is an important step in creating an appropriate security posture of any system, as *availability*, also know as *protection against the threat of denial of service*, is one of the most important goals of computer security. Resource management and control is built in to the zones mechanism as a first-class citizen. Full treatment of this topic, however, is beyond the scope of this chapter.

11.3 Getting Started with Zones

This section introduces how to administer zones; in particular, which zone-administration commands exist and which zone properties and resources are of primary importance. The following example then introduces you to how to create zones and should help you understand the process of creating, installing, and booting a zone. (Note: This procedure does not apply to a linux-branded zone.)

First, you create a non-global zone called *apache1* and start an Apache Web server in it. This will be the only service running in that zone. The only reachable network interface to this machine is therefore configured to be port 80, resulting in a minimized attack surface for that machine.

11.3.1 Zone Administration

Zone administration consists of the following commands:

- zonecfg—Creates zones, configures zones (add resources and properties). Stores the configuration in a private XML file under /etc/zones.

- zoneadm—Performs administrative steps for zones such as list, install, (re)boot, and halt

- `zlogin`—Allows user to log in to the zone to perform maintenance tasks
- `zonename`—Displays the current zone name

The following global-scope properties are used with zones:

- `zonepath`—Path in the global zone to the root directory under which the zone will be installed
- `autoboot`—To boot or not to boot when global zone boots
- `pool`—Resource pools to which zones should be bound
- `brand`—A particular collection of software present in the non-global zones that does not match the software found in the global zone

Resources may include any of the following types:

- `fs`—file system
- `inherit-pkg-dir`—Directory that has its associated packages inherited from the global zone
- `net`—Network device
- `device`—Devices

11.3.2 Creating, Installing, and Booting a Zone for an Apache Web Server

This and the following examples assume that your system already has a directory named `/zone` with sufficient space for zones. This directory can be either a regular directory or a zpool mount point (preferred). Follow the steps to configure your new zone called `apache1`.

The zone uses a shared IP stack, which is the default.

1. Create the zone:

```
# zonecfg -z apache1
apache1: No such zone configured
Use 'create' to begin configuring a new zone.
zonecfg:apache1> create
zonecfg:apache1> set zonepath=/zone/apache1
zonecfg:apache1> add net
zonecfg:apache1:net> set address=10.0.2.100/24
zonecfg:apache1:net> set physical=e1000g0
zonecfg:apache1:net> end
zonecfg:apache1> verify
zonecfg:apache1> commit
zonecfg:apache1> exit
```

2. Install the zone:

```
# zoneadm -z apache1 install
Preparing to install zone
Creating list of files to copy from the global zone.
Copying <7020> files to the zone.
Initializing zone product registry.
Determining zone package initialization order.
Preparing to initialize <1075> packages on the zone.
Initialized <1075> packages on zone.
Zone <apache1> is initialized.
Installation of these packages generated warnings: ....
The file  </zone/apache1/root/var/sadm/system/logs/
   install_log> contains a log of the zone installation.
```

The necessary directories are created. The zone is ready for booting.

3. View the directories in the zone:

```
# ls /zone/apache1/root
bin    etc      home   mnt    platform   sbin     tmp    var
dev    export   lib    opt    proc       system   usr
```

4. Boot your new zone and view your network interfaces:

```
# ifconfig -a
lo0: flags=2001000849<UP,LOOPBACK,RUNNING,MULTICAST,IPv4,VIRTUAL> mtu 8232 index 1
        inet 127.0.0.1 netmask ff000000
e1000g0: flags=1004803<UP,BROADCAST,MULTICAST,DHCP,IPv4> mtu 1500 index 2
        inet 10.0.2.15 netmask ff000000 broadcast 10.0.2.255
        ether 8:0:27:61:75:4
# zoneadm -z apache1 boot
# ifconfig -a
lo0: flags=2001000849<UP,LOOPBACK,RUNNING,MULTICAST,IPv4,VIRTUAL> mtu 8232 index 1
        inet 127.0.0.1 netmask ff000000
lo0:1: flags=2001000849<UP,LOOPBACK,RUNNING,MULTICAST,IPv4,VIRTUAL> mtu 8232 index 1
        zone apache1
        inet 127.0.0.1 netmask ff000000
e1000g0: flags=1004803<UP,BROADCAST,MULTICAST,DHCP,IPv4> mtu 1500 index 2
        inet 10.0.2.15 netmask ffffff00 broadcast 10.0.2.255
        ether 8:0:27:61:75:4
e1000g0:1: flags=1004803<UP,BROADCAST,MULTICAST,DHCP,IPv4> mtu 1500 index 2
        zone apache1
        inet 10.0.2.100 netmask ffffff00 broadcast 10.0.2.255
```

5. Log into the zone and configure it:

```
# zlogin -C apache1
[Connected to zone 'apache1' console]
```

The `-C` command line option to `zlogin` opens the zone console. The key sequence to exit the console connection is ~..

The first time you log into the console, you complete the typical system configuration (selection of terminal type, creation of RSA keys, configuration of network identity with host name and name service, selection of time zone, and choice of root password). This configuration step is omitted here.

```
# ifconfig -a
lo0:1: flags=2001000849<UP,LOOPBACK,RUNNING,MULTICAST,IPv4,VIRTUAL> mtu 8232 index 1
        inet 127.0.0.1 netmask ff000000
e1000g0:1: flags=1000803<UP,LOOPBACK,RUNNING,MULTICAST,IPv4> mtu 1500 index 2
        inet 10.0.2.100 netmask ffffff00 broadcast 10.0.2.255
# ping -s 10.0.2.100
64 bytes from 10.0.2.100: icmp_seq=0. time=0.392 ms
64 bytes from 10.0.2.100: icmp_seq=1. time=0.265 ms
64 bytes from 10.0.2.100: icmp_seq=2. time=0.270 ms
^C
----10.0.2.100 PING Statistics----
3 packets transmitted, 3 packets received, 0% packet loss
round-trip (ms)  min/avg/max/stddev = 0.265/0.309/0.392/0.072
# ~.
[Connection to zone 'apache1' console closed]
```

11.4 The Security Advantages of OS Virtualization

Many organizations avoid potential security issues by deploying only one operating system and application per server. As consolidation strategies are employed to effect better resource utilization, protecting applications and systems becomes paramount. Zone technology provides a variety of security benefits that can help companies host multiple environments and applications on a single server without damaging or exposing one another to security risks.

11.4.1 Isolation and Encapsulation

The idea of isolation can be illustrated with the example of executing applications in sandboxes, such as Java applications within the Java VM sandbox. Damage from an exploited or misbehaving application is then contained and cannot be inflicted on other services. This idea can be employed for standalone services, such as a Web server or for services consisting of an aggregate of middleware, such as typical e-commerce applications within a tiered system architecture, where the different tiers would be isolated from each other. In general, different applications, or aggregates of applications or middleware, can each be run in its own zone.

The encapsulation of single applications or aggregates of applications that jointly make up a network-facing service has additional security benefits.

Many popular security mechanisms such as firewall technology or intrusion detection are applied at the host level, so they are readily applied to zones. In fact, one of the reasons for introducing exclusive IP-stack instances into zones in the first place was to create the ability to apply per-zone packet filtering within a virtual OS.

Concentrating on isolated, encapsulated application environments yield a virtual appliance model. Just like hardware appliances such as load balancers or packet filtering routers in the networking space that cater to specific functions by offering great performance with low administrative overhead, such virtual appliances are specialized to offer just the functionality of the individual application and just the OS support that is necessary for the application to run well. The OS surrounding the application can be hardened and minimized.

The interface that is accessible from the network, the so-called *attack surface*, is minimized and restricted to just what the application needs to expose. For example, a virtual e-mail appliance would only expose the simple mail transport protocol (SMTP) on port 25 to the network, nothing else. Additionally, administrative access could be restricted to local access. Both the smaller trusted computing base and the reduced attack surface improve the security posture of a system. Furthermore, if ISVs embrace this virtual appliance model, much of the burden of securing applications is shifted away from the traditional system administrator to the ISVs. Customers would benefit from the ISVs' ability to provide better-hardened applications.

As previously discussed, each zone has its own characteristics; for example, zonename, IP addresses, hostname, naming services, and root and non-root users. By default, the operating system runs in the global zone. The administrator can virtualize the execution environment by defining one or more non-global zones. Network-facing services can be run in separate zones, thereby limiting the damage possible in the event of security violations. Because zones are implemented in software, they are not limited to granularity defined by hardware boundaries; instead, zones offer sub-CPU resource granularity.

11.4.2 Offering Replicated or Redundant Services Using Zones

The following example demonstrates how to support two separate sets of Web-server user groups on one physical host. Simultaneous access to both Web servers is configured to protect each Web server and system in the event that one becomes compromised.

1. Verify the configuration of your non-global zone `apache1`:

```
# zonecfg -z apache1 info
zonename: apache1
zonepath: /zone/apache1
brand: native
autoboot: false
bootargs:
pool:
limitpriv:
scheduling-class:
ip-type: shared
inherit-pkg-dir: dir: /lib
inherit-pkg-dir: dir: /platform
inherit-pkg-dir: dir: /sbin
inherit-pkg-dir: dir: /usr
net: address: 10.0.2.100/24
        physical: e1000g0
```

2. Create a matching non-global zone `apache2`. Follow the directions for the `apache1` zone, but change the network address. The network address for `apache1` is highlighted in the following output:

```
# zonecfg -z apache2 info
zonename: apache2
zonepath: /zone/apache2
brand: native
autoboot: false
bootargs:
pool:
limitpriv:
scheduling-class:
ip-type: shared
inherit-pkg-dir: dir: /lib
inherit-pkg-dir: dir: /platform
inherit-pkg-dir: dir: /sbin
inherit-pkg-dir: dir: /usr
net: address: 10.0.2.200/24
        physical: e1000g0
```

3. Log in to apache1 and start the Web server application.

```
# zlogin apache1
# zonename
apache1
# cp /etc/apache2/httpd.conf-example /etc/apache2/httpd.conf
# svcadm enable svc:/network/http:apache2
```

4. Repeat step 3 for zone `apache2`.

5. In the global zone, open a Web browser with two tabs and navigate to the following URLs:

   - `http://100.0.2.100/manual/`
   - `http://100.0.2.200/manual/`

Two separate Apache Web servers are now up and running on zones `apache1` and `apache2`.

To the end user, each zone appears as a different system. Each Web server has its own name service:

- `/etc/nsswitch.conf`
- `/etc/resolv.conf`

A malicious attack on one Web server is contained to its zone. Port conflicts are no longer a problem. Each non-global zone uses its own port 80.

11.4.3 Hardening Web-Facing Web Server Using Zones

As of mid 2009, Web page hijacking is a common threat in the Internet at large. Using Solaris zones, we can construct a system that is hardened against the threat of Web page hijacking.

Figure 11.1 illustrates the following idea: a single machine with two network interfaces is connected to the Internet via one interface and to an internal network via the other interface. Two zones are instantiated on this machine. Each zone has exclusive access to one of the two interfaces. The zone (StageZone) facing the internal network is used for staging the production content to be served by the Web server, while the second zone (WebZone) mounts the production content of zone StageZone in a read-only fashion.

11.4.4 A Reduced Set of Privileges for Non-Global Zones

The Solaris operating system implements a set of privileges that provide fine-grained control over the actions of processes. Traditionally, UNIX-based systems have relied on the concept of a superuser called root with the special user identifier: 0. This concept of a superuser has been broken down into discrete privileges. The ability to grant one or more specific privileges that enable processes to perform otherwise restricted operations supplements the concept of superuser in Solaris.

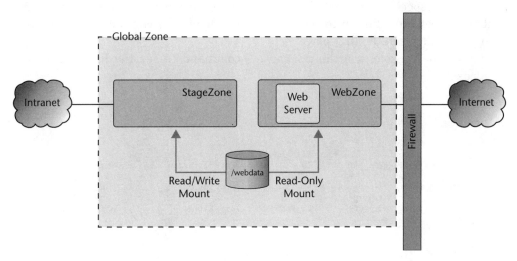

Figure 11.1 System Hardening Against Web Page Hijacking

The single, all-powerful user identifier 0 has been replaced with 68 discrete privileges that can individually be assigned to processes using, for example, the Service Management Facility (SMF), Role-Based Access Control (RBAC), or command line programs such as ppriv.

Processes in the global zone potentially have access to all privileges. In the global zone, use the ppriv -l command to list the privileges that are available.

```
# zonename
global
# ppriv -l
contract_event   contract_observer cpc_cpu          dtrace_kernel   dtrace_proc
dtrace_user      file_chown        file_chown_self  file_dac_execute file_dac_read
file_dac_search  file_dac_write    file_downgrade_sl file_link_any   file_owner
file_setid       file_upgrade_sl   graphics_access  graphics_map    ipc_dac_read
ipc_dac_write    ipc_owner         net_bindmlp      net_icmpaccess  net_mac_aware
net_privaddr     net_rawaccess     proc_audit       proc_chroot     proc_clock_highres
proc_exec        proc_fork         proc_info        proc_lock_memory proc_owner
proc_priocntl    proc_session      proc_setid       proc_taskid     proc_zone
sys_acct         sys_admin         sys_audit        sys_config      sys_devices
sys_ipc_config   sys_linkdir       sys_mount        sys_ip_config   sys_net_config
sys_nfs          sys_res_config    sys_resource     sys_suser_compat sys_time
sys_trans_label  win_colormap      win_config       win_dac_read    win_dac_write
win_devices      win_dga           win_downgrade_sl win_fontpath    win_mac_read
win_mac_write    win_selection     win_upgrade_sl
```

Processes running in a non-global zone are restricted to a subset of privileges. This restricted set does not allow one zone to perform operations that might affect other zones, especially the global zone. This restricted set is mandatory in a zone, so it is a benefit in addition to the more generic benefit of running processes with reduced privileges in the first place.

In the zone console, use the `ppriv -l` command to see the list of available privileges:

```
# zonename
apache1
# ppriv -l
contract_event    contract_observer file_chown     file_chown_self file_dac_execute
file_dac_read     file_dac_search  file_dac_write   file_link_any   file_owner
file_setid        ipc_dac_read     ipc_dac_write    ipc_owner       net_bindmlp
net_icmpaccess    net_mac_aware    net_privaddr     proc_audit      proc_chroot
proc_exec         proc_fork        proc_info        proc_lock_memory proc_owner
proc_session      proc_setid       proc_taskid      sys_acct        sys_admin
sys_audit         sys_mount        sys_nfs          sys_resource
```

The output of these two commands displays that the non-global zone `apache1` is obviously restricted to fewer privileges. Note that this example shows the default set of privileges available to zones.

1. This zone-limiting set can be modified, as there are a number of privileges that can be optionally added, while existing ones can be removed. The following example shows how optional zone privileges are added and how existing zone privileges can be removed.

```
# zonename
global
# zonecfg -z apache1 info limitpriv
limitpriv:
# zonecfg -z apache1 set limitpriv="default,sys_time, !net_icmpaccess"
# zonecfg -z apache1 info limitpriv
limitpriv: default,sys_time,!net_icmpaccess
# zonecfg -z apache2 info limitpriv
limitpriv:
```

In zone `apache1`, the missing privilege `PRIV_NET_ICMPACCESS` causes the command `ping` to fail, while it succeeds in zone `apache2`.

```
# zonename
global
# zlogin apache1 ppriv -e ping localhost
ping: socket Permission denied
# zlogin apache2 ppriv -e ping localhost
localhost is alive
```

2. To further demonstrate the effect of the restrictions, run the `ndd` command to set a driver-configuration parameter; in particular, set the TCP stack into debug mode. Inside the global zone the command succeeds:

```
# zonename
global
# ndd /dev/tcp tcp_debug
0
# ndd -set /dev/tcp tcp_debug 1
# ndd /dev/tcp tcp_debug
1
# ndd -set /dev/tcp tcp_debug 0
```

3. Run the command inside the non-global zone. The command fails. Then, run the command again, this time as an argument to the `ppriv -e -D` debugging command to determine why the command failed:

```
# zonename
apache1
# ndd /dev/tcp tcp_debug
0
# ndd -set /dev/tcp tcp_debug 1
operation failed: Not owner
# ppriv -e -D ndd -set /dev/tcp tcp_debug 1
ndd[4335]: missing privilege "sys_ip_config" (euid = 0, syscall = 54) needed
at nd_getset+0xcf
operation failed: Not owner
```

The missing privilege is `PRIV_SYS_IP_CONFIG`. This privilege allows a process to perform actions such as configuring network interfaces and routes, and accessing parameters for TCP/IP by using the `ndd` command.

11.4.5 Benefits of Exclusive IP Stack Instances

The use of exclusive IP instances enables zones to be used in concert with network-based partitioning for large-scale deployments. In a large-scale deployment, aggregates of applications that work in concert are deployed on physically separate machines. These aggregates communicate with each other over the network. The network connection is typically secured by using IPsec or at least by being encapsulated within VLANs.

Exclusive IP stack instances make per zone IPsec and VLAN access available to applications running in the associated zones. It is also possible to install a packet sniffer inside a zone with an exclusive IP stack, a feature that's not available with a shared IP stack. However, this feature can also be seen as a potential drawback because a successful attacker could be the one who installs a sniffer in a zone!

11.5 Monitoring Events in Zones

Traditional architectures for intrusion detection and auditing provide two options:

- Host-based option: The detection and auditing software runs within the system that is being monitored. This option provides an excellent view of what is happening. However, it is highly susceptible to attack.

- Network-based option: The monitoring software resides inside the network. This option is more resilient to host-based attacks; however, it has limited visibility into what is happening inside the host.

A zones model offers a third option: the monitoring software can be run in the hosting operating system or hypervisor, while the monitored software consists of the application software together with the guest operating system. This approach separates and isolates the auditor from the monitored software, while it maintains excellent visibility into a guest's state.

In the Solaris OS, you can enable auditing on a system and monitor and record what is happening in all zones. The non-global zones cannot interfere.

Other examples of such monitoring include examining the state of processes or threads that run in non-global zones, extending dtrace probes into processes that are running in non-global zones, or monitoring packet-filtering actions in non-global zones that are running exclusive IP stack instances.

11.5.1 Auditing Events in Non-Global Zones

In the following example, auditing is enabled in the global zone. The events in non-global zones, here `apache1`, are recorded in the audit trail.

1. Enable Solaris auditing:

```
# zonename
global
# /etc/security/bsmconv
This script is used to enable the Basic Security Module (BSM).
Shall we continue with the conversion now? [y/n] y
bsmconv: INFO: checking startup file.
bsmconv: INFO: turning on audit module.
bsmconv: INFO: initializing device allocation.
The Basic Security Module is ready.
If there were any errors, please fix them now.
Configure BSM by editing files located in /etc/security.
Reboot this system now to come up with BSM enabled.
```

2. Now, reboot the system for auditing to be effective for all processes:
```
# reboot
```

3. Log into the non-global zone `apache1` and subsequently display the audit record in the global zone. The final entry in the audit file, shaded for your convenience, records the root login to zone `apache1` (IP address 10.0.2.100):

```
# zonename
global
# /praudit /var/audit/20080703221826.not_terminated.unknown
file,2008-07-03 15:18:26.774 -07:00,
header,36,2,AUE_SYSTEMBOOT,na,2008-07-03 15:17:10.301 -07:00
text,booting kernel
header,89,2,AUE_login,,unknown,2008-07-03 15:19:55.310 -07:00
subject,root,root,root,root,root,716,716,0 0 unknown
text,successful login
return,success,0
header,69,2,AUE_login,,unknown,2008-07-03 15:25:06.245 -07:00
subject,root,root,root,root,root,1439,3290887400,0 0 10.0.2.100
return,success,0
```

References

http://opensolaris.org/os/community/zones

http://opensolaris.org/os/community/brandz

Solaris Trusted Extensions Administrator's Procedures. Part No: 819-7309. Sun Microsystems, Inc. 4150 Network Circle Santa Clara, CA 95054, USA. http://docs.sun.com/app/docs/doc/819-7309

System Administration Guide: Virtualization Using the Solaris Operating System. Part No: 819-2450.Sun Microsystems, Inc. 4150 Network Circle Santa Clara, CA 95054, USA. http://docs.sun.com/app/docs/doc/819-2450

Glenn Brunette. *Limiting Service Privileges in the Solaris 10 Operating System*. Sun BluePrints OnLine. A Sun BluePrints Cookbook. Sun Microsystems, Inc. 4150 Network Circle, Santa Clara, CA 95054, USA. May 2005. http://www.sun.com/blueprints/0505/819-2680.pdf

Mark Thacker. *Eliminating Web Page Hijacking Using Solaris 10 Security*. Solaris 10 HowTo Guides. Sun Microsystems, Inc. 4150 Network Circle, Santa Clara, CA 95054, USA. May 2005. http://www.sun.com/software/solaris/howtoguides/s10securityhowto.pdf

Configuring and Using Trusted Extensions

Trusted Extensions extends the Solaris OS by restricting access to information based on the sensitivity of the information. Processes, files, desktop components, and network communications are assigned labels such as PUBLIC and RESTRICTED. The Trusted Extensions policy is based on the following concepts.

- Capabilities that in most UNIX environments are assigned to superuser are available to discrete administrative roles.

- In addition to UNIX permissions, access to data is controlled by special security tags. These tags are called sensitivity labels. Labels are assigned to users, processes, and objects such as data files and directories.

- Users can be cleared to operate in a multilevel desktop environment. In this environment, windows and data at various sensitivity labels can be displayed concurrently while data separation is enforced.

- Administrative roles and trusted processes run in a separate environment called the Trusted Path. This term is used because such applications cannot be interfered with by normal user applications; these applications have no untrusted ancestors.

12.1 Why Use Trusted Extensions?

Many organizations have policies for restricting access to information and for sharing information with others. Whether the data is associated with national security, human resources, financial records, or healthcare, policies are defined that are supposed to limit access to appropriate personnel. For example, there might be rules about labeling printed output, sharing information based on need to know, not making copies, and so on. When these policies are left to the discretion of the individuals who have access to or ownership of the data, there is no guarantee that these policies will be followed.

Strict enforcement of these policies requires a system that implements mandatory access control. Trusted Extensions enforces mandatory policies that are based on the value that is assigned to the data. Every piece of data under the control of the operating system is labeled according to its sensitivity. Data flows that are in violation of the labeling policy are not permitted. Users can share data only with other users and hosts who have been cleared to receive the data. Printed output is automatically labeled. All data on the screen are labeled. Network transmissions are prevented unless the peers are each cleared at the level of the data. Access to removable media is limited to authorized personnel and restricted by labeling rules.

12.2 Enabling Trusted Extensions

Starting with the Solaris 10 05/08 release, Trusted Extensions software no longer is separately installed. Instead, Trusted Extensions is enabled as a service by using SMF. Before enabling Trusted Extensions, you should be aware of several restrictions and assumptions.

Solaris zones are the primary mechanism by which Trusted Extensions implements data separation. Each zone is assigned a unique sensitivity label and requires a custom zone configuration template. Therefore, you must destroy any existing Solaris zones before enabling Trusted Extensions.

Similarly, remove any existing user accounts. Ensure that local root login is enabled (root is not a role).

You create a new labeled zone for each sensitivity label that you want to manage. Using ZFS snapshots and clones saves both time and disk space in this process. You can reserve a 10 G disk slice during your Solaris 10 installation for later configuration as a ZFS pool.

Remote access to the Trusted Path administrative environment is disabled by default. To do the exercises in this chapter, have local desktop access when administering the system.

It is recommended that you have a fixed IP address for your first configuration. DHCP configuration is an advanced topic, and the configuration steps are different for different versions of the Solaris OS.

If you have not already done so, enable the Secure by Default configuration:

netservices limited

To enable Trusted Extensions, you enable the label daemon service and reboot:

```
# svcadm enable -s labeld
# reboot
```

The labeled environment is now enabled but not configured. After logging in as described in the next section, you then configure the system with labels that Trusted Extensions provides. The default label, ADMIN_LOW, is not sufficient to run a multilevel environment.

12.3 Getting Started

After the system reboots, you are presented with a login window that displays the words Trusted Extensions below the Solaris logo.

1. Use the **Options** button to select **Sessions > Trusted JDS.**
2. Then log in as root. You are presented with a dialog box that displays the message of the day and the user attributes of the logged in user (root in this case).
3. Click **OK.** A second dialog box is displayed for selecting the session clearance.
4. Because you want to run in the Trusted Path, simply click **OK** again.

Once the desktop initialization is complete, a window bar appears across the top of the screen. This window bar is called the **Trusted Stripe.**

Figure 12.1 The Trusted Stripe

The Trusted Stripe provides continuous feedback about the label and trustworthiness of the current focus window and displays the label of the current workspace. The window bar displays **Trusted Path.** Notice that the Trusted Stripe cannot be obscured by any application windows.

12.3.1 How Labels Are Used

Although label names and their hierarchy can be customized, this is beyond the scope of this chapter. Trusted Extensions software provides five predefined labels as shown in Table 12.1.

Table 12.1 Trusted Extensions Labels

Label	Purpose
ADMIN_LOW	The lowest label, applied to data that is generally immutable and visible in all zones.
PUBLIC	The lowest label for normal users and their initial label at login. Also used for the label of the public Internet.
CONFIDENTIAL: INTERNAL USE ONLY	The label of your private or corporate network. This label is more sensitive than PUBLIC.
CONFIDENTIAL: NEED TO KNOW	The clearance or upper bound for normal users. This label is more sensitive than CONFIDENTIAL : INTERNAL USE ONLY.
ADMIN_HIGH	The highest label on the system. Used for system configuration. ADMIN_HIGH data must not be visible to normal users.

Two commands are used to display the current label status.

- The `plabel` command displays the sensitivity label of the current or specified process.
- The `getlabel` command displays the sensitivity label of the specified file or directory.

To run either command, open a **Terminal** from the desktop background or from the Main menu. The terminal is also labeled **Trusted Path.**

The sensitivity label of processes that run in the Trusted Path is always **ADMIN_HIGH.** Similarly, the default sensitivity label of all files is initially **ADMIN_HIGH** as well.

```
# plabel $$
ADMIN_HIGH
# getlabel /
ADMIN_HIGH
```

Once you've started the trusted system, you perform three main tasks to create a usable system:

1. Configuring a trusted network
2. Creating users and roles
3. Creating labeled zones

12.4 Configuring Your Trusted Network

Trusted Extensions uses trusted network templates to specify which individual hosts or networks are trusted to transmit explicitly labeled IP packets. If an individual host or a host's network is specified as trusted, then Trusted Extensions automatically includes the sender's label in each packet that is sent to any endpoint on that host. Similarly, Trusted Extensions requires and interprets labels in all packets that are received from a trusted host. The labels are sent using a multilevel protocol called **CIPSO,** so the Trusted Extensions template type is also called **cipso.** You can create multiple cipso-type templates to specify the range or set of labels that are acceptable for specific hosts or networks. The range or set of labels defines the extent to which the systems are multilevel.

By default, remote hosts and networks are assumed to be untrusted. We refer to such hosts as single-level, even though the hosts are unaware of labeling. Because the IP packets of single-level hosts are not explicitly labeled, Trusted Extensions assigns to them a network template with a type of **unlabeled.** The unlabeled type includes a field to specify a default label. In general, you must create an unlabeled template for each of your uniquely labeled hosts or networks.

> **Note**
>
> You might have noticed a console message when the system booted. The message states that your system's IP address is not specified with a **CIPSO** template. When Trusted Extensions is enabled, the kernel automatically assigns a pre-configured **cipso** template to all of the IP addresses associated with any of its local network interfaces. Although not required, it is good practice to use the Solaris Management Console to explicitly associate a **cipso** template with the interface, especially if you want to customize the label range of an interface.

The name of the network template that is assigned to all remote IP addresses is **admin_low.** This template is used to communicate with untrusted systems. This template is generally assigned to remote hosts that provide fundamental services such as DHCP or DNS. In contrast, Trusted Extensions does *not* provide fundamental services to these remote hosts.

To permit access from remote systems that are configured with Trusted Extensions, you must configure each remote system to assign a **CIPSO** template to the peer's IP address. This procedure is discussed in the section on the Solaris Management Console. You can also customize the policy for remote access by **admin_low** hosts.

12.4.1 Using the Solaris Management Console

The creation, modification, and assignment of network templates is done by using the Solaris Management Console. You start the Console by using the **/usr/sbin/smc** command. Initialization takes up to a minute. After initialization is complete, you see a list of Management Tools in the Navigation panel.

1. Select the following entry:

   ```
   This Computer (localhost: Scope=Files, Policy=TSOL)
   ```

   The acronym TSOL is a holdover from the Trusted Solaris product that preceded the development of Trusted Extensions. This acronym is still used in various directory names.

2. Select the **System Configuration** > **Computers and Networks** node.

3. Type the root password. After clicking **OK,** the tool will load.

4. Expand the **Computers and Networks** node by double-clicking to see three entries.

5. Click the **Computer** tool to display your current network configuration.

12.4.2 Construct Remote Host Templates

Your first configuration job in the Solaris Management Console is to restrict the system to network access from trusted systems. Access is restricted by assigning the correct labels to the local system and to any systems with which you and the local system communicate. Some systems are left out of the configuration. Such systems cannot communicate with this system.

1. Under the **Computers and Networks** node, double-click **Security Templates.**

2. The default templates are displayed in the **View** pane. These templates describe the security attributes for hosts that this system can contact.

These lists include **CIPSO** hosts that are running Trusted Extensions and unlabeled hosts.

3. Examine the **cipso** template. View which hosts and which networks are already assigned this template.

4. Examine the **admin_low** template. View which hosts and which networks are already assigned this template.

5. Create a template. Choose **Add Template** from the **Action** menu in the top menu bar. Use the online help for assistance. A **New Template** dialog box appears. Fill it in as shown in Table 12.2.

Table 12.2 Public Template Labels

Template Name:	public
Host Type:	unlabeled
Default Label:	PUBLIC
DOI:	1
Minimum Label:	ADMIN_LOW
Maximum Label:	ADMIN_HIGH
Additional Labels to Accept:	Leave blank

Note

You cannot type in the label fields. Instead, click the Edit button at the right to open the label-builder dialog box. This dialog box is similar to the dialog box that appeared when you logged in. The label that is displayed above the **Label Selection** area currently shows **ADMIN_LOW.**

6. Click the radio button labeled **PUBLIC** to update this entry even though this item appears to be already selected.

7. Click **OK** once to accept the label and click **OK** again to create the template.

8. Now create another template named `internal`. This template is similar to the **public** template except for its name and default label (see Table 12.3).

Table 12.3 Label for the Internal Template

Template Name:	**internal**
Default Label:	CONFIDENTIAL : INTERNAL USE ONLY

12.4.3 Adding Hosts to the System's Known Network

In the **Computers** tool, confirm that you want to view all computers on the network.

If you know the host names and addresses of computers that you want to contact, perform the following task.

1. To add a host that this system can contact, use the **Action** menu and choose **Add Computer.**

2. Identify the host by name and IP address.

3. (Optional) Provide additional information about the host.

4. To add the host, click **Apply.**

5. When the entries are complete, click **OK.**

6. Add a group of hosts that this system can contact. The online help explains how to add groups of hosts by using a network IP address.

12.4.4 Assigning a Security Template to a Host or a Group of Hosts

If you added hosts, assign security templates.

1. Select the **Security Templates** tool again and double-click the **public** template icon.

2. Click the **Hosts Assigned to Template** tab.

To assign the template to a single host, do the following.

1. In the **Hostname** field, type the host's name. In the **IP Address** field, type the host's address.

2. Click the **Add** button. To save your changes, click **OK.**

To assign a template to a group of hosts with contiguous addresses, do the following.

1. Click **Wildcard.**

2. In the **IP Address** field, type the network address.

3. In the **Prefix** field, type the prefix that describes the group of contiguous addresses.

4. Click the **Add** button. To save your changes, click **OK.**

12.4.5 Limiting the Hosts That Can Be Contacted on the Trusted Network

This procedure protects labeled hosts from being contacted by arbitrary unlabeled hosts. When Trusted Extensions is enabled, this default template defines every host on the network (0.0.0.0). By default, every host that is not provided with a **CIPSO** template is defined by the **admin_low** template. This template assigns every system that is not otherwise defined (0.0.0.0) to be an unlabeled system with the default label of **admin_low.** The 0.0.0.0 assignment in the **admin_low** must be replaced with specific entries for every host that the system contacts during boot.

For example, DNS servers, name servers, broadcast and multicast addresses, and routers must be assigned to the **admin_low** template after the 0.0.0.0 wild-card entry is removed. All hosts that are to be contacted at boot time must be specified in the **Computers and Networks** tool.

12.4.5.1 Specifying Unlabeled Hosts That Are Contacted at Boot

Assign hosts to the **admin_low** template.

1. Double-click the **admin_low** template.
2. Click the **Hosts Assigned to Template** tab.
3. Remove the 0.0.0.0 entry.
4. Add each unlabeled host that must be contacted at boot time. Include every on-link router that is not running Trusted Extensions, through which this host must communicate.

12.4.5.2 Specifying Trusted Extensions Hosts That Are Contacted at Boot

Assign hosts to the **cipso** template.

1. Double-click the **cipso** template.
2. Click the **Hosts Assigned to Template** tab.
3. Add each labeled host that must be contacted at boot time, such as your LDAP server and DNS servers. Include every on-link router that is running Trusted Extensions, through which this host must communicate. Make sure that all of your network interfaces are assigned to this template.

12.4.5.3 Setting the New Default Network Label

After you have removed the 0.0.0.0 entry from the **admin_low** template, you must associate the 0.0.0.0 wildcard with a new template.

Open the **public** template and assign the wildcard entry, 0.0.0.0, to this template.

As you will see in the next section, only processes running at the **PUBLIC** label will be able to reach arbitrary hosts, because label equality is required for network connections. Similarly, only arbitrary hosts that are running at the **PUBLIC** label will be able to contact your system.

12.4.6 Configuring Multilevel Network Ports

By default, each zone has its own complete set of network ports for each interface. Because the default network policy for connections is label equality, labeled zones on the same host cannot communicate with each other over the network.

However, multilevel ports, or MLPs, can be configured by using **Trusted Path** administrative tools. When a privileged server binds to an MLP, the server can accept connections from any client whose label is included in the label range or explicit label set that specified in the security template that is associated with the interface.

You can associate an MLP with a network interface that is unique to a zone, or with a network interface that is shared with other zones. When a *port* is specified as an MLP on a shared interface, the port is available only to the zone with which the MLP is associated. For example, to support the multilevel desktop, the X11 server port 6000 is specified as an MLP for all interfaces that belong to the global zone, and to all interfaces that the global shares with the labeled zones.

1. To view the MLP settings for the global zone, select the **System Configuration > Computers and Networks > Trusted Network Zones** tool from the **Navigation** panel.

2. Open the **Properties** for the global zone, as shown in Figure 12.2. Note that MLPs are specified for the multilevel services that the global zone provides. These services include BSD and IPP printing, NFS, the port mapper, and X11.

Do not make any changes to these settings at this time.

12.5 Creating Users and Roles

In this section, you create a role and assign it to a user. Although you create roles and users in the **Trusted Path**, they apply to the labeled zones that you create later.

12.5.1 Creating a Role

Roles are special identities that are used for administrative tasks. Unlike normal users, roles cannot log in to the system. Instead, roles are assumed by authorized users. In the standard Solaris OS, you use the **su(1M)** command. In Trusted

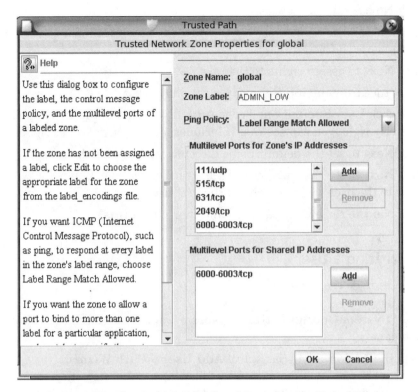

Figure 12.2 The Default Multilevel Ports in the Global Zone

Extensions, you use the **Trusted Path**. For more information about roles and rights management see Chapter 5, "Privileges and Role-Based Access Control."

To create a role, do the following, as shown in Figure 12.2.

1. Select **System Configuration** > **Users** > **Administrative Roles** in the **Navigation** panel.
2. From the **Action** menu bar, select **Add Administrative Role**.
3. Fill in the form with the information shown in Table 12.4.

Table 12.4 Form Information

Role Name:	secadmin
Full Name:	Security Admin
Description:	Security Administrator
Role ID Number:	100
Role Shell:	Administrator's Korn

4. Click **Next.**

5. Type and confirm a password for the role. The password must contain at least one numeric character.

6. Click **Next** to assign rights to the role.

7. Select the **Information Security** right and click **Add.**

8. Then click **User Security** and click **Add**. If you expand the **Information Security** right, you can see that it includes a hierarchy of other rights profiles.

9. Click **Next** to set the default home directory settings for the role.

10. Click **Next** to see the current users assigned to the role. Later, you will assign a role to the user when you create the first user.

11. Click **Next** to review the settings, and then click **Finish.**

12.5.2 Creating a User

To create a user, do the following.

1. Select **System Configuration** > **Users** > **User Accounts** in the **Navigation** panel.

2. From the **Action** menu bar, select **Add User** > **With Wizard.**
    Create a user with the wizard by following similar steps to creating a role. Note that you must create a password here; otherwise the account is locked.

3. After you have finished creating the user, double-click the user to open the **Properties** dialog box.

4. Select the **Roles** tab and assign the **secadmin** role to the user.

5. Select the **Trusted Extensions** tab. Change the **Idle Time** from 5 minutes to 30 minutes.

6. Select the Rights tab and assign the following rights to the user:

    Device Management

    Object Label Management

7. In the extended rights section at the bottom click the **Edit** button for the **Default** privilege set.

8. Locate the **Process Privileges** group in the **Included** list on the right. Select the **proc_info** privilege and **Remove** it. The **proc_info** privilege appears in the **Excluded** list. The user now cannot observe any processes that the user does not own.

9. Click **OK** to dismiss the **Default Privileges** dialog box, and then click **OK** to save the changes.

12.6 Creating Labeled Zones

Now that you have assigned labels to hosts, networks, users and roles, you are ready to assign labels to zones. The **txzonemgr** script provides simple GUI menus to guide you through the steps. The title of this set of menus is *Labeled Zone Manager*.

```
# txzonemgr &
```

12.6.1 Sharing Network Interfaces

Each labeled zone must be able to connect to the X11 server in the global zone. Trusted Extensions provides the ability for the global zone administrator to share one or more IP addresses with all labeled zones. So it is not necessary to specify any networking options when creating labeled zones. Depending on which release of Trusted Extensions is running, you have different defaults and options.

If you are running a release of Trusted Extensions before the Solaris 10 10/08 release, you must create a shared network interface. In the Solaris 10 10/08 release, the loopback interface is shared by default, so it provides connectivity to the X11 server. However, if you want to communicate with remote systems, your zone needs a real interface.

1. Therefore, the first step is to open or double click the Manage Network Interfaces... menu item.

   Your primary interface is displayed (see Figure 12.3). Select the interface and click **OK**. If you have not previously assigned the **cipso** template to this interface by using the Solaris Management Console, you can assign the template in this dialog box. You also have the choice of sharing this interface with all zones, or creating multiple logical interfaces. If you create additional logical interfaces, you can share them later as well.

2. In this exercise, choose to Share the interface. Then click **OK** twice to return to the main menu.

12.6.2 Creating Your First Zone

When you create zones, ZFS provides efficient snapshot and cloning features. However, using ZFS requires planning. You have the following options depending on which release of Solaris your system is running.

- You might already have a ZFS pool available.
- Otherwise, you may be able to convert an unused UFS disk slice into a ZFS pool.
- If neither of the preceding options is available, you can still use UFS.

Figure 12.3 Your Primary Interface Is Displayed

Creating a new ZFS pool from an existing disk slice destroys the data on the slice. If you want to do that, then in a terminal window, do the following:

1. Ensure that the slice is unmounted and removed from /etc/vfstab:

```
#   umount /zone
#   grep zone /etc/vfstab
##/dev/dsk/c1t1d0s4 /dev/rdsk/c1t1d0s4 /zone ufs 2 yes -
```

2. To create a new ZFS pool, use the **zpool** command:
   # `zpool create -f zone slicename`

   where `slicename` is of the form c*n*d*n*s*n*

3. If you do not plan to use ZFS, create the /zone directory.

In the **Labeled Zone Manager**, do the following.

1. Select **Create a New Zone....**
2. When prompted for a zonename, type `public`.
3. A menu of operations displays. These operations can be performed on the zone. Typically, the first or second item is the right choice.
4. Choose **Select Label...** and wait while the system computes all the label combinations.
5. Then select **PUBLIC**, which is at the bottom of the list because it is the lowest available label.

6. Next select **Install....** A window displays the progress of the installation. Installation takes about 15 minutes depending on your hardware. When installation is finished, you are prompted for a hostname for this zone.

7. Because you are using a shared network interface, select the default value, which is the same as the global zone's hostname (see Figure 12.4).

Figure 12.4 Select the Default Value

8. Next, select **Zone Console**. After the console window appears, select **Boot** from the **Labeled Zone Manager**.

   You can follow the **public** zone booting up in the **Zone Console**.

9. If you are prompted for the NFS default domain, select the default and press the F2 key. Ignore the message about being unable to update the root password. The zones have read-only access to the /etc/passwd and /etc/shadow files in the global zone. The zone reboots and initializes its SMF services.

10. Log in as root using the global zone password.

11. Verify that the zone has a network interface by running:

    ```
    # ifconfig -a
    ```

12. Verify that at least one interface is an all-zones interface.

13. Run the following commands:

```
# rm /etc/auto_home_public
# netservices limited
# svcadm disable cde-login
# exit
```

14. From the **Labeled Zone Manager** menu, select **Halt.**

15. If you are using ZFS for your zones, select **Snapshot.** You are ready to create the second zone.

16. Select **Return** to Main Menu.

12.6.3 Creating Your Second Zone

In the following sample procedure, the name of the second zone is **internal.**

1. Select **Create a New Zone...** and type `internal` as its name.

2. Then choose **Select Label** and pick **CONFIDENTIAL : INTERNAL USE ONLY**.

3. If you are using ZFS, choose **Clone** and select the snapshot of your **public** zone as the basis for the **internal** zone. The snapshot should have a name like `zone/public@snapshot`.

4. If you are not using ZFS, you choose **Copy** and select the **public** zone.

5. Choose **Zone Console** and then choose **Boot**. In the **Zone Console**, verify that no errors occur while the zone boots up.

6. Finally, choose **Return to Main Menu** and select the **public** zone again.

7. Boot the **public** zone. You can create additional zones, as Figure 12.5 illustrates.

12.7 Using the Multilevel Desktop

A multilevel desktop, as shown in Figure 12.6, enables you to log in once, and then use different workspaces for activities that require different levels of access. For example, you can log in at the label **PUBLIC,** set your clearance label to **RESTRICTED,** and create workspaces at all labels from **PUBLIC** to **RESTRICTED.** In a labeled network, a **NEED TO KNOW** workspace would receive different emails than a workspace at **PUBLIC.** Your access in a **NEED TO KNOW** workspace would be different from that in a **PUBLIC** workspace.

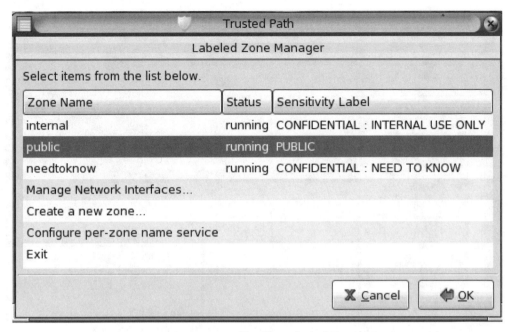

Figure 12.5 Zones Listed in the Labeled Zone Manager

You are now ready to try out the multilevel environment. Your choices begin at the login screen. You must choose a trusted desktop, then review and confirm messages from the trusted system.

1. Log out as `root` and log in as your new user.

   You have a choice of **Trusted CDE** or **Trusted JDS** sessions.

2. For this exercise, choose **Trusted JDS.**

   The **Message of the Day** window displays your name, rights, roles, and label range.

3. Click **OK.** A dialog box displays to select a new clearance.

4. You can simply click **OK,** or you can uncheck the **NEED TO KNOW** label and select **INTERNAL USE ONLY.**

After dismissing the clearance dialog box, the GNOME desktop initializes. The Trusted Stripe and the nautilus background appear. Your workspace labels initially have the label **PUBLIC.**

12.7.1 Changing Your Workspace Label

Each workspace has a label. The label applies to actions that you initiate from the front panel or background menu. You can change the label of a workspace by using

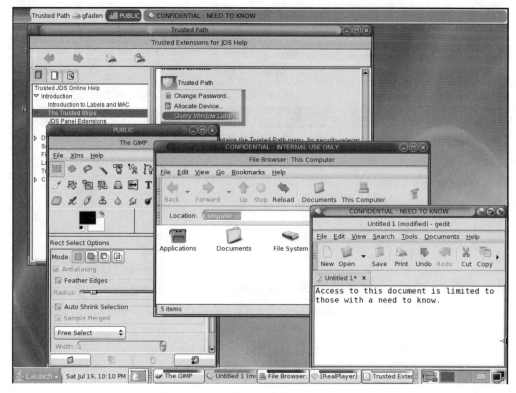

Figure 12.6 The Multilevel Desktop

the **Change Workspace Label** item. This item can be selected from either of two menus.

- A menu in the Trusted Stripe region displays the workspace icon. When you click on this region, the Change Workspace Label menu displays.
- Or, you can right-click on a workspace in the panel workspace applet.

If you select a label with no corresponding labeled zone, an error message appears. However, the label is still applied. If a zone of that label is later booted, you can activate that workspace by refreshing the label or by selecting **Terminal** from the **Launch** menu.

12.7.2 Moving Windows into Other Workspaces

Windows can be moved between workspaces even if their labels are different from the workspace. The workspace label is simply the default for starting new applications. The label does not apply to existing applications. You can move windows by dragging them in the panel workspace applet or by using the window manager menu. When you change the label of an existing workspace, any existing windows remain in that workspace and retain their original labels.

12.7.3 Copying and Pasting Between Labels

Only authorized users can cut and paste across label boundaries. Because the user was assigned the **Object Label Management** rights profile, the required authorizations are granted. However, all such actions are mediated by the **Trusted Path** and must be confirmed by the user. Such actions are auditable and are configurable per user. You can also grant a user the authorization to upgrade information, but not to downgrade it. Drag-and-drop across labels is not currently supported in Trusted JDS. In Trusted CDE, you can drag-and-drop between uniquely labeled File Managers.

12.7.4 File System Protection

In Trusted Extensions, each mount point is labeled according to the zone that owns the mount point.

In the **internal** zone, open a **Terminal** and run the following command:

```
$ /usr/demo/tsol/getmounts.sh
```

This script displays the labels of all of the mount points in the invoking zone.

- The mount points that are listed as **ADMIN_LOW** are shared read-only from the global zone.

- The mount points that are owned by the zone are labeled **CONFIDENTIAL : INTERNAL USE ONLY** and are only writable by processes in that zone.

- You might also see that the mount point `/zone/public/export/home` is labeled **PUBLIC.** This mount point is read-only in the internal zone and is writable only in the **public** zone.

The file manager **nautilus** can also be used to display the label of any file or directory.

Open the **Properties** dialog in the current file or directory and select the **Permissions** tab. The **File Label** field is at the bottom.

12.7.5 Observing Processes

A user in a zone cannot observe the processes in other zones. To demonstrate this, do the following.

1. Open a Terminal window at the **PUBLIC** label, and run the command: `prstat -Z`.
2. Now bring up another Terminal at the **CONFIDENTIAL : INTERNAL USE ONLY** label and run the command `prstat -Z`. Note that the process numbers are distinct. Furthermore, only the current user's processes are visible.

12.7.6 Assuming a Role

Assuming a role in Trusted Extensions is done by using the **Trusted Path** menu. The name of the user who can assume a role is displayed in the Trusted Stripe next to a hat. To assume a role, do the following.

1. First, switch to an unused workspace.
2. Then, click the user name in the Trusted Stripe. The secadmin role is available.
3. Select the secadmin role and type the role's password. After the system authenticates the role, the workspace label is associated with the Trusted Path, and the workspace takes on the role's identity.

The system protects the **Trusted Path** by preventing normal user windows from being moved into this workspace. The system similarly prevents the user from assuming a role in a workspace unless the workspace is initially empty.

12.7.7 Accessing Devices

The Trusted Path also provides a menu item for allocating devices.

Select the **Allocate Device** menu item from the Trusted Path. The **Device Manager** appears with a list of available devices.

The list is updated when USB devices are hot-plugged. Normally, users are not permitted to allocate devices, but this user was assigned the **Device Management** rights profile.

When a device is allocated it is only made available to the current user at the label of the current workspace. Administrators can restrict the label range at which individual devices can be allocated. Because this user was granted the authorization to manage devices, the **Administration** dialog box is available. To see what you can customize and restrict per device, select the audio device and click **Administration > Properties** (see Figure 12.7).

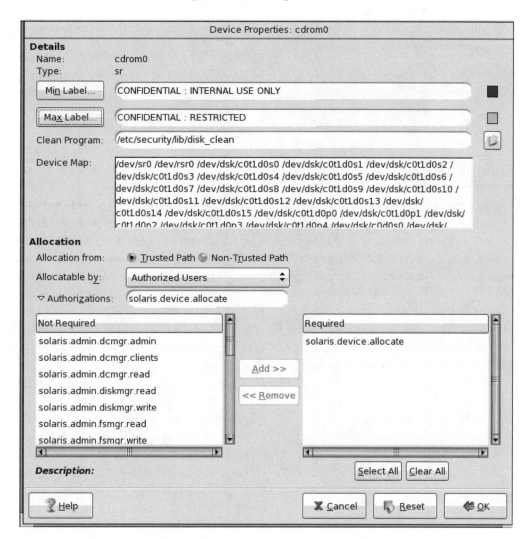

Figure 12.7 The Audio Device in the Administration Dialog Box

12.7.8 Accessing Your Network

If you followed the procedure for assigning network templates, the default label for remote hosts is **PUBLIC**. Therefore, you are limited to accessing your network from the **public** zone. Even though the **internal** zone is sharing the same interface as the **public** zone, applications in the **internal** zone cannot connect to any remote systems, except to remote systems that have been explicitly assigned the **internal** network template, or a **cipso** (label range from **ADMIN_LOW** to **ADMIN_HIGH**) template.

To display the network template that is associated with a remote host, type a command similar to the following:

```
$ /usr/sbin/tninfo -h www.sun.com
IP address= 75.5.124.61
template = public
```

Summary

Trusted Extensions can be configured to provide strong separation for a wide variety of environments including workstations, laptops, Sun Ray servers, Sun Rays, NFS servers, network guards, and Web servers. A single chapter cannot describe all of the configuration options and features of Trusted Extensions. For extensive documentation, see the *Trusted Extensions Collection* at http://docs.sun.com/app/docs/coll/175.9.

Index

informIT.com THE TRUSTED TECHNOLOGY LEARNING SOURCE

PEARSON

InformIT is a brand of Pearson and the online presence for the world's leading technology publishers. It's your source for reliable and qualified content and knowledge, providing access to the top brands, authors, and contributors from the tech community.

✦Addison-Wesley   **Cisco Press**   EXAM/**CRAM**   **IBM Press.**   **QUE·**   **PRENTICE HALL**   **SAMS** | Safari✝

LearnIT at InformIT

Looking for a book, eBook, or training video on a new technology? Seeking timely and relevant information and tutorials? Looking for expert opinions, advice, and tips? **InformIT has the solution.**

- Learn about new releases and special promotions by subscribing to a wide variety of newsletters.
  Visit **informit.com/newsletters**.

- Access FREE podcasts from experts at **informit.com/podcasts**.

- Read the latest author articles and sample chapters at **informit.com/articles**.

- Access thousands of books and videos in the Safari Books Online digital library at **safari.informit.com**.

- Get tips from expert blogs at **informit.com/blogs**.

Visit **informit.com/learn** to discover all the ways you can access the hottest technology content.

Are You Part of the IT Crowd?

Connect with Pearson authors and editors via RSS feeds, Facebook, Twitter, YouTube, and more! Visit **informit.com/socialconnect**.

informIT.com THE TRUSTED TECHNOLOGY LEARNING SOURCE   **PEARSON**

 ✦Addison-Wesley   **Cisco Press**   EXAM/**CRAM**   **IBM Press.**   **QUE·**   **PRENTICE HALL**   **SAMS** | Safari✝

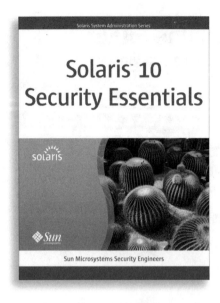

Solaris System Administration Series

Solaris 10 Security Essentials

solaris

Sun

Sun Microsystems Security Engineers

A04 – 682 – 5813 → Jeja

FREE Online Edition

Your purchase of **Solaris™ 10 Security Essentials** includes access to a free online edition for 45 days through the Safari Books Online subscription service. Nearly every Prentice Hall book is available online through Safari Books Online, along with more than 5,000 other technical books and videos from publishers such as Addison-Wesley Professional, Cisco Press, Exam Cram, IBM Press, O'Reilly, Que, and Sams.

SAFARI BOOKS ONLINE allows you to search for a specific answer, cut and paste code, download chapters, and stay current with emerging technologies.

Activate your FREE Online Edition at www.informit.com/safarifree

> **STEP 1:** Enter the coupon code: HQJLYFA.

> **STEP 2:** New Safari users, complete the brief registration form.
> Safari subscribers, just log in.

If you have difficulty registering on Safari or accessing the online edition,
please e-mail customer-service@safaribooksonline.com

Safari
Books Online

Addison Wesley · AdobePress · ALPHA · Cisco Press · FT Press · IBM Press · lynda.com · Microsoft Press · New Riders

O'REILLY · Peachpit Press · QUE · Redbooks · SAMS · SAS Publishing · Sun microsystems · Wharton School Publishing · WILEY